THE FORGOTTEN VCs

THE VICTORIA CROSSES
of the
WAR IN THE FAR EAST DURING WW2

'When you go home don't worry about what to tell your loved ones and friends about service in Asia. No one will know where you were, or where it is if you do. You are, and will remain, "The Forgotten Army".'
Attributed to General Bill Slim

THE FORGOTTEN VCs

THE VICTORIA CROSSES
of the
WAR IN THE FAR EAST DURING WW2

Brian Best

Frontline Books

THE FORGOTTEN VCS
The Victoria Crosses of the War in the Far East During WW2

First published in 2018 by Frontline Books,
an imprint of Pen & Sword Books Ltd,
47 Church Street, Barnsley, S. Yorkshire, S70 2AS.

Copyright © Brian Best, 2018

The right of Brian Best to be identified as the author of this work has been asserted by him in accordance with the Copyright, Designs and Patents Act 1988.

ISBN: 978-1-52671-797-9

All rights reserved. No part of this publication may be reproduced, stored in or introduced into a retrieval system, or transmitted, in any form, or by any means (electronic, mechanical, photocopying, recording or otherwise) without the prior written permission of the publisher. Any person who does any unauthorized act in relation to this publication may be liable to criminal prosecution and civil claims for damages.

CIP data records for this title are available from the British Library

Printed and bound by TJ International
Typeset in 10.5/12.5 Palatino

Pen & Sword Books Limited incorporates the imprints of Atlas, Archaeology, Aviation, Discovery, Family History, Fiction, History, Maritime, Military, Military Classics, Politics, Select, Transport, True Crime, Air World, Frontline Publishing, Leo Cooper, Remember When, Seaforth Publishing, The Praetorian Press, Wharncliffe Local History, Wharncliffe Transport, Wharncliffe True Crime and White Owl.

For more information on our books, please visit
www.frontline-books.com
email info@frontline-books.com
or write to us at the above address.

Contents

Introduction		vii
Glossary		ix
Acknowledgements		xi
Chapter 1	The Protagonists	1
Chapter 2	The Malayan Campaign	11
	Scarf, Arthur; Cumming, Arthur Edward; Anderson, Charles	
Chapter 3	The Fall of Singapore	24
	Wilkinson, Thomas; Magennis, James; Fraser, Ian	
Chapter 4	Defeat in Burma	44
	Singh, Parkash	
Chapter 5	The Chin Hills	55
	Ghale, Gaje	
Chapter 6	Second Arakan Campaign	58
	Horwood, Alec George; Hoey, Charles Ferguson; Singh, Nand	
Chapter 7	Wingate's VC Chindits	69
	Cairns, George; Allmand, Michael; Pun, Tul Bahadur; Blaker, Frank Gerald	
Chapter 8	The Battle of Imphal	86
	Hafiz, Abdul; Turner, Hanson Victor; Lama, Ganju; Thapa, Netrabahadur; Rai, Agansing	
Chapter 9	The Siege of Kohima	98
	Harman, John; Randle, John	
Chapter 10	The Follow-Up – Arakan Singh, Ram Sarup;	113
	Ram, Bhandari; Singh, Umrao; Shah, Sher; Knowland, George; Gurung, Bhanubhakta; Raymond, Claud	
Chapter 11	Marching South	135
	Chib, Prakash Singh; Singh, Gian; Judge, Karamjeen Singh; Din, Fazal; Weston, William Basil; Gurung, Lachhiman	
Chapter 12	Australia's War	150
	Kingsbury, Bruce; French, John; Newton, William; Kelliher, Richard; Derrick, Thomas; Chowne, Albert; Kenna, Edward; Sukanaivalu, Sefanaia; Rattey, Reginald; Partridge, Frank; Mackey, John; Starcevich, Leslie; Gray, Robert	
Bibliography		194
Index		196

Introduction

When my father died twenty years ago, little did I think that I would use my interest in military history to write books on the subject. Furthermore, I never thought I would be asked to write a book about the fighting in the Far East, including, in large part, the Forgotten Army and its exploits in the Burma Campaign, the longest fought by the British Army in the Second World War.

When he left school, my father went to work for the Burma Oil Company in London. Still a young man, he was sent out to Burma and India in 1935 just before the former separated from the latter and granted a new constitution calling for a fully elected Burmese assembly. This probably meant little to my father as it did to most men of his generation and, like them, he enjoyed the life of a pukka colonial. Not a bad step up for a lad from Charlton, south-east London. I have photographs of Dad relaxing with colleagues and sipping *chotapegs* on a veranda in the Karen Hills, or posing in his shorts and a solar topee with his servants. He picked up enough of the Urdu language to get by – mostly issuing orders – until he returned to the head office in 1938. After he married my mother in 1940, he was called up and sent for training at Catterick, where it was discovered he had experience of Burma and a smattering of the language. This was enough for him to be assigned to the Indian Army. So, as my mother was preparing to give birth to me, Dad made the long sea voyage to India where he did his officer training (OCTU) at Arangaon in the western state of Maharashtra. It would not be until 1946 that he would meet his son.

One of his fellow officer cadets was called Albion Harman, who came from an extraordinary family. His father was a wealthy entrepreneur who owned Lundy Island off the north Devon coast. His younger brother was John Harman, who was destined to be awarded a posthumous Victoria Cross for outstanding gallantry at Kohima in 1944. It was this connection and John's story that started my interest in the

INTRODUCTION

Victoria Cross that has lasted for more than fifty years. I also have tenuous connections with Harman's regiment, the 4th Battalion, The Royal West Kent Regiment. On the thirty-fifth anniversary of the Battle of Kohima I was asked by the regiment to interview several of the veterans of that epic battle with a view to incorporating it into a recruitment film, which sadly did not materialise. I have kept the notes of their incredible experiences and some will be mentioned in the chapter about Kohima.

When Dad was commissioned, he joined the Queen Victoria's Own Madras Sappers and Miners. After some jungle training, the regiment was shipped east to the Indian border in time for the start of the Second Invasion of the Arakan as part of the XVth Corps. In command of a mixed bunch of Sikhs, Gurkhas and Jats, Dad's involvement in the advance was purely supportive – his speciality was the docks along the Arakan coast.

Years later, at my request, he did apply for the medals for which he was entitled. This included the unique Burma Star. Rather in the fashion that the 'Old Contemptibles' of the First World War are well-regarded, so another slightly derogatory term bestowed on the men who served in Burma – the Forgotten Army – can now be proclaimed with pride.

Brian Best,
Rutland, 2017.

Glossary

Army Group	The largest military command deployed by the British Army, commanded by a general or field marshal and containing 400,000 to 600,000 troops.
Army	A military command controlling several subordinate corps, commanded by a lieutenant general and containing 100,000 to 200,000 troops.
Corps	A military command controlling two or more divisions commanded by a lieutenant general and containing 50,000 to 100,000 troops.
Division	An infantry or armoured formation commanded by a major general and containing 10,000 to 20,000 troops.
Brigade	A formation containing several battalions commanded by a brigadier and consisting of 3,000 to 6,000 troops.
Regiment	A unit controlled by a lieutenant colonel and consisting of 500 to 900 troops.
Company	A sub-unit of a battalion commanded by a major or captain and consisting of eighty to 150 troops.
Platoon	A sub-unit of a company commanded by a lieutenant and consisting of fifteen to thirty troops.
Squad	A sub-unit of a platoon commanded by a sergeant and consisting of eight to twelve troops.

Indian Army Ranks and the Equivalent British Rank:

Sepoy	Private
Lance Naik	Lance Corporal
Naik	Corporal
Havildar	Sergeant
Havildar Major	Sergeant Major
Jemadar	Lieutenant
Subadar	Captain

GLOSSARY

The XIVth Army (14th or Fourteenth Army) was a multinational force commanded by Lieutenant General William 'Bill' Slim. It was composed of units from the armies of India, Britain, East and West Africa. It was the Second World War's largest Commonwealth army with nearly a million men by late 1944. At different periods it was composed of four corps:

    IV Corps
    XV Corps
    XXXIII Corps
    XXXIV Corps

A total of thirteen divisions served with the army:

    British 2nd Infantry Division
    British 36th Infantry Division
    Indian 5th Infantry Division
    Indian 7th Infantry Division
    Indian 17th Infantry Division
    Indian 19th Infantry Division
    Indian 20th Infantry Division
    Indian 23rd Infantry Division
    Indian 25th Infantry Division
    Indian 26th Infantry Division
    11th (East African) Infantry Division
    81st (West African) Infantry Division
    82nd (West African) Infantry Division

Acknowledgements

I would like to thank the following individuals: Tom Johnson, Steve Snelling, Anthony Staunton, Harry Willey, Laurence Parker, Robert Mewett, Reg Woollard, Molly Fudge and Nigel Holmes.

Part 1

The Protagonists

The Japanese

When Japan defeated the Russian fleet at the Battle of Tsushima in 1904, the British were the first to applaud the victory against one of their main rivals. The Imperial Japanese Navy grew to be the third largest in the world after the Royal and American navies. In 1902 the two countries signed the Anglo–Japanese Alliance, which was twice renewed before the First World War. However, within twenty-five years this spirit of friendly co-operation had changed radically. Japan experienced increasing isolation, exacerbated by a political crisis that resulted in the assassinations of two prime ministers. The 1920s and 1930s was a time of turmoil and fear in the country.

In 1931, the Japanese took control of mineral-wealthy Manchuria and, besides a half-hearted Chinese reaction, the military began to behave autonomously and influence events in Japanese politics. An attempted coup in 1936, which saw several government ministers assassinated, gave the military even greater power to the extent that an act was passed stating that only serving officers could become military ministers.

The military began to impose its thinking on children's education and primary schools became tools of the state. They were given the title of 'National People's Schools' and reflected their mission of training loyal subject for the Japanese empire. When they graduated, the students were taught vocational skills that would aid in future major militaristic expansion.

The ancient term *bushido* referred to the *samurai* way of life and was loosely akin to the concept of chivalry in Europe. During pre-war and the Second World War the Japanese military sought to use *bushido* to present war as purifying and death as a duty. *Bushido* would provide a spiritual shield to let soldiers fight to the end. Although the original *bushido* called for the *samurai* to be aware of death it was not meant for one to waste one's life in a pointless suicide. This concept was corrupted by the military establishment, which identified *bushido* as the sacrificing of one's life for Japan.

Another scheme of national bonding was the introduction of emperor-based ideology. Before Emperor Hirohito ascended the Japanese throne in 1926, an emperor wielded no political power. He was regarded as a figurehead and leader of the Shinto religion but the military saw in the new emperor another way of binding the Japanese people into manageable and obedient followers of their extreme patriotism. After the war Hirohito claimed not to have had any influence on the actions and behaviour of the military but it was he who had chosen the hard-line General Hideki Tojo as prime minister and was complicit in Japan joining Nazi Germany and Fascist Italy in forming the Axis Powers. To the public he was regarded as a deity who had descended from the gods who created Japan. The Japanese were taught to lay down their lives for the Emperor, rather in the way that today's brainwashed fanatical Islamists are prepared to die for a warped cause.

After the First World War, Japan perceived the apparent decline of Europe as a world power and saw herself as a natural leader for all of east Asia. With the slogan 'Asia for the Asians', Japan began supporting the anti-colonial movements in India and South-East Asia. With the Fall of France in 1940 and the emergence of the Vichy Government, Japan was able to use its alliance with Germany to occupy French Indo–China.

Japan had gone to war with China in 1931 but the fighting was localised, centring mainly in Manchuria. In was not until 1937 and the start of the Second Sino–Japanese War that Japan made great inroads into the country. The ordinary Japanese soldier underwent a harsh training that brutalised him. The so-called 'Rape of Nanking' saw the Japanese perpetrate the most appalling crimes against the population, which was mirrored countless times during the Second World War. Gone was the Japanese Army much admired by the world in 1905 to be replaced by an arrogant force holding its subject populations and prisoners in utter contempt. The Japanese soldier believed in a spiritual essence that could overcome all obstacles. It was called *seishin* or strength of will, which gave him a sense of invincibility that would allow him to defeat even the more technologically and numerically superior foes.

Although the Japanese Army had modernised, its equipment was not on par with those of its enemies. It lacked enough artillery and its tanks were too light. Although it gained a reputation for leaving snipers behind to kill as many of the enemy as possible, these were not good shots. The Arisaka rifle was almost as tall as the average Japanese solder, which affected his aim considerably. The Japanese machine-guns were inferior to the Bren gun, but still accounted for many casualties. The one weapon that was most effective was the one-man grenade launcher, widely used during the Burma Campaign.

The Great Powers demanded that Japan withdraw from China but were actually powerless to do anything about it. The United States, in particular, was a strong supporter of China and had not enjoyed good relations with Japan. It had been wary of Japan since the 1900s, viewing her as an economic threat but happy, nonetheless, to provide it with most of its oil. In order to force Japan to withdraw it imposed a 100 per cent embargo on the sale of oil, which would have crippled the country's economy. Tokyo saw this as a blockade to counter Japanese military and economic strength and, with the possibility of a war with the United States, began stockpiling around fifty-four million barrels of oil.

Without a declaration of war, the Japanese launched a sudden carrier-borne attack on the American Pacific Fleet at Pearl Harbor. The date chosen was 7 December 1941 to coincide with attacks on Hong Kong, the Philippines, Malaya, Dutch East Indies and Singapore. The plan was that the Americans would be unable to react for at least half a year, giving Japan enough time to grab oil from the Dutch East Indies and rubber from Malaya.

The main targets were to sink or cripple America's aircraft carriers, so delaying any retaliatory action until Japan had completed her conquest of South-East Asia. Poor intelligence resulted in the sinking and damaging of several old capital ships, but no aircraft carriers. By good fortune, all the American carriers were at sea on exercise.

The unleashing of a determined Imperial Japanese Army on South-East Asia found the West's colonies in a state of unpreparedness. Victory after victory gave the Japanese a sense of invincibility. They were encouraged in the main by the indigenous populations of the colonies they had purportedly liberated, who were anxious to throw off the European yoke. They sold the idea of a perverted version of the European Union with its Greater East Asia Co-Prosperity Sphere. It would not take long, however, before the natural arrogance, inherent racism and brutality of the Japanese was exposed, but by then it was too late.

The Americans

On 8 July 1853, a squadron commanded by Commodore Matthew Perry of the United States Navy sailed into Tokyo harbour. Perry, on behalf of the United States government, demanded that Japan open her ports to American merchant ships. Having no navy with which to defend itself, Japan agreed to the ultimatum. For the Japanese it was the end of the ancient system and the start of an economic boom. Over the following decades, the Japanese economy expanded at the expense of the traditional Shogunate. In its place was a new centralised government with the Emperor as its symbolic head.

With the help of French and German instructors, the Japanese developed a modern army along European lines. The Imperial Japanese Navy was modelled on the lines of the Royal Navy, who supplied advisors to train the fledgling naval establishment. Having opened up Japan to the rest of the world, America developed a great wariness of Japanese economic success. Furthermore, the US was opposed to Tokyo's expansionist policies and did all it could, short of war, to thwart them. Relations between the two countries became increasingly tense after the invasion of Manchuria and the seizure of much of China in 1937–39.

In 1940, President Roosevelt approved military aid to Generalissimo Chiang Kai-shek's Nationalist Army and supplied experienced personnel including a retired aviator from a flying circus, Clair L. Chenault, who commanded the American Volunteer Group 'The Flying Tigers', the American Military Mission to China (AMMISCA) under Brigadier General John Magruder and Lieutenant General Joseph Stilwell, head of the China–Burma–India theatre and known as 'Vinegar Joe'. America's support was not entirely altruistic. It was hoped that the Nationalist Army would occupy a large number of enemy troops that would otherwise have been involved in the defence of the many Pacific islands that the Americans would have to overcome.

The Chinese Nationalist Army had been driven from all major seaports and forced to retreat south-west to Chungking, on the upper Yangtze gorges some 700 miles from the coast. Here Chiang Kai-shek established the Army's headquarters and new capital of the republic. The Chinese Army was hardly a united unit, with many sections governed by former war lords. Another obstacle was the ongoing fight between the Nationalists and Mao-Tse Tung's communist Army. General Stilwell was scathing about the way that American war material was being used in this civil war instead of against the Japanese.

Another huge problem that became almost insurmountable was the means of supplying American aid. With the coastal ports controlled by the Japanese, and French acquiescence allowing Japan to occupy Indochina, this left the nearest port of Rangoon in southern Burma, which was some 14,000 miles by sea from America. Once material was delivered to Rangoon, it then involved a train journey to the north to Lashio, followed by a tortuous journey on the Burma Road into Kunming in the Chinese province of Yumman. Commanding the army in Yumman was a war lord named General Lung Yun, who had used the Burma Road to amass a fortune from shipping opium and taxing the traffic. This came to an end when the Japanese Army swept into Burma; Rangoon was the first important target it attacked and, at a stroke, this cut off aid to China via the Burma Road.

The severing of the vital link now involved America, which was supporting and supplying Chiang Kai-shek's Nationalist Army with material to continue its fight against the Japanese in China. Unlike the mutual support in the European theatre of the war, there was American resentment for what it saw as supporting the British Empire in Burma and India. Two divisions of the Nationalist Army, unable to reach China, were marooned on the Assam border and under Stilwell's command.

Stilwell proved to be an uncompromising critic of the British Indian Army High Command and expressed the view that the British soldier had behaved in a cowardly manner against the Japanese invader. The open contempt between the two allies meant that there was not to be the close co-operation between the two countries that largely existed on the Europe front. Stilwell was also scathing about his Chinese commander, Chiang Kai-shek, who he thought, correctly, was corrupt and hoarding American Lend-Lease supplies in order to fight his communist rivals.

This left Major General George Stratemeyer, commanding Eastern Air Command, to use his fleet of transport aircraft to ferry material over the eastern end of the Himalayas, colloquially known as 'the Hump'. Not only was this dangerous but also it could not deliver sufficient supplies. The alternative was to link up with the old Burma Road. This strategic route employed the railway that ran north from the port of Rangoon, through Mandalay to Myitkyina. Running parallel was the road that branched off at Mandalay, through Lashio and over the Chinese border into Yunnan Province and Chiang Kai-shek's headquarters at Chungking. If the road and railway was severed at Rangoon it would starve the Chinese Army of vital American supplies.

The original Burma Road linking Burma with south-west China was 717 miles long, with its terminals at Kunming in China and Lashio in Burma. It was built to convey supplies to China during the Second Sino–Japanese War in 1937. Under Stilwell's command, a new road was hacked through the mountains from Ledo in Assam, through the important town of Myitkyina to link up with the old road at Wanddingzhen in the Chinese province of Yunnan. This was accomplished in January 1945, a little too late to make a difference.

With the fall of the British colonies of Malaya and Singapore, her understandable focus was on Germany. Australia now looked for an ally to help keep the Japanese from threatening their homeland. For the Americans, Australia was perfectly situated as a base from which to start their advance on Japan. Over the following years, thousands of American servicemen arrived, trained and moved on to take part in the South Pacific War. The Commander in Chief was General Douglas MacArthur, a vain, outspoken but brilliant soldier, who virtually sidelined his hosts, making it clear that he wanted American-only troops to carry the war north to the Philippines.

A natural resentment grew between the two allies as Australia was tasked with clearing the Japanese from the island countries to her north; Papua New Guinea and later Bougainville and Borneo. For the most part these were mopping up operations as by 1943 the Japanese had become isolated, with supplies and reinforcements denied them by the Allied navies and air forces. However, any suggestion that the Japanese had lost their fanatical fighting spirit was quickly dispelled in the tough campaigns the Australians fought in the jungles. The battles on the Kokoda Trail and Milne Bay still resonate in today's Australia. In the course of three years, the Australians were awarded eleven Victoria Crosses.

The British

Japan had been an ally of the West at the beginning of the twentieth century. The British had even sent Royal Navy instructors including the torpedo expert, Arthur Knyvet Wilson VC, to help build its navy. The British Army had a great admiration for the Imperial Army. After the First World War, senior officers and military attachés were advising the British government not to object to Japanese expansion in China. Britain's rather muted response to Japanese aggression was similar to Neville Chamberlain's 'Peace in our Time' reaction to Nazi Germany's expansion into Czechoslovakia and Austria. Still recovering from the losses of the First World War, the Great Depression, and a reduction in spending on equipment and personnel for her armed forces, Britain was in no position to seek another war.

The Japanese reaction to Britain's perceived weakness was contempt. It took a fellow fascist, Benito Mussolini, to voice what many critics felt, that Britain was 'a decrepit, weary nation which would inevitably give way to a youthful and virile power'. Japan's actions in China and indifference towards Britain were signals to the rest of Asia that Britain would count for less and less in the Far East.

The outbreak of the Second World War and the fall of the European democracies saw Britain standing alone with every chance of being invaded. The fact that it was not was down to several factors; the evacuation of the British Expedtionary Force (BEF) from Dunkirk, the Battle of Britain, the destruction of the flotilla of the *Kriegsmarine*'s new destroyers in the Battle of Narvik, the shift of fighting to North Africa and material supplies from the United States. With her eyes fixed on events in Europe, Britain was totally unprepared to add Japan to the list of enemies. Also, financially Britain could not afford war with Japan. With the British defence policy resting on Singapore, Winston Churchill was confident that the Japanese would not dare to take on such a formidable fortress.

In the confusion of the swift and sudden attacks by the Imperial Army, the weakly defended colonial countries were soon overrun; the Dutch in Indonesia, the French in Indo-China and the British in Malaya. Burma was starved of air cover and could call on only eight old Curtiss Mohawk fighter planes stationed at Calcutta. There were no bomber squadrons and the only armour were old carriers and armoured cars used for training. There were just two British battalions stationed in the country; 1/Gloucester Regiment and 2/King's Own Yorkshire Light Infantry. The local regiments were the Burma Defence Force and the Burma Rifles, both of which were woefully short of equipment.

The invasion of Malaya and the threat to Singapore, Britain's main military base in South-East Asia, caused many of the troop ships bound for the North African campaign to be diverted to defend the 'Gibraltar of the East'. Many arrived as Singapore fell. The Royal Navy sent two of her most powerful battleships to ward off the threat of Japanese landings on the east coast of Malaya. Instead, in a brief encounter with Japanese dive bombers and torpedo planes, the sinking of HMS *Prince of Wales* and HMS *Repulse* eliminated Britain's sea power and her main Far East base at Singapore soon fell. About 80,000 British, Indian and Australian troops became prisoners of war, joining the 50,000 captured in Malaya. Churchill called the fall of Singapore on 15 February 1942, the 'worst disaster and largest capitulation in British military history'.

With the United States now involved with fighting Japan and the main command structure shifting to Australia and New Zealand, Britain was ill-prepared to give much support in manpower or equipment. The German threat was of the greatest concern while events on the other side of the world received scant priority. When Burma was invaded, it was considered very much an Indian Army affair. The campaign was the last great adventure of Britain's imperial Army. Only two British divisions fought in Burma and only one in thirteen of all ground troops was British Army; Gurkhas, East and West Africans, Sikhs, Jats, Baluchis, Madeassis, Dogras, Rajputs, Punjabs and others made up the balance and all were volunteers.

The prevailing view was that Burma was nothing but a buffer between the Japanese troops and India. In Churchill's view, it was not worth fighting in Burma other than to defend the line on the Indian border.

India and its Army

When the Second World War began in September 1939, Britain made India a belligerent without consulting her elected councils. The first the Indian public learned of this was the announcement by Lord Linlithgow, the Viceroy, that war had broken out between His Majesty and Germany. In 1935, the Congress Party had won seven out of eleven provinces and this high-handed approach by the British caused much anger. Jawaharlal Nehru later wrote that: 'One man, and he a foreigner, plunged four hundred millions of human beings into a war without the slightest reference to them.' They responded by declaring that India would not support the war effort until it had been granted complete independence. In 1942, the Congress Party was so sure that Britain could not win that it sponsored mass civil disobedience to support the 'Quit India' campaign. The British authorities responded by imprisoning the entire Congress Party leadership, including Mahatma Gandhi.

The Indian political establishment was far more concerned with the constitutional future than about the war. Even at this early period, there was heated disagreement about whether there should be a united India favoured by the Congress Party or, as the Muslim League demanded, as separate Muslim state. It was against this background that the Indian Army had to operate.

In 1939, the Indian Army was an experienced force, having fought many campaigns on the North West Frontier. It had also performed well in the First World War, having been withdrawn from the mud and misery of the Western Front to fight in the Middle East. The British High Command had no plan for the expansion of India's forces, which numbered about 130,000. The British Army had some 44,000 men serving in India at that time. Their role was to maintain internal security and guard against the perennial threat from Russia through Afghanistan.

Following the Indian Mutiny in 1857–58, the British largely recruited the martial races from western and north-western areas, such as the Punjab, which had shown loyalty during this brutal conflict. There were twenty regular Indian infantry regiments and ten Gurkha, which comprised of two battalions. During the war, the Gurkhas raised a further two battalions each, while the Indian regiments raised up to fifteen each. The Indian Army supplied a brigade each for Singapore, the Persian Gulf, the Red Sea, Egypt and Burma. By the start of the Second World War, Indians were starting to be granted King's Indian Commissions and by the end of the war there were nearly 14,000 Indian serving officers. Although the size of the Army expanded dramatically from 194,373 in 1939 to 2,499,909 in 1945, it was initially bedeviled by a lack of equipment and modern weapons.

When the Japanese invaded Burma, there were only two incomplete and inadequately trained formations in the country; the 1st Burma Infantry Brigade and the 17th Indian Infantry Division. The British Indian Army was to go through a fractious and humiliating two years until the Japanese overreached themselves in 1944 at Imphal and Kohima. In 1942, there was a devastating famine in Bengal, largely brought about by a series of crop failures, a cyclone and the cutting off of rice supplies from Burma. Other contributing factors were the high number of refugees escaping from the Japanese in Burma and the intractable attitude of India's other provisional governments in helping Bengal by supplying surplus foodstuffs.

The 'Quit India' campaign gathered pace and there were large demonstrations by the population for independence, which called on the overstretched British troops to control them. The Congress Party incited anti-Allied feeling, campaigning against recruiting for the Army and the support for the war. Armed gangs attacked railways in Bengal and Bihar, halting the flow of supplies to the Burma front, and it was several weeks before the situation was brought under control.

Subhas Chandra Bose, a former National Indian Congress leader, formed an alliance with Japan to recruit captured Indian soldiers into the Indian National Army (INA). After the fall of Singapore, a British warrant officer, Charles Steel, was captured before being made to slave on the Burma–Siam railway. He recorded that: 'About a quarter of the captured Indians, mostly Sikhs, saw the Japanese as a means of gaining independence from their British masters and became willing collaborators and enthusiastic gaolers.'

Despite all the anti-British pressure in India, there was little backlash when it came to recruiting and that says something for the inner strength of the Indian Army. Why would Indian and Nepalese soldiers be willing to fight and die for a foreign cause? The answer is mainly the regimental system, which worked so well for the British Army. The Indian soldier, once he had 'eaten the salt', or taken the oath that binds him to his regiment, is bound by its code to never bring shame on his comrades or family. Many of the recruits were from peasant stock and took the oath seriously, resulting in gallantry bordering on the suicidal.

Also, the quality of officers had improved enormously since the pre-Mutiny days. Men who passed out in the top thirty at Sandhurst during the 1930s would be offered a commission in the Indian Army. Despite this, the outbreak of the war found the Indian Army at its weakest. The commissioning of junior officers was increased but it would take at least eighteen months for them to perfect their Urdu in order to converse with their soldiers. All troops would have to be trained to fight an entirely different war than they previously expected.

The British Indian Army faced enormous problems just to remain along its 700 mile-long Burmese border. These were lean days but also it afforded an opportunity to build up support with the construction of military roads with labour mostly recruited from the Manipur tea plantations, and the construction of bases, hospitals and airfields. The most pressing priority was to build a new Army.

Chapter 2

The Malayan Campaign

> Singapore, alone of cities in the Far East, gave its inhabitants the illusion of security. Aeroplanes droned overhead during the day ... There was hardly an hour of the day when one looked up into the sky and failed to see an aeroplane of some description ... There were frequent fire practice when the big naval guns that protected the island would hurl their shells many miles out to sea ... The fighting men of many different peoples were to be seen walking the streets of Singapore city ... Singapore seemed stiff with troops ... Singapore was an island. But that did not make it a fortress.
>
> Ian Morrison, The Times' Far East correspondent, describing pre-war Singapore

In the spring of 1940, Britain was on the brink of being invaded by Germany. The BEF had had been pushed out of continental Europe, abandoning most of her weapons and equipment in the retreat to Dunkirk. All eyes were on what Germany would do next. The history of that fraught time shows that Germany had long-term plans to invade the Soviet Union, which happened on 22 June 1940, and regarded Britain as a spent force that could be dealt with later. In Britain it was a nervy period during which her services had to be increased, strengthened and re-equipped.

The collapse of France and Italy's entry into the war focused Britain's attention on the Middle East; in particular the Suez Canal. The Commonwealth countries of Australia, New Zealand and in particular India were called upon to supply troops to combat the Axis Powers in Libya, Egypt, Somalia, Ethiopia and Iraq. Little thought was given to the increasing threat appearing in the Far East.

In 1940, President Roosevelt signed the Export Control Act prohibiting the export of essential defence materials including steel and oil to Japan. The British and Dutch followed suit in an effort to halt a Japanese invasion of China. This put Japan in an untenable position and, thanks to the Americans breaking the Japanese diplomatic code, they learned of the probable consequences. The Japanese Foreign Minister, Teijiro Toyada, responded in his communication with Japan's US Ambassador:

> Commercial and economic relations between Japan and third countries, led by England and the United States, are gradually becoming so horribly strained that we cannot endure it much longer. Consequently, our Empire, to save its very life, must take measures to secure the raw materials of the South Seas.

Faced with the choice between economic collapse and withdrawal from its recent conquests, the Japanese Imperial General Headquarters began planning to seize the oil from the Dutch East Indies (Indonesia) and tin and rubber from Malaya. In Burma they did not plan to overrun the country, but to capture Rangoon, thus cutting supplies to China via the Burma Road. Japan's strategy was to seize these key objectives and establish a defensive perimeter to defeat Allied counter-attacks and negotiate a peace treaty. An essential part of the plan was to attack the US Pacific Fleet at Pearl Harbor, sinking or badly damaging the aircraft carriers, to give Japan time to complete its defensive perimeter.

Without a declaration of war, the Japanese launched a sudden carrier-borne attack on the American Pacific Fleet at Pearl Harbor. The date chosen was 7 December 1941 to coincide with attacks on Hong Kong, the Philippines, Dutch East Indies, Malaya and Singapore. The main targets were to sink or cripple America's aircraft carriers, so delaying any retaliatory action until Japan had completed its conquest of South-East Asia. Although the attack sank and damaged several old capital ships, all the American carriers were at sea on exercise. The raid's commander, Admiral Yamamoto, is reputed to have said: 'I fear all we have done today is to awaken a great, sleeping giant and fill him with a terrible resolve.'

In November, the British became aware of the large-scale build-up of Japanese troops in French Indo-China. Japan explained it away as part of its operations in China. After the French surrendered to Germany, the country was governed by Vichy France, who gave fellow-Axis Japan access to airfields and naval facilities. Japan also coerced the Thai government to let it use the country as a springboard for the invasion of neighbouring Malaya.

The former General Officer Commanding Malaya, Major General William Dobbie (1935–39), warned London of the country's inadequate defences and requested reinforcements, both on the ground and in the air. His recommendations were ignored. The 300–500 aircraft requested was rejected as the priority was for Britain and the Middle East. This left twelve obsolete Brewster Buffalo aircraft in northern Malaya and eighty-three in Singapore facing 439 Japanese. It was further believed that Singapore, with its strong naval presence, and the thick jungle covering most of the Malay peninsular would deter any invasion.

At the time of the Japanese invasion, the air cover had been increased to four squadrons of Blenheim Mk.I and Mk.IV light bombers and the obsolete Buffalos, Vickers Vildebeest and some Fairey Albacore bi-planes. These were hardly a match for the new and nimble Japanese Zero and Oscar fighters.

On Sunday, 7 December 1941 the Japanese attacked Pearl Harbor. Later on the 7th (8 December Far Eastern Time) the Japanese invaded targets in the Western Pacific and South-East Asia. One of the targets was Kota Bharu on the eastern coast of Thailand near its border with Malaya. The Japanese launched an early morning amphibious landing, thus heralding the start of the Asia–Pacific War.

The following day, a pilot of 62 Squadron performed the first Victoria Cross act of the war, but it took until peace came before it was recognised.

ARTHUR SCARF VC

Arthur Stewart King Scarf was born in Wimbledon in south-west London on 14 June 1914. He attended King's College in Wimbledon between 1922 and 1931. One of his masters recalled him as:

> A pleasant boy, maybe not frightfully bracing, but a fine ordinary chap. He never reached the Rugger XV, but played a steady unsensational game in the second team and he was mad about aeroplanes.

A comment of faint praise, but one that pointed to the young Scarf's future. When he left school, he joined an insurance company which he found 'suffocating'. He applied to join the Royal Navy as he enjoyed sailing, but his lack of academic qualifications ruled him out from joining that service. Not deterred, he applied to join the RAF, which at that time was looking for flying personnel. In 1936, he was accepted for pilot training. Rather like his education at King's College, his progress was pedestrian rather than spectacular but he emerged as a competent and reliable pilot.

Scarf graduated on 11 October 1936 and was posted to 9 Squadron at Scampton, Lincolnshire, as a pilot flying the lumbering Handley Page Heyford bomber. There followed a number of moves flying different types of aircraft until, in February 1938, he joined 62 Squadron, which was converting to the more modern Bristol Blenheim Mk.I light bomber.

In August 1939, the squadron was ordered to Singapore for what seemed a quiet posting. Scarf rejoiced in the RAF nickname of 'Pongo' and attained the rank of squadron leader. In February 1941 the squadron changed bases and moved north to Alor Star on the west coast, about 20 miles from the Thai border. There was a hospital adjacent to the airfield where he fell in love with and married one of the nurses named Elizabeth, who he called 'Sal'.

The Japanese had signalled their intention to invade through Thailand and Alor Star was on the expected route they would take. On 8 December 1941, the Japanese came ashore on the beach at Kota Bahru in Thailand and prepared to advance down the Malay peninsular. The five squadrons that were stationed in the north headed for the beachhead but, due to heavy rainstorms, the attack was aborted. Flying offshore, they managed to sink a transport and damage another vessel.

The Japanese filled the Thai airfields close to the border with squadrons of bombers and fighters. Elements of this force attacked Alor Star just as 62 Squadron had returned to be refuelled and rearmed. In the aftermath of this attack, just two Blenheims escaped damage but the ground crew managed to patch up a few more, which the following day were able to fly 45 miles south to Butterworth airfield.

On 9 December, the remnants of Nos. 34 and 62 squadrons were lined up at Butterworth ready to attack the Japanese-held airfield at Singora. 'Pongo' Scarf was the first airborne and circled waiting to be joined by the rest of the squadrons. At that moment a formation of Japanese bombers appeared and dropped bombs on the assembled Blenheims on the apron below, destroying them all.

Rather than abandoning the mission, 'Pongo' decided to make a solo attack on Singora. Flying low, he headed for the border and was soon greeted by enemy fighters.

His mid-upper gunner, Flight Sergeant Cyril Rich, managed to keep the fighters at bay by expending seventeen drums of .303 ammunition. Finally, they reached their target and 'Pongo' flew low over the airfield, dropping his bombs while Rich sprayed the parked aircraft with machine-gun fire.

By now the Japanese were fully alerted and the Blenheim was under constant attack. Riddled with cannon fire, it was inevitable that the crew would fall victim. It was 'Pongo' Scarf who took the brunt of the enemy fire. His left arm was shattered and his unarmoured seat could not stop further rounds wounding him in the back. He slumped forward and his navigator, Flight Sergeant Paddy Calder, called to Rich to come help. With Rich holding him upright, 'Pongo' remained conscious enough to fly the bomber to the nearest airfield, his old base at Alor Star.

With Calder and Rich's help, he managed to crash-land in a paddy field about 100 yards from the hospital. The two crew members lifted 'Pongo' on to the wing as medical staff rushed to help bring him into the hospital. What happened next is best explained by Peter Elphick in his book *Singapore – The Pregnable Fortress*:

> From that event sprang one of the Singapore myths.
>
> The story went that Scarf's wife, Elizabeth, known as 'Sally', was a nurse at Alor Star hospital and that he died in her arms after she volunteered two pints of blood for a transfusion. It made a romantic, if very sad tale.
>
> It is not known who invented the story, but it appears in several books. Sally Scarf did nothing to discredit the story, and why should she? – it made such a tellable tale. Sally was indeed a nurse at Alor Star, but she, along with all the other military wives in the north, had been sent south the day before her husband's death. It was especially necessary to get her away from the front line as she was well into pregnancy.
>
> One of the nurses, Phyllis Briggs, wrote in her diary: 'Suddenly an ambulance arrived; it was Pongo Scarf, a young RAF officer we all knew well. His plane crash-landed in a field nearby. Pongo was badly wounded. He was given a blood transfusion but his condition was hopeless. His wife, Sally, was one of our nursing sisters, but during the previous day had left Alor Star with the rest of the Service wives, so poor Pongo died without seeing her again.
>
> 'I was determined to see that he should be properly buried. We managed to get a coffin from the jail. Another sister came along with me in my Morris 8 and we followed the ambulance bearing the coffin to the local cemetery where a grave had been dug. On my way we met two army padres driving towards us. I stopped the car and asked them would they come with us to say a prayer, so later when I saw Sally I could tell her that we had done all we could.'

Owing to the chaotic nature of the Malayan campaign, Scarf's Victoria Cross was not gazetted until 21 June 1946. His Cross was presented to his widow, Sally, on 30 July 1946 and is now on display at the Royal Air Force Museum at Hendon.

While Pongo Scarf and his fellow flyers were contesting the skies above the Malay peninsular, the men of the 3rd India Corps were fighting an unequal battle against a superior-trained Japanese Army. The 8th Indian Infantry Brigade was swept aside by the enemy troops who landed at Kota Bahru and similarly the 11th Indian Infantry Brigade was forced to retreat from Jitna. It foretold of a depressing series of defeats that pushed the British Indian Army southward.

In April 1941, the 2nd Battalion, 12th Frontier Force Regiment was sent from India to Singapore. With the increasing pressure from the Japanese invasion, the regiment was sent to join the 22nd Indian Infantry Brigade in the protection of the airfield and road link at Kuantan on the east coast. As was the case with all the regiments involved in this campaign, few were fully trained and none were familiar with jungle fighting. In the course of the defence of Kuantan, a Victoria Cross was awarded to the commanding officer of the 2/12 Frontier Force who, despite his wounds, fought on and collected his wounded to bring them to safety.

ARTHUR EDWARD CUMMING VC

Arthur Edward Cumming was born in Karachi on 18 June 1896 the son of a serving Indian Army officer. After his education, he followed his father and entered the Indian Army in 1916 at the age of twenty. In 1917 he joined the 53rd Sikhs and on 7 November 1918 he was awarded the Military Cross for gallantry in Palestine for his part at Megiddo, the battle that finally defeated the Turks.

In 1919, the 53rd Sikhs was renamed the Frontier Force Regiment and Cumming was promoted to captain and then major in 1933. He remained a one-regiment soldier and was promoted to lieutenant colonel in command of 2/12 Frontier Force in March 1941. The following month he was posted to Singapore.

When the Japanese started their invasion, Cumming's command was sent to Kuantan, about halfway down the east coast, to join the 22nd Indian Infantry Brigade. The brigade was thinly spread as they defended a front of thirty-two miles covering the Kuantan airfield, which became the Brigade's HQ, and the road link inland to central Malaya and the capital, Kuala Lumpur. It was about fifty miles off the coast of Kuantan that the pride of the Royal Navy, HMS *Prince of Wales* and HMS *Repulse*, were sunk on 10 December 1941.

The expected Japanese attack started on 29 December and, after being briefly held up, pushed the brigade south across the Kuantan River. The defenders held the line until 3 January, when they attempted to withdraw. The Japanese chose to launch an all-out attack as the brigade started to retreat, causing great confusion, and a rout seemed inevitable. Colonel Cumming moved his regiment to the airfield, where he established his own HQ and attempted to cover the brigade's retreat. The airfield was surrounded by a barbed-wire perimeter fence that the Japanese attacked in waves, hurling firecrackers and firing blindly in the hope of panicking the defenders. The tactic had worked with other inexperienced Indian units but the Frontier Force was made of sterner material. As the Japanese surged around them in the dark, they were able to lob their grenades into the packed ranks, causing many casualties.

Cumming gathered about forty men from his Battalion Headquarters and went on the counter-attack. This group was made up of runners, signallers and clerks who responded to their commanding officer's urging. During a lull in the attacks, they counted forty-two dead Japanese around them.

Cumming took the opportunity to visit the southern flank to assess the situation. Joined by his adjutant, Captain Ian Grimwood, they examined the wire fence and in the moonlight they saw what they thought were coconut windfalls caught on the wire.

On closer inspection they realised that the windfalls were the heads of Japanese soldiers climbing the wire. Unholstering their Webley .455 revolvers, they blazed away, but six Japanese managed to get over the wire and attack the two officers. In the mêlée, the enemy were killed but not before bayoneting Cumming twice in the stomach.

The spirited but doomed defence was described in the history of *The Frontier Force Regiment*:

> There seemed abundant ammunition and the leading enemy waves suffered heavily. Then ammunition began to run short, but in Colonel Cumming's Bren gun carrier were five more boxes. This was now backed up to the trench and Cumming managed to throw them down. As he was getting out of his carrier the driver, Sepoy Albel Singh, handed him a tommy gun, a weapon he had not previously used. However, he turned it on a swarm of Japanese and got back into the trench.

The yellow swarm started another attack from the rear, but stopped at a grass hut behind the position, some climbing on the roof, some inside and some crawling under the raised floor. Cumming told the Subadar-Major to open rapid fire; all the Japs in the hut were slaughtered.

It was now 9pm – Cumming ordered the Subadar-Major to begin the withdrawal, while he went forward to 'C' Company to order its withdrawal. While on the way, he was three more times wounded and fainted. When he came to, the driver told him there was a roadblock in the cutting on the line of withdrawal, and there were now several wounded men in the back of the carrier ... The cutting was held by the Japs, who had put a tree across the road. Cumming told Albel Singh to charge the cutting as the tree was held up by the bank and there was room for the carrier to pass under it.

A mine exploded under the carrier and blew it into the air, but it came down with tracks undamaged and went on. A shower of grenades was thrown from the bank, but these bounced off the rabbit-wire that covered the top of the carrier and burst harmlessly in the road. Machine-gun fire was opened in front and several bullets passed through the carrier ... Rifle fire was also opened and some of the wounded men were wounded afresh. Cumming's right arm was shattered. Finally an armour-piercing bullet pierced the carrier and hit Albel Singh in both thighs. Nevertheless he drove on through the roadblock and the carrier reached Brigade Headquarters, where he and the CO were evacuated to hospital.

Cumming was sent south by rail to the main hospital in Singapore. It says something for his powers of recuperation for he passed himself fit enough to take command of the combined remnants of 2nd and 4th Battalions of 9th Jat Regiment, who had been badly mauled at the Battle of Jitra on 11–12 December.

The relentless Japanese drive on Singapore resulted in events that shamed the British, Australian and Indian nations. As the Japanese crossed to the island, many soldiers deserted and, in the aftermath, commanding officers blamed each other for the debacle.

Cumming discharged himself from hospital, despite being swathed in bandages, and re-joined the 15th Indian Brigade, now reduced to the size of a battalion, to take command of the Jats. They were deployed along the ill-defined Kanji–Jurong line that ran north–south a few miles west of Singapore City.

During early morning fighting, Cumming lost touch with two of his companies, which had been overrun along with the battalions either side of him. He was unaware of this and it was not until he led his remaining 250 men west to a small scrub-covered hill, which was his second objective, that he realised something was wrong. He sent out patrols that confirmed his worst fears; they were completely cut off by the enemy.

When he learned that General Percival and his staff had surrendered to General Tomoyuki Yamashita at the Ford Motor Factory on 15 February, Cumming had other ideas. Leaving his dwindling command to surrender, he led a party of nine British and three Indian officers through the Japanese lines to the coast.

Finding a *sampan* that would take them off the island, the small party sailed to Sumatra. In the weeks before the fall of Singapore, two officers seconded to the Special Operations Executive (SOE) had set up a chain of food and water dumps for just such a situation. Using trusted locals, those refugees in small boats that reached the mouth of the Indragari River could travel halfway across the island and then walk overland to the port of Padang on the west coast. Here Cumming and his companions managed to catch a small Dutch steamer crowded with fifty evacuees and, avoiding Japanese naval patrols, sailed the eight days to Colombo in Ceylon.

Many others who had left Singapore by ship were not so lucky. Of the forty-four vessels that set out for Sumatra, forty were sunk by the Japanese Navy with the loss of about 4,000 lives.

Cumming was able to complete his hospital treatment in the peace of Ceylon. When he was well enough he was promoted to temporary brigadier and given command of 63rd Indian Infantry Brigade, 17 Indian Division, which had suffered greatly in the retreat through Burma in 1942. Cumming joined them at Tiddim on the Burma–India border, where they were involved in sending out patrols to attack the over-extended Japanese Army.

In 1943, he was awarded the Order of the British Empire (OBE) and in 1944 he was moved to the other side of India to command Dehra Dun Sub-Area. One of the largest internment camps was located in this region where German, Austrian and Italian nationals were detained. One of the prisoners who escaped was the Austrian mountaineer Heinrich Harrer, who wrote a best-selling book, *Seven Years In Tibet,* later made into a film.

Brigadier Arthur Cumming retired in 1947. He was appointed Volunteer Superintendent of Police in Cyprus during 1956–59. He was living in Edinburgh when he died on 10 April 1971 and cremated at Warriston Crematorium, Edinburgh. His medal group is displayed at the Imperial War Museum.

The relentless Japanese advance of 9 miles each day pushed the Allies back to Malaya's southern-most state of Johore. One of the reasons for the swift advance was pedal-power. Although the Japanese had landed without bicycles, they commandeered those belonging to the bicycle-mad Malays. This enabled them to move quicker that the defence-minded British Empire military and to appear behind their positions. This caused the British to be constantly in retreat to avoid being encircled. Japanese air superiority caused havoc among the green troops, who became totally demoralised by the almost continuous strafing and bombing.

Apart from the performance of Arthur Cumming's Frontier Force at Kuantan, the only spirited opposition came from the Australian 2/19th Battalion, whose commander was awarded the Victoria Cross.

CHARLES ANDERSON VC

Charles Groves Wright Anderson was born on 12 February 1897 at Newlands, Cape Town, South Africa. He was the third of five children born to Alfred Anderson, an English-born auditor and later newspaper editor, and his Belgian-born wife Emma (née Trossaert). In 1900, the family moved to the East Africa Protectorate (Kenya) and farmed at Mount Margaret near Nairobi.

In 1907, Anderson was sent to England to be educated at St Brendan's College, Bristol. In 1914, on completion of his education, he returned to Africa and joined the local volunteer force at the outbreak of the Great War. In 1915, he joined the Calcutta Volunteer Battery, which had been sent from India to serve in the East Africa Campaign.

On 13 October 1916, Anderson was commissioned as a temporary lieutenant in the 2nd Battalion, 3rd King's African Rifles. It was soon apparent that he displayed outstanding leadership qualities in the lengthy pursuit of General von Lettow-Vorbeck's German-led Askaris. Anderson was awarded the Military Cross for his part in the fighting at Namacurra in Portuguese East Africa (Mozambique) in July 1918. He was demobbed in 1919 with the rank of temporary captain and returned to the family farm. He later served as chairman of the Kenya Settler's Association in the Rift Valley district.

Anderson suffered from myopia and increasingly had to wear stronger glasses, but this did not deter him from his passion for big game hunting. In 1931, he married Edith Marian Tout, the niece of Sir Frederick Tout, a prominent solicitor and cattleman from New South Wales, Australia. During a visit to his wife's home country, Anderson was sufficiently impressed that he decided to migrate with his family and purchase a 2,000-acre grazing property near Young, close to Sir Frederick Tout's property.

In March 1939, he joined the Citizen Military Forces and was appointed captain in the 56th Battalion (Riverina Regiment). He was promoted to major in October and transferred in July 1940 as second-in-command of the 2/19th Battalion, Australian Imperial Force (AIF). In early 1941, the battalion was on the way to Singapore and on 1 August he was promoted to lieutenant colonel in command of 2/19th. Although he was bespectacled and softly spoken he soon commanded respect. He was one of the few officers who had experience of jungle fighting and trained his men in bayonet use and snap shooting, which he had employed in his hunting of big game.

Lieutenant General Arthur Percival, GOC Malaya Command, had overseen the erosion of his command until only Johore State lay between the Japanese and Singapore. The 2/29th Battalion had put up a good fight on 14 January at Gemes, when it had destroyed six enemy tanks, which was captured by a newsreel cameraman. This brief respite did little to halt the Japanese progress, where the imminent danger lay to the west along the Maur River. In command of this area was Brigadier Horacio Duncan of the 45th Indian Infantry Brigade. His HQ was a bungalow at Bakri and few miles south of Maur that was destroyed by a low-level air attack and the entire staff were killed or badly wounded. Miraculously, Duncan survived but was so severely concussed he was unable to assume command.

The 2/19th arrived at Bakri of 18th January and Anderson found that he had assumed command of the brigade. That evening Bakri came under fire from the Japanese Guards Division, which had landed south of Maur. Gathering together the remnants of the 45th Brigade and 2/29th AIF, they resisted the Japanese attacks but all the time sustaining casualties. On the 20th, Anderson decided to make a fighting withdrawal to the bridge at Parit Sulong. From there he hoped to reach the important crossroads at Yong Peng and the Australian lines.

Along the way, the column had to fight its way past two roadblocks. The first was not astride the road but on a low ridge of rubber trees that dominated it. Pinned down by enemy fire, Anderson called for his men to charge and to sing *Walzing Matilda*. The solders did go forward but not at a charge. They crept closer until they were within grenade-throwing distance and killed some of the enemy.

Anderson then led some men to silence a couple of machine-gun nests. Stalking them as he did as a big game hunter, he destroyed the nests and shot two Japanese with his Webley revolver. The second barricade was constructed from gutted transport vehicles that a 25-pounder managed to demolish, allowing the column through. The defenders were soon despatched by axes and grenades.

It took two days to travel the eleven miles to Parit Sulong and the all-important bridge. To their dismay the Japanese had arrived on the other side and blocked it. Anderson ordered further attacks on the bridge but his weakened force was unable to break through. Anderson radioed General Gordon Bennett, the commander of 8th Australian Division at Yong Peng to come to their aid.

Bennett's reply was discouraging:

> Regret there is little prospect of any attack to help you. Special party, if successful, should have appeared before this. Twenty of your men and many Indians have already returned through the jungle to road which is at present in our possession. You may at your discretion leave wounded with volunteers, destroy heavy equipment and escape. Sorry unable to help your heroic effort. Good luck.

Trapped, Anderson was forced to abandon his badly wounded in the hopes that the Japanese would care for them. The only way left to reach Yong Peng, on the main arterial road to Singapore, was through thick jungle. Ordering his men to disperse in small groups and try to reach their destination, Anderson's men left the bridge and the 150 badly wounded and melted into the jungle.

Tragically, the Japanese chose to behave in a brutal and inhumane way towards the helpless wounded. In what became known as the Massacre of Parit Sulong, they bayoneted, shot or doused in petrol and burned all but two of the wounded. These two managed to escape and tell of the harrowing fate of their comrades.

The men began to trudge their way seven miles through the jungle to Yong Peng. There was a track that led past a disused tin mine that was not blocked by the Japanese and the survivors managed to re-join the main body of the AIF. Only 400 of the 2/19th and 2/29th, together with a few soldiers from the 45th Indian Brigade, got back to safety to Yong Peng; less than a quarter of the number at the start of the battle. The troops had been under constant fire for six days and the heroic performance of the 8th Division at Maur and Gemas was in marked contrast to the behaviour of the raw recruits on Singapore.

Anderson was sent to Johore Baharu, opposite Singapore Island, to reconstitute his depleted command but was almost immediately struck down with dysentery and hospitalised. He did not manage to re-join the 2/19th until 13 February. The previous day it was announced that he had received the Victoria Cross; the only Australian commander in the Second World War to be so honoured. This good news was tempered by the surrender of Singapore two days later.

Anderson went into captivity. In May, he was first sent by crowded prison ship up the Tenasserim strip in Burma to repair an airstrip. From there he was moved to work on the notorious Burma–Siam Railway, where he was in charge of 3,000 Australians working the northern section of the railway. Like the Colonel Toosey, in charge of prisoners working on the infamous Bridge over the River Kwai, Anderson negotiated (slightly) better treatment for his men and his conduct lifted the prisoners' morale. He was finally freed after the Japanese surrender and repatriated in November 1945.

Anderson received his Victoria Cross on 8 January 1947 in Sydney from the Governor General of Australia. He returned to farming and took over a large property that his wife had inherited. He became an advocate for rural issues and the rehabilitation of returning servicemen. He also entered politics and served on various joint committees.e became H He retained his military links and became honorary Colonel of the 56th and later 4th Battalion. At the invitation of the old British 17th Division, he visited the Muar–Parit Sulong battlefield.

At the age of ninety-one, Anderson passed away at his home at Red Hill, Canberra, on 11 November 1988. His funeral was conducted with full military honours.

Chapter 3

The Fall of Singapore

As the Japanese were poised to attack Singapore, the naval dockyard had become a ghost base. The incessant bombing had forced the naval ships to leave. The only ones left were small patrol vessels and a motley collection of steamships preparing to evacuate civilians to Batavia.

THOMAS WILKINSON VC
Born on 1 August 1898, at West Bank, Widnes on the northern bank of the River Mersey, Thomas Wilkinson was the youngest of five brothers. His father was the captain and part-owner of the sailing sloop *Irene,* which sailed the Mersey and the adjacent canals. Leaving the local school when he was fourteen, he was employed as a grocer's errand boy until he joined his brothers and worked as a cabin boy and deckhand on his father's vessel. This was employed to carry salt along the Mersey and the canals from Northwich in Cheshire to the Widnes chemical factories; later to merge into Imperial Chemical Industries.

With the outbreak of the First World War, Tam as he was commonly named, joined the Merchant Navy and served as quartermaster on the Blue Funnel ship *Alcinous*, which was converted to a troopship. After the war, he travelled to the Far East and was employed by Jardine in Hong Kong to sail with its Indo–China Steam Navigation Company. Moving up the promotion ladder, he successfully sat for his Master's Certificate around 1936 and was given command of SS *Hang Sang* plying the China coast. His chief officer, John Littler, wrote of him:

> He did not drink, which was remarkable in China. He was tremendously keen on physical fitness and he was universally liked … he had contracted TB when he first arrived in China and this would explain his abstemious and non-smoking nature.

Wilkinson was on home leave when the Second World War broke out and he returned to China to offer his service to the Royal Navy. Many Merchant Navy officers volunteered at the beginning of the war and were commissioned in the Royal Navy Reserve. One such was Richard Stannard, who won the VC during the Norwegian Campaign in 1940. These Merchant Navy men were not the sort you find in the ward room on HM vessels, having never undergone Royal Navy training, but were nonetheless highly experienced seamen. Wilkinson, from a Lancastrian working-class background, had travelled the China Sea for nearly twenty years and was an invaluable asset to the Navy.

Temporary Lieutenant Wilkinson was given command of *Li Wo,* a 1,100-ton flat-bottomed passenger steamship built for the Indo–China Steamship Navigation Company in Hong Kong in 1938 for service on the Yangtze River. She was commandeered by the Royal Navy to be used as an auxiliary patrol vessel. She was armed with an old 4-inch gun mounted on a platform at the bow, two machine-guns and a depth charge thrower. She was sent to Singapore, where she undertook routine patrols around the island's waters.

With a Japanese victory all but inevitable, evacuation of civilians was ordered by sea to Batavia (Jakarta), the capital of the Dutch East Indies, and so far unoccupied by the Japanese. This mini-Dunkirk was a hazardous undertaking as the Japanese had command of the sky and her Navy the sea. Shortly before the surrender, HMS *Li Wo* was ordered by the Navy to sail to Batavia with eighty-four men, mostly naval reservists, including several survivors from the *Prince of Wales* and *Repulse,* five soldiers, two men from the RAF and sixteen Malays.

Loading lorries with provisions, Chief Petty Officer Charlie Rogers took the party to Keppel Harbour, where *Li Wo* was riding at anchor about a mile offshore. Included in their ranks was Leading Seaman Tom Parsons, who recalled:

> Once aboard, CPO Rogers was given an order by Sub Lt Stanton to detail all ratings for their Action Stations and duties. Being that I was the only Gunlayer rating, I was appointed Gunlayer of the 4-inch gun.

Li Wo sailed out of Singapore in the early hours of 13 February and having paused before passing through the Durian Strait minefield in daylight, set course for Batavia.

Her progress was far from smooth. During the afternoon, around 13.20 hours, *Li Wo* was subjected to the first of a series of attacks carried out by Japanese aircraft.

Parsons, writing from memory recalled:

> The first day at sea we were attacked by enemy aircraft on four occasions and every one of those four attacks was by a single aircraft only. They were fighter-bombers who [sic] dropped one bomb and then flew off. Thanks to the skill of Lt. Wilkinson ... all bombs missed.

On the following day, he recalled two further air attacks, the first by a single fighter-bomber, which dropped one bomb and missed, and the second, about two hours later, involving two aircraft, each of which failed to score a hit with their single bombs. In the course of the latter action, Parsons replied with the 4in gun and his one shot was close enough to deter any further attack.

Of course, it is not unusual for two accounts of the same action to differ. In his book, *Stand By to Die*, an account written by A.V. Sellwood in 1962 based on the recollections of Lieutenant Ron Stanton, *Li Wo* was attacked by fifty-two aircraft in one raid, which varies wildly from the accounts by Parsons and Rogers. As far as both Parsons and Rogers were concerned, the mass attacks in the book were pure invention that did not stand up to the barest scrutiny. Parsons insisted:

> If we had been attacked by 52 planes, we wouldn't have lasted five seconds let alone five minutes. *Li Wo* was a small, insignificant vessel of 1000 tons, so can anyone believe that a commanding officer would deploy 50 aircraft on a mission to sink such a small ship and not succeed in sinking her? *Li Wo*'s old 4-inch gun had a maximum elevation of no more than 60 degrees and with just two Vickers Lewis guns (one port and one starboard) what chance would any ship with only those armaments have to fight off 52 Jap planes?

Wilkinson anchored for the night near a small island, and in the morning *Li Wo* steered first for Singkep Island, where Wilkinson hoped to see out the hours of daylight before making a dash across the Banka Straits, then known as 'bomb alley'.

In the event, *Li Wo* left earlier than intended having survived a low-level bombing attack by two aircraft. A little under three hours later an enemy seaplane appeared but did not attack. According to Parsons, it was:

> A Jap reconnaissance plane, with no bombs, as we were a sitting target.

> We then immediately got under way again. Between 4.30pm and 5pm, we sighted smoke on the horizon. It was a convoy. The captain asked if anyone could recognise any Jap warships. I told him I could as I (had) served on the China Station (1936–38) and was familiar with the silhouettes of Jap warships. I was told to come to the bridge. I did so, and he handed me his telescope. I recognised one Jap light cruiser and two Jap destroyers. Without looking any further, I told him: 'Japanese.' He asked me if I was certain. I replied: 'Yes sir, without any doubt.' With that, I was told to return to the gun …

Parsons then said he made a point of checking the ammunition available to him. According to him, it consisted of six semi-armour piercing shells, four graze fuse shells, three anti-aircraft shells and three practice shells. Parsons was adamant that the reference to there being only thirteen practice shells – originally made by F.G. Ritchie, Singapore's deputy superintending sea transport officer, and repeated in Wilkinson's VC citation – was entirely erroneous and misleading. He insisted that no captain worth his salt would go to sea without live ammunition. Parsons added:

> Prior to the attack on the Jap convoy, the only action the *Li Wo* fought was against single fighter-bomber aircraft and on one occasion against two fighter-bombers. In addition to four 'graze fuse' shells, six live armour-piercing shells were standing upright on deck, one in each rack, aft of the breakwater on the port side. Three AA shells stood on the starboard side … I thought, 'Christ, is that all we have?' realising the hopelessness of the situation. I then reported this to the captain, from the gun to the bridge … and I then resumed my action station, sight and range set, waiting to open fire.

Manning the gun with him, according to his recollection, were: Leading Seaman Bumett (breech worker), Leading Seaman Hadley (sight-setter), an unknown stoker (trainer) and Leading Seaman Bennet, Leading Seaman Bentley, Leading Seaman Wilcox and another unnamed stoker providing ammunition supply. A ginger-haired New Zealand sub-lieutenant, who he later discovered to be Edgar Neil Derbridge, later joined them as rammer and, he stressed, the captain of the gun was Chief Petty Officer Charlie Rogers.

According to Parsons, as *Li Wo* closed on the Japanese convoy, Tam Wilkinson addressed the team manning the 4in gun from the bridge. Parsons remembered:

I have never ever forgotten those words. They have always been clearly imprinted on my mind. He said, 'Ahead of us is a Jap convoy. I am going to attack it. I am going to take as many of those Jap bastards with us as possible.' In reply, Parsons observed, 'Look, sir, we have only 13 high explosive shells that can do any damage. We have no range finder ... It will be gunlayer firing, gunlayer's control. I think it will be best if we use the blank practice shells to find our range and target'. He thought for a moment and then said, 'it might be a good idea and then it might not be. If we can get in close without being recognised it will be a shot wasted.' We loaded a semi-armour piercing shell and I ordered that the three AA shells be set at fuse two, and I would aim at the super structure.

We opened fire. Our first shot was over the target. I ordered fix sight, rapid salvoes. I know that at least three of our five remaining shells hit our target, a troop transport. Soon that ship was blazing furiously. By now, we were right amongst the convoy, but our ammunition was expended. I will always remember a RAF sergeant who manned the twin Vickers Lewis machine-guns on the starboard side. His devastating fire wiped out the four-man gun's crew of the second target which the *Li Wo* rammed and sank. That RAF sergeant was unknown, unrecognised.

Steam was now escaping from the *Li Wo* and we were stationary. We soon came under fire from those Jap warships (but) their gunnery was really lousy. Shell after shell screamed overhead. We could not hit back. All we could do was take it. How long it was before they hit us, I don't know. Looking back, it seemed ages, but in reality it must have been five to 10 minutes and when they did find the range it was all over. The *Li Wo* listed to starboard and sank stem first ...

Parsons was hit in the chest and Rogers suffered a leg wound. Parsons was the only one to state that the vessel rammed was not the one set afire. Rogers insisted it was and *Li Wo* had also inflicted considerable damage to the guns, crew and bridge complement of at least three smaller ships as well as the transport that was set afire, rammed and eventually abandoned. In Rogers' account, *Li Wo* had deliberately rammed the damaged ship, from which she fired at the small river boat. His report of the action continues:

We hit her at top speed amidships and became interlocked – our bows being buckled back. We were now really at close quarters. A machine-gun duel took place, which was fast and furious, with many men being killed or wounded. The Li Wo gunners eventually wiped out two guns which caused the Japanese to abandon ship, which by this time was well ablaze.

In the course, of this desperate fight the Japanese light cruiser, *Yura*, one of the convoy escorts, circled round behind *Li Wo* and closed in at high speed for the kill:

> We eventually became disentangled from the crippled Japanese ship and set course away from the cruiser, noted Rogers. The cruiser opened fire … and we then noticed that the enemy destroyer that had been heading for us from the opposite direction was turning away. No doubt she knew that we were at the mercy of the cruiser as we were out-gunned and out-ranged.

Even so, *Li Wo* continued to resist, helped in part by the wayward firing of the enemy gunners. Rogers recalled some of the Japanese salvoes falling as far as 300 yards wide. As the range closed the riverboat was increasingly hit, causing many casualties. Eventually, after about the ninth salvo, Wilkinson accepted the inevitable and ordered the survivors to abandon ship. All who were able jumped overboard:

> The last sight I had of the *Li Wo* as she started on her last voyage to the bottom of the ocean was something I shall never forget. Her Ensigns were still flying and the Captain was standing on the bridge and, although she was listing to port, she was still under way. Then, suddenly, she disappeared …

Li Wo might have gone, but the ordeal of those members of her crew and passengers still struggling for their lives in the midst of the Japanese convoy was far from over. With no land in sight, the survivors searched for anything in the water that might keep them afloat:

> Eventually, in the distance, a lifeboat was sighted, bobbing up and down in the swell. Leading Seaman Thompson and myself struck out towards it, but as we were approaching it, we noticed a ship from the convoy coming towards us. We swam away as fast as possible and, on glancing back, saw the ship ram the lifeboat.

Around this area were about thirty men struggling for their lives, little realising that the worst was yet to come:

> The Japanese were not content to leave us to our fate, but circled around and opened up a murderous attack with machine-guns, hand-grenades, coal and wood. It was just plain 'cold-blooded murder'. Amidst the hell, men could be heard crying out for mercy, but still the Japanese continued their 'sport'. I lay on my back with my arms out-stretched and luckily no more shot came in my direction.

After what seemed an eternity, the ship moved off, leaving the ones who had cheated death once more to their fate. The nine survivors made toward the half-submerged lifeboat.

> Lt Stanton had a bullet hole through the back of his head. Another officer was wounded in the stomach and had part of his hand shot away. PO Huntley had his foot blown off and was in a very bad condition. We helped each other into the lifeboat, which was now submerged to the gunwale, and tried to make the best of a bad situation. There were no oars, food or medical supplies. All we could do was let the boat drift. As we drifted, we saw the ship that we had crippled. It was drifting and still on fire. We spent a very cold night, and as dawn broke, one of the officers, whom I had been holding in my arms, died from his severe shrapnel wounds. I informed Lt Stanton, who helped me take off his lifebelt and put him over the side …

There followed two days of drifting without food and in shark-infested waters before the survivors glimpsed their first sight of land, about sixteen miles away. At one point, a Japanese destroyer approached them, but it departed after no more than a cursory glance. By then, the boat was barely afloat and Stanton, together with another officer, decided to risk swimming towards the destroyer – a distance Rogers estimated at two miles.

That left six men: Rogers, Petty Officer Huntley, Leading Seamen Wilden and Spencer, a Malay called Tel, and an unnamed soldier. That number quickly became four following the death from wounds of Huntley and the loss of the soldier overboard. Spencer then decided to make an attempt to swim ashore, leaving just Rogers, Wilden and the Malay to take their chances with the tides. Rogers wrote:

> As luck would have it, another partly submerged boat drifted towards us just before dark. We swam towards it and found that it was a Naval whaler, split down the centre, but preferable to our boat because it had oars and a sail. We boarded her, rigged her for sailing,

and had just picked out a sight of land to sail for, when we heard yells and shouts. They came from two rafts we had not previously seen. On one raft there were three men, on the other, four men. They were also survivors from the *Li Wo* and we were glad to find that they had a tin of biscuits with them. I could only let a few on board the whaler and then we took the rafts in tow. We were helped by a strong wind which sprang up, but the boat was submerged to the gunwale, so we were actually sitting in water all the time.

During the night, a Japanese patrol boat came close, but with the survivors slipping quietly over the lee side they failed to detect them. Rogers added:

My aim was to reach the land ahead of us, but the tides were so strong that we could only drift with them. At about 2am, we sighted land straight ahead, so I put six men on the oars and we started rowing for our lives. We were still rowing four hours later, but I knew we were getting nearer to the shore.

Rogers' party, who by now included Parsons, struck land on Banka Island, not far from a point where a force of Japanese was landing. For the time being they were ignored. A little after dawn a small group, led by Rogers, and including Leading Seamen Parsons and Wilcox and A.B. Smith, ran into a Japanese patrol and were promptly taken prisoner.

The *Li Wo* survivors were marched to Muntok, where a school had been converted into a temporary prison camp. There, Stanton and Thompson later joined them. According to Sellwood's account, they had reached shore via a raft and a British launch, which was operating under Japanese parole. The two officers who had swum off with them had also reached Banka island safely only to be murdered by bandits.

Cruel captivity followed, during which disease and malnourishment claimed more of *Li Wo*'s gallant company. It was not quite the end of the heroic saga. Towards the end of February 1942, Tom Parsons joined a small band of prisoners set on making a break for freedom. After numerous adventures, the four-strong party led by Lieutenant Colonel John Dalley, a senior Malayan policeman given command of a force of Chinese irregulars during the Singapore fighting, succeeded in reaching Java. They were betrayed and recaptured but fortunately they were able to convince their interrogators that they were fugitives from Singapore. They said that their ship had been sunk rather than confess to being escapers, for whom the punishment would have been almost certain death.

Sent first to Glodok Jail in Batavia, Parsons was later moved to Tanjong Priok prison camp before eventually winding up at Palembang No.2 camp, where he was among hundreds of PoWs set to work on building an airfield. Parsons saw no other *Li Wo* survivors for another three years until May 1945 when he was moved to Palembang No.1 camp, where his remaining crewmates had been transferred. His reunion proved a short one. Three days later, he was among a party shipped to Singapore and Changi jail, where he remained until the end of the war.

Repatriated to England in October 1945, Parsons was discharged from the Navy the following June as being unfit for further service. A few months later, he heard a news announcement on the wireless that Lieutenant Thomas Wilkinson, RNR, had been awarded the Victoria Cross. His Cross was presented to his brother, William, by the King at Buckingham Palace on 28 January 1947. It is now displayed in the Lord Ashcroft Gallery at the Imperial War Museum.

The defeat in Johore made the fall of Singapore inevitable. On 8 February 1942, the Japanese landed in darkness on the north-west of the island. Their main attacks were made down the Kranji Creek and Pasir Laba, where the Australian 19th and 29th Battalions bore the brunt of the assault. It took just seven days for the Japanese to roll back the British defenders before all the forces surrendered on 15 February.

The Fall of Singapore was the greatest military humiliation since General Cornwallis surrendered to the Americans on 18 October 1781 at Yorktown. Many factors contributed to this shameful defeat; poorly trained soldiers led by uninspiring commanders, absence of air cover and the sense that the population was witnessing one of the great tragedies of the war.

General Percival has been selected as the man who lost Malaya and Singapore. This was only partly justified. He cut rather a ridiculous figure, being tall and thin with prominent teeth and a weak chin. He was lacking in vigour and conviction and was regarded as a completely negative person. Nonetheless, his record showed him to be a courageous soldier; he had won the DSO and Bar and the MC in the First World War. He would have made an adequate commander in peacetime but was out of his depth in the situation in which he found himself. The Australian commander, General Gordon Bennet, was temperamentally unsuitable for a semi-diplomatic command and was as scathing about British officers as he was of Australian regulars. He caused further controversy when he relinquished his command in order to escape from Singapore. The fellow high command officers were hardly better and it was largely left to the battalion commanders to put up any resistance.

The British capitulated a mere seventy days after the Japanese invaded Malaya. This landed the victors with the problem of what to do with 130,000 men they had captured; something for which they had not prepared. In the short-term, the prisoners were marched off to the barracks complex at Changi, where they waited until their captors decided what to do with them. Having shunned the Geneva Convention, the Japanese made use of such a captive workforce by sending them to build the Burma–Siam Railway or work in mines as slave labourers.

Throughout the Malaya/Singapore campaign, the British lost about 8,780 killed or wounded and a total of 130,000 captured. Those Indians who were captured made for rich recruitment by the Japanese-sponsored pro-Independence Indian National League led by Rashi Bihari Bose. Of the 40,000 Indian soldiers who went into captivity in Singapore, 30,000 volunteered to join the newly established Indian National Army commanded by Subhas Chandra Bose. About 7,000 fought with the Japanese Army in Burma, some were prison guards, but the majority were shipped to the South Pacific and used as labourers, suffering as much as the Allied prisoners.

The following three years were ones of terror for the ordinary population of Singapore. The *kempeitai* (secret police) established a 'purge through purification' programme that claimed the lives of between 25,000 to 50,000 ethnic Chinese in Singapore and Malaya. Schools were established and the population was forced to learn Japanese. Radio and newspapers proclaimed only pro-Japanese propaganda and listening to Western news was punishable by death.

During this terrible occupation, there was retaliation by an Allied commando group called Z Force. In September 1943 the unit, led by Major Ivan Lyon, managed to infiltrate Singapore Harbour and sink and damage seven ships. The following year it repeated the act of sabotage when it sank three ships. Unfortunately, Major Lyon and thirteen men were killed in the fighting that followed and ten others were captured and executed.

Nearing the end of the war, their exploits were not in vain as another daring attack by a small X-Craft submarine penetrated the Japanese defences and sank a heavy cruiser, resulting in two VCs being awarded.

JAMES MAGENNIS VC
During the Second World War only three junior ratings were awarded the Victoria Cross: Able Seaman William Savage at St Nazaire and

Leading Seaman Jack Mantle on board the auxiliary cruiser HMS *Foylebank* at Portland. Both died in action, which left Leading Seaman James Magennis as the only junior rating to win a VC and survive the war.

It is nearly seventy years since that remarkable day in Ebor Street, Belfast, when everyone celebrated his achievement, but few people in the city now remember James Magennis. For a brief time he brought both sides of the religious divide together. When Magennis returned to Belfast in 1949, the euphoria at the end of the war had evaporated and Northern Ireland was once again setting hard into its old ways.

James Joseph Magennis was born in the Catholic area of West Belfast on 27 October 1919. His home in Ebor Street was in one of the many side roads that spread from the Falls Road and Springfield Road, both of which became all too familiar to the British public during the Troubles of the 1970s and '80s.

Belfast in Magennis's childhood was going through great political, religious and sectarian agitation. Although the First World War was over, Ireland was still in a state of turmoil. The Anglo–Irish Treaty of 1922 divided the country into a six-county Northern Ireland and a twenty-six county Irish Free State (later, Republic). This did not stop the unrest; Belfast was a hotbed of sectarian tensions and many from both sides lost their lives.

James, or Mick as he became better known, attended St Finian's School on the Falls Road. He did not join in the team sports of Gaelic football or hurling but significantly excelled at swimming; something that played a part in him becoming a Royal Navy frogman. At the age of fifteen Magennis enlisted in the Navy and travelled to the Suffolk training establishment of HMS *Ganges* near the port of Harwich. After nine months of arduous training, First Class Boy Seaman Magennis qualified and, on 6 March 1936, joined the battleship HMS *Royal Sovereign* at Portsmouth.

After just three weeks at sea, he was transferred to the cruiser *Dauntless* and, when he reached Ceylon, he was drafted again to join the 7,550-ton cruiser *Enterprise*. The following year he gained promotion to able seaman and transferred to the old First World War aircraft carrier *Hermes*. However, after serving on board four ships that had been built during and just after First World War, Magennis was at last to get a new one.

With the outbreak of war, Magennis was drafted to the newly built 1,670-ton destroyer, HMS *Kandahar*. After months of patrolling in the North Sea, *Kandahar* had her first encounter with the enemy. She left Greenock with her sister ship, HMS *Kelly*, commanded by Lord Louis Mountbatten, and several other vessels.

As dusk was falling on 9 May 1940, there was a tremendous explosion. A torpedo smashed into *Kelly's* plates on the forward boiler-room and burst with a terrifying blast. A great lick of flame roared up into the night, the mast head silhouetted black and stark against its flare. Men lay dead, dying wounded and stunned. *Kelly* canted over to starboard in a cloud of hissing steam and smoke with a great hole torn in her side from her keel almost to her upper deck.

Then out of the blackness, a German E-boat appeared going at forty knots. The whole boat hit the *Kelly's* sloping deck, then disappeared in the darkness astern and sank.

At dawn the following dawn, *Kandahar* put her stern alongside *Kelly* and took off the wounded. Magennis recalled his feelings in 1969 in an interview:

> Fear is a word people never mention to me, as though they don't think I could ever be afraid. But fear came to me when the smoke of battle had died down; when all that lingered was a dawn mist that hung like funeral crepe ... and death. The action was over. Enemy E-boats had torpedoed *Kelly*. Her sister ship *Kandahar* was edging alongside to take off the injured. It was a sight of the dead and dying that struck real fear into me for the first time in my life. It made me sick. It paralysed me. I remembered the remedy my old gunners mate gave for everything – 'fight it'.

The crippled ship was towed back to the River Tyne, where she was repaired. On 21 February 1941, in company with sister ship *Kimberley* and the cruiser *Manchester,* she captured the German blockade runner SS *Wahehe* off Iceland.

On 22 May 1941, *Kandahar* was again involved in rescuing survivors. This time they were from the destroyer HMS *Greyhound,* sunk during the Battle of Crete. Under heavy air attack, *Kandahar* was forced to abandon its rescue attempt with many of the survivors still in the water. In another incident during this incessant aerial onslaught, the destroyer *Juno* was hit and broke in half. Magennis showed his mettle when he repeatedly dived into fuel oil and burning diesel to bring out shipwrecked men.

Two of *Kandahar's* sister ships were lost that day; *Kashmir* and the renovated but unlucky *Kelly*. After seeing much action in the Mediterranean theatre, *Kandahar's* luck, too, ran out. On 19 December 1941, she struck a mine and the crew were ordered to abandon ship. HMS *Jaguar* was on hand to rescue the crew and later sank the stricken *Kandahar*.

When Magennis finally returned to the UK, he learned that he was to be drafted to the cruiser HMS *Belfast*. To his great annoyance, he found himself sent to the HMS *Defiance* in Devonport for torpedo training as a step to entering the Submarine Service. Magennis heard that new smaller submarines were being built and that they were looking for volunteers for special service. The little boats were to be called X-craft and carried four crew members, one of whom was to be a diver. Magennis volunteered for special service on 15 March 1943 and was sent to the high security training facility at Loch Striven in Scotland.

The X-craft were 50ft in length, 35 tons in weight with a diameter of 5½ft. There was only 5ft headroom, so Magennis, at 5ft 4in, could cope reasonably comfortably. The sub could dive to 300ft and had a steaming capacity of 1,200 miles.

For months, they practised diving and doing dummy attacks on friendly warships when they anchored in the loch. Then in September 1943, six X-craft left their Scottish base towed by a mother submarine and headed out into the North Sea. Their destination was Altenfjord in the Arctic Circle in northern Norway and their target was the 44,000 ton German battleship *Tirpitz*.

Magennis was on board *X-7* with Lieutenant Phillips and Stoker Luck as the passage crew. Three or four times in twenty-four hours the little boats had to surface to ventilate. During the passage, they stayed 40ft deeper than the mother submarine, *Thrasher*. There were problems on route. *X-8* broke her tow and it took fourteen hours before it was fixed again. She then suffered buoyancy problems and was scuttled. *X-9* also broke her tow and tragically was never seen again.

X-7's crew experienced their own problems and after eight weary days they got the signal to surface off Altenfjord. There they swapped places with the operational crew, commanded by Lieutenant Geoffrey Place, and were taken on board HMS *Thrasher*.

Tirpitz was to be attacked by *X-5*, *X-6* and *X-7*, with *X-10* attacking *Scharnhorst*. *X-7* and *X-6* managed to drop its charges beneath *Tirpitz* before being forced to scuttle their craft and surrendering. *X-5* did penetrate the anti-torpedo nets but did not press home its attack and was lost, presumably destroyed. Both successful X-craft commanders, Geoffrey Place and Donald Cameron, were awarded the Victoria Cross.

Meanwhile, *Thrasher* remained at the entrance to Altenfjord for two days. She surfaced boldly and sneaked up the fjord as far she could. A flashing light led her to rescue the crew of *X-10*, which had mechanical problems and had had to call off her attack and return to sea. As it happened, *Scharnhorst* was not at anchor in Altenfjord.

For his efforts in the gruelling outward journey, Magennis received a Mention in Despatches.

In late 1943 and early 1944, six new X-craft were built and began to arrive by train at Loch Cairnbawn. These new craft were to be used in tropical waters and were called XE instead of just X. They were slightly longer and had a type of air conditioning in them to cope with condensation in the tropics. The new XE craft were to be sent on a top secret mission against Japan. Magennis was promoted to leading seaman and was accepted as a diver. Up until then, only officers were allowed to be divers.

As part of the training team, Magennis helped new officers on midget submarines. One of these was Lieutenant Ian Fraser and they immediately struck a rapport. After six months of hard training, the crews of the six XE-craft were ready for their next mission.

IAN FRASER VC

Ian Edward Fraser was born at 79 Uxbridge Road, Ealing, Middlesex, on 18 December 1920, the son of Sydney, a marine engineer, and Florence (née McKenzie). Within six months, the family moved to Malaya, where Sydney was employed as an engineer.

Fraser was educated at several schools in Liverpool and briefly at Peasenhall Village School in Suffolk. From 1933 to 1935, he attended High Wycombe Royal Grammar School. He chose a seaman's life and trained on HMS *Conway*, the Merchant Navy training ship in the Mersey. In 1938, he joined the Blue Funnel Line as a cadet and went to sea in *Tuscan Star* and *Sydney Star*. Just before the outbreak of the Second World War, he joined the battleship *Royal Oak* as a midshipman Royal Naval Reserve for what he thought would be four month's training. Instead, with the start of hostilities, he served on the destroyer HMS *Keith*. He was in the destroyer *Montrose* at Dunkirk and in another destroyer, *Malcolm*, when she and other escorts sank *U-651* in the Atlantic on 29 June 1941. He ended his career in surface ships when he volunteered for submarines. His small stature earned him the nickname 'Titch' and he fitted in well in the cramped environment of a submariner.

On 1 April 1942, he joined HMS *Sahib* in the Mediterranean and was awarded the Distinguished Service Cross for his part in the sinking of *U-301* and several Axis supply vessels. It was a bout of horseplay during a post-patrol party that saved Fraser from spending the rest of the war as a prisoner of war. A thrown heavy brass ashtray broke a bone in his foot and he was unable to go out on patrol, during which *Sahib* was lost and all but one of her crew were made prisoners of war.

In 1943, Fraser was promoted to first lieutenant and given command of the old submarine *H.44*. While it was undergoing a refit, Fraser married his childhood sweetheart, Melba Estelle Hughes. By early 1944, Fraser had become bored with the mundane duties assigned to the ageing *H.44* and in March 1944 volunteered for training in the new weapon, the X-craft. Only 50ft long and a pressure hull of just 5ft 6in diameter, X-craft carried a crew of four. Instead of torpedoes, she carried two large underwater side charges each weighing 4 tons, which could be released under the keel of an enemy ship and detonated by a clockwork time fuse. The X-craft had been used successfully against *Tirpitz* and there were still plenty of enemy targets left.

After months of training in Loch Cairnbawn, Fraser was ready to take command of *XE3*, which was launched at Rothesay on 27 November 1944 by his wife. *XE3* was unofficially named *Sigyn*, a character from Norse mythology. Incidentally, Fraser named his house *Sigyn* after the war.

By this time, the Germans had been pushed back to their own border and the threat from the *Kriegsmarine* had been all but neutralised. The war against Japan seemed far from over, so the 14th Submarine Flotilla was loaded aboard its depot ship, HMS *Bonaventure*, and, on 21 February 1945, sent to South-East Asia. Its route to the Far East took it across the Atlantic to Trinidad, where the crews practised in tropical conditions. They then passed through the Panama Canal to San Diego and across the Pacific to Brisbane, arriving on 27 April having steamed 14,888 miles.

The general opinion was that they were too late and that there were no targets for the miniature subs. However, the Americans did need someone to cut the under-sea telecommunication cables running from Saigon and Hong Kong. The divers had practised cutting their way through anti-submarine nets but needed to train in cutting cables. Tragically, during the training off the Great Barrier Reef, two officer divers lost their lives through oxygen poisoning.

HMS *Bonaventure* was ordered to sail, first to the Philippines and then North Borneo. Finally, the crews received their orders to cut the cables. *XE5* could not cut those off Hong Kong, but *XE4* had been successful in cutting them off Saigon.

There was an additional target; the 10,000-ton cruisers *Takao* and *Myoko*, anchored in the Johore Straits between mainland Malaya and Singapore Island. Even though they would be vulnerable if they left the shelter of Singapore, they made formidable floating gun batteries with which to defend the Straits. Each with a complement of 630 crew, they were both heavily armed and had extra armoured plating. They were

THE FALL OF SINGAPORE

anchored in shallow water close to the Singapore side of the Johore Straight and it was thought that the Japanese had placed them there to guard the Causeway against an attack by British troops approaching from Malaya.

In what was called Operation *Struggle*, *XE1*'s target was to destroy *Myoko*, while *XE3*'s mission was to sink *Takao*. The two craft were lowered over the side of *Bonaventure* and attached to their mother submarines, *Start and Stygian*. The distance from Borneo to the target was some 650 miles. The towing boats with the XE-craft sailed on 26 July 1945 and it was four days later that the towing crew and operational crew changed places about 40 miles off Singapore. On the *Tirpitz* mission, Magennis had been passage crew, but now he was the operational crew and one of the most experienced divers. The rest of the crew were the navigator, a New Zealand sub-lieutenant named 'Kiwi' Smith and Engine Room Artificer Charlie Reed was the engineer.

The two X-boats slipped their tows and Fraser stayed on the surface, trimmed well down, using his diesel engines and making about 5 knots, presenting as low a silhouette as possible. In the early hours of 30 July, the tiny submarine hugged the coast until she reached the narrows of Kuala Johore. The *Takao* lay three miles up the straight by the causeway, the only connection between Singapore Island and the mainland.

By 07.00 hours on 31 July, and without sleep all night, Fraser took *XE3* to the seabed for three-quarters of an hour and all the crew took Benzedrine tablets. Now they had to make good time and race against the tide to reach *Takao* before she lay on the bottom of the harbour.

At 09.30 hours, Fraser peered through the periscope and sighted the boom, from which the wire mesh hung and which Magennis expected to have to leave the sub to cut. However, they had their first slice of luck when it was clear that the boom was open and they slipped undetected through the boom gate.

Creeping slowly along the curved channel, Fraser gave Magennis the order to put on his frogman suit. They had been below now for some seven hours and the air was hot and clammy. Fraser clearly remembered the events of the day:

> I felt sorry for poor Magennis, as he struggled as best he could into the thick rubber suit – a job difficult enough in the open air with plenty of space and an assistant, but here, in the confines of an X-craft control room, twenty times harder. When I next looked at Magennis, the suit was half on, his face red and streaming with sweat, and his long hair dangling like a pair of horns over his eyes. His chest fairly heaved as he panted for breath in the oxygen-scarce

atmosphere of the boat and the muscles of his arms gleaming and rippled as he pulled the tight rubber neck piece up under his arms.

Fraser gave the order to submerge to 40ft and helped Magennis to dress. Then he gave the order to bring her up again to periscope depth. There, exactly in the position shown on Fraser's chart, was the *Takao*. As they edged towards the huge warship, Fraser swung the periscope and had the shock of seeing a boat full of Japanese sailors going ashore just 40 or 50ft away. One of the sailors was trailing his hand in the water and it was a miracle that the sub was not detected.

XE3 touched the bottom and the *Takao* keel both fore and aft was touching the seabed, with an opening in the middle. On Fraser's first try, he was brought up short. He could have dropped the charges as with previous missions, but instead he tried again and was successful in putting the X-craft right in the middle of the big ship. They were sitting on the bottom, with *Takao*'s keel a foot above their heads.

Magennis was ready. He fitted his hood on and entered the wet and dry compartment. The door closed and the compartment started to flood as the pumps transferred water from the ballast tank. Then Magennis tried to raise the hatch above his head, but found that it hit the cruiser's bottom and did not leave enough room for him to get through.

Taking a deep breath, Magennis took off his breathing set and found that he could squeeze through the gap with it removed. Outside, he replaced his breathing apparatus, something that had never been attempted before by a diver. He found *Takao*'s bottom one mass of barnacles, weed and razor sharp shells, on which he tore his hands to pieces and ripped his suit, starting more leaks. Magennis later said of this part of the operation:

> My first impression was how murky the water was. The bottom of the target resembled something like an underwater jungle and I had to clear a patch of undergrowth and barnacles off six places in order to make sure the magnetic limpets would stick on. Getting them on was quite like my old training days when I stuck many dummies under our own ship. It took me about three-quarters of an hour altogether before I got back to *XE3*.

When finished, he closed the hatch and started to drain down. Lieutenant Fraser had great difficulty in freeing the midget submarine from under the enemy's keel and managed this by blowing his ballast tanks. This resulted in *XE3* surfacing momentarily. They then settled back on the seabed a short distance from *Takao*. Fraser then gave the order to release both side carriers, the two tons of Amatol explosive and the empty limpet mine carrier. The Amatol fell away correctly, but the empty carrier was still attached to the sub. The carrier had apparently become flooded during the delay and, unless released, the craft was in dire peril with no possibility of escape. The limpet mine carrier had to be released from the outside.

Despite being covered in sweat and weak with exhaustion, Magennis prepared to go outside again. Both Fraser and Reed volunteered, but Magennis said that it was his job. He left the submarine for a second time and, with a large spanner, managed to release the limpet mine holder. He gave the thumbs up for the last time and climbed back into the wet and dry compartment and closed the lid.

XE3 slipped out across the bank and, in another race against the tide, headed back to sea. Fraser successfully navigated the strait and at 21.00 hours, passed the boom, which was still open. After another mile, they surfaced and opened the hatch, which went with a whoosh as they had been building up pressure inside.

At 23.50 hours they were picked up by their parent submarine and they were able to rest for the first time in fifty-two hours. The crew of *Stygian* heard a huge explosion and saw a big glow over Singapore Island, which lifted everyone's spirits.

Their sister X-craft *XE1* was unable to attack *Myoko*. Instead, the crew dropped their Amatol charges under *Takao* as well. When they reached base, arrangements were made for *XE3* and *XE4* to return to sink *Myoko*. Fortunately, this was aborted when the news came of the Japanese surrender.

Magennis was drafted to HM Submarine *Voracious*, which was stationed in Sydney. One November morning, he got a message that Lieutenant Fraser wanted to see him. Holding out his hand, Fraser congratulated his diver with the words, 'You have won the Victoria Cross'. Fraser, too, had been awarded the VC, while 'Kiwi' Smith received the DSO and ERA Reed, the CGM.

Fraser and Magennis received their VCs from the King on 11 December 1945 alongside Colonel Charles Newman, the leader of the commando raid on the dry dock at St Nazaire in 1943.

While Magennis's family and neighbours were overjoyed at the news of the award, the politicians in Belfast were thrown into a quandary. The Unionists, who ran the city, were embarrassed that a Catholic Navy man had been awarded the highest decoration for bravery. They had to acknowledge the fact with a civic ceremony, but they stopped short of offering Magennis the Freedom of the City. On the other side, the Nationalists were trying to make political capital, but at the same time being scornful that Magennis was a member of His Majesty's Navy.

A fund was set up and a substantial sum was donated. However, Magennis's final years in the service were not happy ones. He was reduced in rank and served time in Portsmouth's Detention Quarters for drunkenness. In 1949, he was demobbed and returned to Belfast, but settling into civilian life after fifteen years of service was far from easy. It was made even harder to cope when his son, David, was killed by a trolleybus.

By 1952, Magennis had lost his job and the fund he had received was exhausted as he had generously shared it among his family and friends. Shortly afterwards, he was forced to sell his Cross for £75 to a dealer, who agreed to donate it to the Belfast Museum. Unfortunately this was not done quietly but in front of a journalist and photographer. Magennis later recalled that moment:

> The dealer had promised to keep quiet about it, but after a few weeks he announced publicly he would present it to the Belfast Museum. My name was on it and everyone knew it was my VC. What a stink it caused; what a blow up. The world protested. I received hundreds of letters condemning me. Some were sympathetic; others, rude and scurrilous ...

This was the beginning of a period of re-evaluation for Magennis. The people of Belfast did not seem to hold him in high regard, some even tried to downgrade his act of bravery. He realised that the limelight he had basked in was gone forever. It was clear he was not wanted in Protestant Unionist East Belfast and neither was he wanted in Catholic Nationalist West Belfast. They only thing was to go to England.

On 7 February 1955, Magennis and his family moved to Rossington near Doncaster, where he found work as an electrician at the local coal mine. Here he found the comradeship of the Yorkshire miners very much akin to his early experiences in submarines.

In the late 1950s, the Magennis family moved to Bradford and Mick lived here for the remainder of his life. After years of suffering from chest problems, he finally died of acute bronchitis on 12 February 1986. This brave sailor was cremated and his ashes scattered in the Garden of Remembrance at Shipley, West Yorkshire. His Victoria Cross medal group, along with the diving suit he wore under *Takao*, are on display in the Lord Ashcroft Gallery.

In addition to the Victoria Cross, Ian Fraser was appointed Officer of the US Legion of Merit. Any hopes he had of remaining in the Royal Navy disappeared when it became clear that he was not going to be offered a permanent commission and he took his discharge in 1947.

Back in civilian life, Fraser used his expertise and contacts to form his own company, Universal Divers. To finance the company, he organised a troupe of frogmen to re-enact their wartime experiences in X- craft in a 20,000 gallon glass-sided tank, which appeared at such venues as Belle Vue, Manchester, and Liverpool's Shakespeare Theatre. This unashamedly traded on Fraser's VC and he was fiercely criticised for commercialising the award.

With the exploration of North Sea oil, Fraser's company was much in demand and became a great success. In 1975, he sold his company to the Blue Star Line and stayed with the new company, Star Offshore Services, until his retirement in 1982. He became a JP and was vice-president of the Merseyside Branch of the Submarine Old Comrades Association. Since 2002, he had been the vice-chairman of the VC and GC Association. He died on 1 September 2008 at the age of eighty-seven.

Along with Magennis's group, Fraser's VC is on display in the Lord Ashcroft Gallery at the Imperial War Museum.

Chapter 4

Defeat in Burma

Burma, or as the Honourable East India Company initially called her, 'Further India', was a country that was annexed in stages until it became a British colony after the Third Anglo–Burmese War of 1886–89. Elongated in shape, it is larger than France and its four main rivers from west to east are the Irrawaddy, Chindwin, Sittang and Salween.

In 1853, a new king, Mindon Min, took power in Upper Burma and maintained good relations with Britain. When he died in October 1878, his crown passed to his twenty-one-year old son, Thibaw. There were older heirs but Mindon Min's premier, the supposedly moderate Kinwun Mingyi, thought that Thibaw would be easily dominated. How wrong he was, for in February 1879 the new king and his palace guard had eighty of Thibaw's close relatives and the premier executed to remove rival claimants. This was regarded as normal in Burma when a new king came to the throne, but what really galvanised the British to intervene was a perceived threat from the French.

In 1883, Thibaw sent a Burmese official mission to Europe to negotiate political and commercial treaties to offset British influence in Burma. The mission was well received in France, arousing British alarm. The possibility of France, which already ruled Indo-China, moving closer and possibly threatening British India was unthinkable. The Anglo–French struggle for India was still fresh in the mind and Britain felt the need of a buffer country between India and Indo-China. Similarly, it needed Afghanistan to keep the Russians at a distance on its western border.

The British occupied Lower and Upper Burma without much opposition and exiled Thibaw and his family to India, where he died in 1916. Under colonial rule the country flourished, but only to the betterment of the British. The great expansion of rice cultivation found a ready market and accounted for half the world's supply. The export of hardwood from the vast forests in the north accounted for seventy-five per cent of the world's teak and the mining of rubies and wolfram along with the expansion of the oil fields elevated Burma's exports to new heights. All this rapid exploration brought prosperity to Burma yet, despite this wealth, it was still regarded as an Indian backwater.

In 1939, the population of Burma numbered about seventeen million with most people living in the lowland area around Rangoon and Mandalay. The rest of the country was mostly occupied by hill tribes; the Karens and Shans lived along the border with Thailand and China; the Kachins lived in the north above Myitkyina with the Nagas, Chins and Shans inhabited the hills bordering India.

There were never that many British in Burma, mainly because of the oppressive climate; heat, humidity and monsoon, combined with a wide range of tropical diseases. Nevertheless, the new colonists managed to destroy the traditional Burmese social system in the way that only an industrial society can overwhelm a purely peasantry-based people. Despite Britain building railways and developing river transport, which should have benefitted the indigenous population, Burma's neighbour, India, flooded the country with its workers. The immigration of millions of Indians who served as clerks, merchants, labourers and, provocatively, money-lenders, exacerbated the growing resentment felt by the Burmese, who found themselves at the bottom of the pecking order; humiliated and poorly treated. As George Orwell wrote in his book *Burma Days*: 'Burma's relationship with the British Empire is that of slave and master.'

In 1937, the rising tide of resentment led to Britain separating Burma from India and granting her a new constitution, with an elected assembly giving the Burmese people many domestic reforms. This only seemed to embolden the protesters and there was a wave of strikes and protests the following year. The next three years brought simmering discontentment until the Japanese invaded South-East Asia to the acclaim of most Burmese.

The twenty-nine Victoria Crosses awarded for the Burma Campaign between 1943 and 1945 were all outstandingly extraordinary, yet most are unknown today. Of the twenty-nine, eighteen were posthumous, being awarded for acts that almost defy belief. Recipients who should have been dead of their wounds summoned up enough of their remaining life to fulfil their gallant acts. Eleven Indians were awarded the VC, six of which were posthumous, which was all the more amazing given the mounting discontent in their homeland.

Subhas Chandra Bose, a former National Indian Congress leader, formed an alliance with the Japanese to recruit captured Indian soldiers in Malaya into an army of liberation called the INA (Indian National Army). Although he found enough recruits, Bose's force never amounted to much and as the Allies' successes in 1944–45 increased, many of his soldiers were only too pleased to swap sides again. The Japanese had alienated many members of the INA by denying them equipment and supplies or by using them as labourers and porters rather than fighting troops.

By the end of March 1945, the soldiers of the British Indian Army were so rejuvenated by their unstoppable push to eject the Japanese from Burma that they quickly turned on any captured member of the INA and many were shot. Bill Slim was alarmed enough to issue an order that the turncoat INA prisoners should be shown due consideration as prisoners of war and not killed out of hand.

The activities of the INA caused enough concern for the British to mount a propaganda programme in the Indian regiments starting with greater co-operation among the European officers and Indian troops. The British intelligence departments coined the acronym 'Jiffs' (Japanese–India Fifth Column) to describe the INA. Stories were circulated of Japanese atrocities on prisoners of war linking them with the INA. An even greater emphasis was placed on the bravery of Indian troops, as borne out by the number of Victoria Crosses they received.

The actions performed by the British, Indians and Gurkhas were inspired by *esprit de corps*, comradeship and a desire to kill a hated enemy. The nine VCs of the British regiments were all posthumous, as were the four from the Punjab regiments. At a time when India was clamouring for independence and anti-colonial feeling was rife, the men of the Indian Army had displayed a loyal and united front in fighting the Japanese.

On 14 December 1941, the Japanese and Thai Army (Japan had signed a treaty with Thailand, whose Army joined forces with Japan), crossed the frontier of Southern Burma at the Tenasserim strip on the Malayan Peninsular and took the border crossing of Victoria Point, (now Kawthaung). After a break of a month, the Japanese consolidated its position and, instead of advancing up the Tenasserim strip, they switched their attack to the east of Rangoon with the aim of cutting the road and railways north of the city. The Japanese had occupied countries that could supply her needs; oil from the Dutch East Indies, rubber and tin from Malaya. At this point Japan had no great wish to move into Burma except to capture Rangoon and stop the Chinese being supplied via the Burma Road.

The 17th Indian Division, which had been trained and equipped for fighting in North Africa, was sent with its new commander, Major

General 'Jacky' Smyth VC, to try and prevent the Japanese taking Rangoon. For twenty-two days its men were pushed back from a series of defensive positions. They had been bombed and machine-gunned by not only the Japanese but also, in error, the RAF. Finally, part of the 17th found themselves at a railway bridge and the only crossing over the Sittang River. The 800-yard-wide river was the last defendable position before Rangoon. The enemy thrust was relentless and cut around the flanks of the retreating 17th. General Smyth had already crossed the bridge with a third of his division and was faced with the dilemma of sacrificing the other two-thirds by blowing up the bridge or allowing the Japanese to capture it.

For the soldiers stranded on the east bank, the sound of the explosions was followed by disbelief and fury. With the centre span of the bridge destroyed, about 3,500 troops had to try and cross the river with anything that floated or take a chance swimming. The Japanese no longer had to press towards the bridge but focused their efforts on wiping out the remaining retreating troops concentrated in a defensive 'box' at Mokpalin, within hearing distance of the bridge. After several hours, the order came to evacuate. Very few soldiers could swim, so improvised rafts were floated. With the Japanese firing from the bank, many were killed in the water and on the mud flats.

Once the depleted 17th reached Rangoon it was found that it had lost 5,000 men killed, captured or missing, and all their weapons and equipment taken. The Sittang Bridge disaster was the defining moment that spelt the end of British rule in Burma. With twenty per cent of the Army's fighting strength gone, Rangoon soon fell on 7 March 1942. Smyth was dismissed and replaced by Major General D.T. 'Punch' Cowan, who managed to bring the remnants of the 17th back to India.

Lieutenant General William 'Bill' Slim, the new commander of the 50,000-strong Burma Corps (Burcorps – a combination of 1st Burma and 17th Indian Division), arrived and staged several successful offensives but these were only delayed the enemy's inevitable victory. The retreating Burcorps had no alternative but to turn north towards the Indian frontier where there were no land links. Instead it would be a debilitating slog over the jungle-covered hills with precious few trails. Their progress would be made even more harrowing by an estimated 400,000 Indian and Anglo–Burmese refugees fleeing from the Japanese. Many thousands of these wretched fugitives were murdered by a vengeful Burmese population or succumbed to starvation and disease as they struggled back to India.

Fighting rear guard actions and operating a scorched earth policy, including the destruction of the Yenangyaung oil fields, the 12,000 remnants of Burcorps reached Assam, India, on 20 May 1942. Of these, barely a sixth was anything but sick; British and Indian losses numbered 13,597, almost half missing. Resembling scarecrows, starved and in rags, Slim's regiments assembled along the frontier just as the monsoon broke. They had retreated through some of the worst terrain in the world covering some 800 miles in three-and-a-half months; the longest retreat in the history of the British Army. Slim visited them in their rough tented accommodation in Imphal and expected to be greeted by exhausted men suffering from low morale. Instead they cheered him. He later wrote:

> To be cheered by troops whom you have led to victory is grand and exhilarating. To be cheered by the gaunt remains of those you have led only in defeat, withdrawal and disaster is infinitely moving and humbling.

In the north, the Burma Road was cut when the 55th Chinese Division was forced back towards the Salween River on the Chinese border, where it blew the Huitong Bridge. This effectively became the front line from 1942 to late 1944. During the summer, the transport aircraft of the United States Army Air Force (USAAF) flew 13,000 Chinese soldiers over the Himalayas back to Yunnan province. General Joseph 'Vinegar Joe' Stilwell was placed in command of the Northern Combat Area Command (NCAC), based in Ledo on the border between Assam and Burma. On 1 December 1942, the Commander-in-Chief, General Sir Archibald Wavell, agreed that Stilwell should take over and be in command of the building of the Ledo Road from Assam and link up with the original Burma Road at some point beyond Myitkyina. With the help of the Chinese Army, it was hoped to clear the Japanese from this vital area.

Much of the border was jungle-clad mountains with innumerable fast-flowing rivers that acted as a barrier against the now-exhausted Japanese, who stopped at the Chindwin River to rest and resupply. There was one vulnerable area that offered the Japanese the opportunity to invade India; the Arakan. Situated on the west coast of Burma, this province provided small ports and airfields for the Japanese. Any invasion into India would net the Japanese the important ports of Chittagong and Cox's Bazaar and put them in range of Calcutta.

Wavell took advantage of the monsoon to re-equip and reinforce his depleted army. Roads and airstrips were built and the beginnings of a properly organised army began to take shape. The Army of Burma had ceased to exist and the troops were incorporated into IVth Corps, based at Imphal. General Sir Harold Alexander, the General Officer in Command in Burma, was recalled to London and command of XVth Corps passed to Slim in India.

The monsoon broke and this curtain of rain saved India for the Japanese were no better prepared than the British to fight through five months' downpour.

*

The south-west monsoon lasts from mid-May until mid-October, dumping 200in of rainfall on the coastal area of Arakan. The onset of the monsoon was the only piece of good luck for the British Indian Army and gave it some respite. The five-month long pause presented Slim the chance to start to reorganise his command. From 1940, a quarter of a million trained troops of the Indian Army had been sent west to the Middle East and North Africa to fight the Germans and the Italians. This left an ill-trained and poorly equipped army much reduced by sickness and exhaustion.

General Archibald Wavell had been the Commander-in-Chief Middle East and successfully pushed the Italians back through Libya to the point of expelling them from the country when he was ordered to halt and send troops and equipment to Greece. He disagreed with Churchill but reluctantly acquiesced. The result was a disaster that left Wavell open to a counter-attack by the newly arrived *Afrika Korps*, who pushed the British back to Egypt. The failure of Operation *Battleaxe* in June 1941, gave Churchill the excuse to replace Wavell with General Claude Auchinleck. In effect the two generals swapped command and Wavell became Commander-in-Chief India. He found that he had again inherited a command that was undermanned and inadequately equipped.

After the retreat from Burma, he was again put under pressure by Churchill and the Chiefs of Staff in London to mount an offensive for which he was ill-prepared. General Wavell was aware how stretched the Japanese Army was and that a small-scale operation ninety miles into the Arakan would boost morale as well as capture the port of Akyab on the Mayu Peninsular. In charge of the operation was Lieutenant General Noel Irwin, Commander-in-Chief Eastern Army in India. He had a series of disagreements with Lieutenant General Slim, appointed commander XV Corps from 9 June 1942. XV Corps commanded 14th Indian Light Division, which was stationed on the border with the coastal province of Arakan. It had been raised and trained in Quetta in Balochistan to serve in the desert regions of Iraq and Persia and was quite unprepared for jungle warfare.

Irwin informed Slim that the headquarters of Eastern Army and XV Corps were to exchange places for the offensive. This meant that

Eastern Army HQ would take direct command of the offensive, while XV Corps HQ would move to Ranchi in Bihar to restore civil unrest and train fresh troops for later combat in Burma. Irwin did, however, retain XV's 14th Indian Light Division commanded by Major General Wilfred Lloyd.

The objective of the incursion was to advance about ninety miles down the coast, occupy the Mayu Peninsular and take the port and airfield at Akyab on Akyab Island. Appeals for landing craft to take the port were not answered so a purely land-based operation began on 17 December 1942 after a lengthy build-up. Spearheaded by Lloyd's 14th Indian Division, the advance crossed into the Arakan. The Japanese had had plenty of time to prepare well-entrenched strongpoints in a terrain that suited defence. Arakan was a region of steep jungle-covered hills sharply descending to paddy fields, scrub and swamp interspersed with steep-banked tidal creeks. The objective was reduced to a thrust down the Mayu Peninsular to Foul Point and then ferrying the troops across to Akyab Island.

Moving down either side of the north–south Mayu Range and along the eastern bank of the Mayu River, the forward patrols had almost reached Donbaik, ten miles above Foul Point. The difficult conditions slowed the transport of supplies, which had given the Japanese time to bring additional troops to the area. It was not until 6 January 1943 that the advance resumed but the Japanese repelled all attempts to take Donbaik. The third attack involved the meagre support of eight lightly armoured Valentine tanks instead of the fifty requested. These were soon destroyed by close-range anti-tank fire.

On 18 March, General Irwin reinforced the attack with the 2nd British Division and the 71st Brigade of the 26th Indian Division but to no avail. Penetrating the outer Japanese defences, they were met with heavy enemy fire from the well-sited underground bunkers. They were furthermore hit in the flank by a counter-attack that caused the British to draw back up the Mayu River and escape the trap at Rathedaung. The Japanese were relentless and managed to straddle the Mayu Range. To avoid encirclement, the British retreated further north to the port of Maungdaw. On 20 March, Wavell ordered the abandonment of the operation and the holding of a defensive line along the twelve-mile road between Maungdaw and Buthidaung.

There Irwin's troops halted and counted the cost in casualties; both combat and particularly malaria. The troops had been shaken and suffered a lowering of morale. Lloyd was dismissed by Irwin for ordering the withdrawal of his isolated 47th Indian Brigade back across the Mayu Range. Irwin rescinded the order but the 47th was forced to retreat in small groups, abandoning all its equipment and ceasing to be a fighting force.

The Japanese cut the Maungdaw–Buthidaung Road causing the British and Indian troops to destroy their transport and retreat. Slim had belatedly been restored to command XV Corps but when Irwin ordered that Maungdaw should be held at all costs, Slim decided that the port was not prepared for a siege and that the exhausted troops of the Indian Division could not be expected to resist. On 11 May the port was abandoned and XV Corps and the rest of the invading force returned to the Indian border. Irwin and Slim blamed each other for the abortive operation but it was Irwin who was removed from his command. Slim was promoted to command the new multi-national XIVth Army (also referred to as the 14th or Fourteenth Army), later to gain fame as the 'Forgotten Army'.

The premature invasion had been a terrible blow to British prestige but it also acted as a catalyst for major reforms in the Anglo–Indian Army that laid the foundation for the string of Allied victories in 1944–45.

PARKASH SINGH VC

The debacle of the first incursion into the Arakan did produce two outstanding heroic acts performed by one soldier – Havildar Parkash Singh.

Singh was born on 31 March 1913 into a Sikh farming family in Sharikar in the Lyallipur district of Punjab, in what later became Pakistan. As a schoolboy he was somewhat unruly but the schoolmaster tolerated his behaviour as he was an exceptional athlete; he went on to hold the All India 800m record. He managed to matriculate and was offered a scholarship by the headmaster of the government college at Lyallipur, but Parkash had other ideas. In 1936, he tried to join the Viceroy's Police but as there were no vacancies, he enlisted in the 8th Punjab Regiment. As with all Indian Army regiments, the mixture of races meant that the companies were divided according to religion; two companies of Muslims and one of Jat Hindus. Parkash joined the 5th Battalion made up of Punjab Sikhs.

When he joined, the 8th Punjab was serving on the North West Frontier. There was almost continual unrest from the various tribes, which was further exacerbated by the political and religious teachings of Mirza Ali Khan, better known as the Fakir of Ipi. Singh was part of the 30,000 force that was deployed to this troublesome region. He saw his first action when his company was besieged by hostile tribesmen, losing some sixty men including their commanding officer.

Parkash was soon promoted to havildar (sergeant) and the 8th Punjab became part of the 14th Indian Light Division under the command of Major General Lloyd. Singh's regiment was on the west side of the advance down the Mayu Peninsular and had almost reached Donbaik, ten miles north of Foul Point at the tip of the peninsular. The terrain was so rugged that the most effective vehicles were the four-man armoured Bren gun carriers. These tracked carriers were vulnerable, being lightly armoured and open, so that an accurately thrown grenade could disable the crew.

On 6 January 1943, the frontal attack on Donbaik had been repulsed and a withdrawal ordered. It was here that Singh performed his first gallant act. The Bren gun carrier Platoon of 5/8th Punjab was attacked by a strong Japanese patrol near Donbaik. The platoon commander, Lieutenant Bert Causey, was wounded and forced to retire, handing over the command to his havildar. Singh noticed two other carriers were bogged down in a *chaung* (a tidal creek) and taking very heavy enemy fire. He immediately drove to rescue the helpless crews, calling on them to abandon the vehicles and run for safety while he laid down covering fire. When his gunner was wounded, he took control of the gun and, driving with one hand, charged towards the enemy and drove them from their positions. As he returned, he picked up the stranded crews, coming under heavy fire, but he succeeded in bringing the eight men to safety.

Another unsuccessful assault on 19 January ended with the same result. The battalion's carriers came under heavy anti-tank fire in the same area and several were destroyed. The crews were given up for dead but once again Singh was on hand to rescue his comrades. Driving down to the beach under intense enemy fire, he found three badly burned British soldiers lying in the shelter of the burning carrier. Picking up each wounded soldier and laying them in his carrier, Singh drove back and passed his cargo to the stretcher bearers.

Singh then realised that his officer was missing and, despite being advised not to return, he replenished his ammunition and drove back down the beach into the intense enemy fire. He found his wounded officer and driver in their badly damaged carrier, too badly injured to be moved. Despite being ordered by his officer to go back and save himself, Singh rigged a makeshift tow chain which connected to the damaged carrier. As he did this he saw a group of Japanese soldiers break cover from some bushes just 200 yards away. Realising there was no time to get away, Singh seized his Bren gun and began hosing the advancing enemy, killing two or three and wounding others. The remainder dashed back to cover.

There was yet another snag; the damaged carrier was still in gear and the wounded men were unable to put it in neutral. Still under fire, Singh jumped into the vehicle and pulled the lever into neutral. Once secure, the towed carrier began its return only for the single tow chain to cause the damaged carrier to yaw wildly from side to side.

Singh got out and walked on the seaward side of the vehicle in order to change the attachment point for the chain. Two more anti-tank shells hit the carrier but fortunately not the tracks. After what must have seemed like hours – it was forty minutes – both carriers managed to reach their lines. Singh's very gallant actions, entirely on his own initiative, were an inspiration to all ranks both British and Indian. He was recommended for both actions and it was suggested he should receive the VC and Bar, something that was rarely given, but this was overturned. His citation appeared in *The London Gazette* on 13 May 1943 and he was invested with his Victoria Cross by the Viceroy, Lord Linlithgow, at the Red Fort, in Delhi, in August 1943. This was one of the last acts performed by the outgoing Viceroy, who was succeeded in October by Archibald Wavell.

Singh was promoted to jemadar (the lowest commissioned rank) on 15 August 1943 and continued to fight in the Burma Campaign. A further promotion to subadar (captain) followed on 1 November 1944. On his return home, the government of Punjab granted him sixty-four acres of land. He then entered into an arranged marriage with a suitable girl who had never seen him before. Fortunately the marriage turned out to be a long and happy one.

The migration that followed India's independence and partition in 1947 led to the largest movement of a population in human history. Families were uprooted from their homes and travelled both west and east to a divided Muslim Pakistan, or south to a Sikh or Hindu India. Inadequately policed, or even thought through, the mass pogrom resulted in the worst period of communal violence the world has witnessed. In March 1947, Lord Ismay, the Chief of Staff of the Viceroy for India, Lord Louis Mountbatten, likened India to 'a ship on fire in mid-ocean with ammunition in the hold'. Mountbatten pleaded with the leaders of the Hindu and Muslim leadership that they should form a united country but this was turned down and the violence continued unabated.

Singh, his new bride and family decided that they belonged to India. As a born leader, he was put in charge of all the wives and children to undertake this dangerous journey. Although there had been harmless rivalry between the diverse companies in the Punjab Regiment, they actively supported each other in a jam. While the Muslims and Hindus were massacring each other in their thousands, his Indian Army comrades helped Singh and his family to safety. Along with other Sikh comrades, they managed to travel by train and they made their way to Jalandhar, Punjab. On the journey, they were frequently fired upon by Pathans and several of their number were killed. A compensation board allotted 64 acres to replace the land that he had left behind.

Singh transferred to the Sikh Regiment and was appointed to a Short Service Regular Commission as a lieutenant and, in 1952, to a Regular Commission. He retired in 1969 with the rank of major to become a prosperous potato farmer.

He enjoyed robust health until a badly treated dental infection caused cardiac problems. He travelled to the UK for heart surgery at the Old Court Hospital, Ealing, London, but died of complications on 23 March 1991. He was cremated on 28 March at the Golders Green Crematorium and his ashes returned to his home village in the Punjab. His medals are on display in the Lord Ashcroft Gallery in the Imperial War Museum.

Chapter 5

The Chin Hills

After the beaten XV Corps retreated back to India, another confrontation took place to the east in the Chin Hills, which was the only part of Burma left in British hands. As early as December 1942, the Japanese had occupied the small river port of Kalemyo on the Chindwin and began probing north towards the strategically important village of Tiddim. On 24 May 1943, they occupied No.2 Stockade, one of a series of clearings in the Kennedy Peak area; the others being Fort White and No.3 Stockade. These were about thirty miles from Tiddim and one of a line of staging posts constructed by General White's expedition into the Chin Hills during the Third Burma War of 1889–90. The 2nd/5th Gurkha Rifles and a company of the 1st/4th were sent to eject them, but to do this they had to occupy the heights of Basha Hill that dominated No.2 Stockade.

Basha Hill consisted of three ridges; Basha East, West and Centre. It was found that West and Centre were unoccupied but the enemy had dug in on Basha East. On 26 May, the Gurkhas attempted to take the Japanese position but heavy machine-gun fire stopped them just 200 yards short of their bunkers.

Another attack went in the following day and thanks to an outstanding act of gallantry and determination, the ridge was taken.

GAJE GHALE VC
Born either on 1 August 1918 or 1 July 1922, Gaje Ghale was one of the fourteen children of Birkham Ghale and Mainli Ama in the village of Barpak. Ghale worked as a shepherd until he was old enough to enlist as a boy soldier in the Gurkha Rifles. After training, he was appointed to the 5th Gurkha Rifles and sent to his posting in Waziristan during the confrontation with the Fakir of Ipi during the late 1930s. From 1939 to 1942, he served as an instructor at the Regimental Centre at Abbotabad.

Ghale was sent to Burma in time to taste defeat as the 48th Indian Brigade endured its long and dispiriting retreat from the Sittang Bridge back to Assam. As part of the 17th Indian Division, his regiment took up positions in the Chin Hills of Manipur, where the construction of the road to Tiddim was started. In March 1943, the 5th Gurkhas repulsed a strong Japanese attempt to force them out of the Chin Hills. Following this, probing patrols discovered that the enemy had moved closer to Tiddim and occupied a vital position that dominated the nearby stockades. After the failure to take Basha East on 26 May, another attempt was made the following day.

'D' Company 5th Gurkhas, consisting of only two platoons, was led by Captain V.E. Dennys and supported by men of the 4th Gurkhas, as it advanced along the knife-edged ridge but the heavy enemy fire caused them to swing to the left. The War Diary and Intelligence Summary described what happened:

> Fierce firing broke out on both sides including enemy mortars and artillery ... Captain Dennys was seen leading D Coy up the hill ... Under very heavy enemy automatic fire and grenades, D Coy. under the inspired leadership of Captain Dennys, advanced, were halted and advanced again, were again halted and finally a charge up a steep slope assaulted and drove the enemy out of their positions killing several as they ran away ... However, enemy snipers were still hiding in the trees. Three of these were seen and disposed of, but one certainly remained and he shot Captain Dennys through the left calf muscle ... In this attack, the conduct of Capt. Dennys, Subadar Padambahadur Gurung, Havildar Gaja Ghale and Naik Dilbahadur Thapa had been outstanding.

Ghale had been promoted to acting havildar on the 26th as a result of the many casualties among the platoon commanders in the first attack. It may have been this elevation that drove him to perform his outstanding act. Approaching the Japanese positions along the bare 5-yard wide ridge with precipitous flanks on either side, the havildar let out the Gurkha battle cry 'Aayi Gurkhali!' – the Gurkhas are upon you! – and, ignoring the heavy fire, led his platoon forward. He was the first to enter the Japanese strongpoint and in the ensuing hand-to-hand fighting a grenade exploded close by and he was wounded in the chest, arm and leg. Covered in blood, he continued to throw grenades with his good arm. The surviving enemy turned tail but soon returned to counter-attack.

Ghale refused to retire for medical treatment and stayed to fight off the new assault. With the position held, the wounded man allowed medical attention. The Gurkhas had sustained seventy-one casualties but suffered just seven fatalities. The Japanese suffered greatly in the brief but fierce fight. The battalion commander, however, decided that they were too weak to hold their position against a much superior enemy and ordered his men to retire to Kennedy Peak, leaving a light screen at Fort White. The Japanese made another attempt in November, capturing Fort White and occupying virtually the whole of the south-eastern Chin Hills.

Ghale was recommended for the Victoria Cross and it was proposed to present it at the Regimental Centre at Abbotabad. The regimental bahun (the religious advisor) said the date was inauspicious and should be postponed. The date and venue were changed and Ghale received his Cross on 6 January 1944 from Field Marshal Lord Wavell at a parade beneath the walls of the Red Fort in Delhi. He was also promoted to jemadar on 28 August 1943. After independence, he remained in the 5th Gurkhas and was promoted to subadar major. In 1962–63, he served with the United Nations in the Congo during the civil war.

He was a frequent visitor to London for the Victoria Cross and George Cross Association gatherings. Large and jolly, he became as broad as he was tall. On his retirement from the Army as honorary captain, he received the Star of Nepal from the Nepalese Prime Minister. He also attended the opening of the Gurkha Museum at Winchester and was one of the six VCs to meet the Queen when she visited Nepal in 1986. He was married and had four sons and four daughters. This fine soldier died in Delhi on 28 March 2000. His medals are on display in the Lord Ashcroft Gallery of the Imperial War Museum.

Chapter 6

Second Arakan Campaign

Taking the advantage that the monsoon gave, the Allied High Command was overhauled. General Wavell was elevated to Field Marshal Lord Wavell, the new Viceroy of India. In June 1943, his place as Commander-in-Chief was taken by Field Marshal Claude Auckinleck, but his direct participation in the war in Burma was removed and given to the new command named South East Asia Command (SEAC). The supreme commander was the charismatic Admiral Lord Louis Mountbatten, who toured the front delivering upbeat talks to lift the troops' flagging morale. He repeated what he had told their commanders:

> If the Japs try their old dodge of infiltrating behind you and cutting your line of communication, stay put: We will supply you by air. There will be no retreat.

Mountbatten expected them to fight on during the monsoon to catch the enemy on the hop and assured them of a first-class medical set-up. He added:

> Who started this story about the Jap Superman? I have seen the Japs in Japan. Millions of them are unintelligent slum-dwellers, with no factory laws, no trade unions, no freedom of speech, nothing except an ignorant fanatical idea that their Emperor is God. Intelligent free men can whip them every time.

The shake-up removed some under-performing senior commanders but fortunately one important leader was not replaced; Lieutenant General William Slim was to be a priceless asset as the XIVth Army retook

Burma. Mountbatten later said: 'Personally, I consider Slim was the finest general the Second World War produced.'

Having spent 1943 training and re-equipping, the High Command decided once again to the take war into Burma and this time they were well prepared. In Manipur, Slim's XIVth Army had prepared to meet an expected Japanese build-up to invade India through the Arakan. The Japanese High Command's plan, known as Operation C, sought to split open the British front and separate the eastern half of the sector from the west. They would then aim to take the port of Chittagong and to incite a general uprising against the British. The main blow would be to smash the Allied centre, taking Imphal and Dinapur. There was one snag: in just one year, Japanese airpower had been overtaken by the Allies, who were able take on their fighters, launch bombing raids and drop supplies to their forces even in the deepest jungles, and with very little opposition.

The XV Indian Corps under the command of Lieutenant General A.P.F. Christison advanced to take the small port of Maunglaw and through it they hoped to bring in supplies by boat from Calcutta. The Japanese were in a very strong position to block any attempts to take the Mayu Peninsular. They reinforced the Maunglaw–Buthidaung Road with underground bunkers and machine-gun positions covering each other with cross-fire. The sixteen-mile-long road ran through two tunnels bored through the Mayu Range, which were a vital artery of communication. British patrols reported that the approaching hills were heavily fortified and that a large force was being assembled.

The first British soldier to be awarded the Victoria Cross had survived an escape from the Germans and made his way to the Dunkirk beaches. His gallantry in leading a 'forlorn hope' charge against the enemy resulted in him being recommended for the Cross.

ALEC GEORGE HORWOOD VC

Alec George Horwood, or John as he preferred to be named, was born in Deptford in south-east London on 6 January 1914. His father, George, had been a former mayor of the borough during the 1920s. When he left school in the 1930s, Horwood worked as a clerk at Hartley's jam factory in south London. He was also a keen cyclist, captaining the Bath Road Cycle Club and winning the annual cup so many times that he felt obliged to withdraw from the event. He also joined the 1/6th Battalion, The Queen's West Surrey Regiment (Territorial Army), and was one of the first to be called up at the outbreak of the Second World War in 1939.

Horwood endured the inactivity of the bleak winter of the Phoney War in northern France, but in the spring of 1940 the British Expeditionary

Force became engaged in Belgium. Despite finding good defensive positions along the banks of the many canals and rivers, the BEF was constantly outflanked by the Germans. A wedge was driven between the British and their French allies and the BEF was pushed back towards the coast.

In the fight to stop the German progress through Belgium, Sergeant Horwood was captured at the Battle of Escault as he helped a wounded comrade. On 26 May, the captives were moved to a collection point at a military barracks near Antwerp in preparation for a lengthy incarceration as prisoners of war. Horwood found a window that could be opened and, together with Captain A.R. Trench of his regiment, managed to climb out and head for a nearby wood. They had to swim a wide ditch before hiding among the trees until the coast was clear. Trench wrote a report of their journey, which was remarkable for its endurance and determination.

Walking through the woods, they came upon an empty house and were able to change into civilian cloths and take some food. On 27 May the pair walked to Antwerp, which was full of Germans, but they found some friendly Belgians who hid them in a sports hall. They were given food and a map with directions to Knocke, where they hoped to meet a Frenchman who could help in their escape. The Belgians noticed the two men were wearing regulation Army boots and persuaded them to remove the hobnails from the soles.

On 28th they left Antwerp and two days later reached Knocke, but found that their contact had returned to France. They spent another night in a barn and the next day walked to Ostend, hoping to find a boat. The town had been heavily bombed and they observed that the Germans had established a staff headquarters. With no chance of finding a boat, they walked down the coast to Nieuport, where they found their route blocked by the wide Yser River. Shouted at by a party of Germans on the opposite bank, they walked inland, found a boat in a small creek and decided that this was the best way to reach their own lines. They spent the night in an abandoned house, where they found more clothes (they had taken to wearing two of everything to combat the cold nights) and went to sleep. They were disturbed later by two armed Germans who were looking for loot but who ignored them.

At midnight, stocking up with water and food, they rowed out into the main river and let the current carry them to the sea. When they were about a mile from the beach, they started rowing south-west towards Dunkirk, where they hoped to find the British Army. It was now 2 June and they could hear distant gunfire. They spotted a Royal Navy destroyer, HMS *Basilisk*, but found she had been burnt out and abandoned. Boarding her, they picked up a couple of lifebelts and carried on down the coast.

About seven miles from Dunkirk, they watched a large air raid on the beach and town. When the raid stopped, their rowed to shore and found they had arrived among the retreating French Army. Explaining who they were, they were driven to British Headquarters, narrowly missing being hit by a German shell that exploded close by. From Dunkirk, they caught a transport and arrived in Dover on the morning of 2 June.

For their gallant escape Trench was awarded the Military Cross and Horwood the Distinguished Conduct Medal. Later in 1940, Horwood was commissioned and became a lieutenant but almost immediately transferred to the 1st Northamptonshire Regiment in India. He arrived as the regiment was deployed as part of the 20th Indian Division of XV Corps on the Arakan Front.

On 20 December 1943, the Northamptonshires had moved into the Kaladan Valley, at Kyauchaw, north of Buthidaung, one of the main objectives of the invasion. The battalion's task was to capture an isolated Japanese bunker position on the track from the Chindwin River, a staging post for the build-up of the anticipated attack on Imphal. With the increase in Allied airpower, the Northamptonshires waited 3 miles away until the Japanese position was bombed. After several days' wait, the cloud cover lifted sufficiently for the raid to take place. Moving forward, they heard automatic firing, which suggested the bombing had not destroyed the enemy bunker. This was indeed the case and the battalion had difficulty getting near the strongpoint and suffered mounting casualties.

Horwood was the mortar platoon commander and frequently exposed himself to sniper fire as he went forward to ascertain the location of the machine-gun nests and bunkers. The regiment was pinned down for a couple of days and unable to close with the Japs. Lieutenant John Hopkins recalled:

> I kept losing men from these wretched grenade attacks, occasionally bursts of rifle fire, and then John Horwood in the afternoon said, 'Look. I am sure these chaps would run if we got at them. We ought to attack them.' I said, 'Well, I've got only twelve men left.' He said, 'Well, that's no good, I'll go and see the CO and see what I can do,' and he went back. He came back later and he said, 'I've borrowed a platoon of Gurkhas,' and these Gurkhas came up and started getting organised to put in the attack, fixing bayonets, and out came their kukris suspended from their wrists.

On 20 January, with Bren gun support, Horwood led his group of Gurkhas but, at the point of taking the position, he was hit by a burst of automatic fire and killed as he was stopped by the barbed wire in front of the Japanese bunker. The attack then fizzled out. Another officer remarked that:

> It was a rather hopeless thing, I suppose, but he was extremely brave man, a gallant chap ... He saw no reason why we should all be hanging back as we might have been, he was determined to have a go himself.

His action is reminiscent of that made by Colonel H. Jones at Goose Green; a suicidal charge that came to naught.

The outcome was that the Northamptonshires took the Japanese position two days later and Horwood was recommended for the Victoria Cross. This was presented to his widow by the King on 5 December 1944 at Buckingham Palace. His medal group is displayed in the Lord Ashcroft Gallery, Imperial War Museum.

The Japanese were confident that they could use similar tactics they used in the first Arakan invasion; namely encircle the two Allied divisions as they moved either side of the Mayu Range and cut off their communications. It would then be easy to destroy them piecemeal, and they would have air cover thanks to the reappearance of the famed Japanese Zero fighter. However, the newly arrived Spitfires of the Third Tactical Air Force proved too strong for them. After a week, sixty-five Zeros had been shot down with the loss of just three Spitfires. The Japanese had also budgeted for enough food to last seven days, during which time they expected to be in India. In contrast, the almost uninterrupted sorties by Troop Carrier Command dropped some 3,000 tons supplies to the encircled forces, ranging from petrol and food to cigarettes and beer.

Crossing the Mayu Range was a narrow track known as the Ngakedauk Pass, or as the British called it 'Okedoke Pass', which was improved by Indian engineers. This led to the 7th Division HQ known as the Admin Box, a one-mile square area where about 8,000 administrative clerks, signallers, sappers, ordnance and medical units were based. There were two battalions of infantry and a dozen batteries of artillery to defend the area. It was certainly not designed as a fortress, being surrounded by a ring of hills, from which the Japanese raided.

In one terrifying incident they overran a field hospital, slaughtering the wounded and medical staff. Isolated as it was, Admin Box was steadily supplied by the Dakotas of Troop Carrier Command. All these support personnel were issued with weapons and helped to fight off the Japs as they came down from the hills. The mini-siege lasted from 5 to 23 February, when the Japanese pulled back, starving and exhausted.

In order to clear a particularly troublesome Japanese position that threatened both the Ngakedauk Pass and the Admin Box, a British county regiment, the Lincolnshires, attached to 26th Indian Infantry Division, was called upon to take it. It resulted in success and the awarding of the Victoria Cross to one of its officers.

CHARLES FERGUSON HOEY VC

Charles Ferguson Hoey was born on 29 March 1914 at Duncan on Vancouver Island, British Columbia. His father, Ferguson, came from County Tyrone in Northern Ireland and emigrated to Canada with his wife Mary (née Simpson). Charles was educated at the local grammar school and showed a great interest in the military (his maternal grandfather was Major General Charles Rudyard Simpson). When he was sixteen, he volunteered for the 62nd Field Battery, Canadian Militia. His main aim was to join the British Army and in 1932 he sailed to England and enlisted in the Royal West Kent Regiment. In 1935 he won a cadetship and entered the Royal Military College, graduating in December 1936.

Hoey was commissioned in the 2nd Battalion Lincolnshire Regiment, which had been his grandfather's regiment. The following year, the regiment was sent to India and he served on the North West Frontier. With the outbreak of war with Japan, Hoey was promoted to major, transferred to the 1st Battalion and sent to the Burmese front. After jungle training he took part in several patrols in the Arakan area.

In July 1943, he led his company of forty men behind enemy lines for a raid on the small port of Maungdaw. It was regarded as a hush-hush operation for he returned with documents and photos. In the course of the raid they killed twenty-two Japanese before finding their way back through the lines. For his leadership in this successful operation, Major Hoey was awarded the Military Cross. His citation read:

> On 5 July 1943, Major Hoey was in charge of a force sent to raid Maungdaw, Burma. Throughout the raid he showed outstanding powers of leadership and though delayed by several accidents on the way, succeeded in getting his force into Maungdaw and inflicting casualties on the enemy. Throughout the operation he showed a complete disregard for his personal safety and remained

completely imperturbable in face of all difficulties and dangers. His personal example was an inspiration to all his men and contributed to a great extent to the success of the operation. The force succeeded in hitting at least 22 Japanese for certain. The majority were killed. Owing to the skilful handling of his force, Major Hoey only sustained three casualties, of other ranks, wounded. Major Hoey's determination, courage and skill during the whole operation were beyond praise.

The 1/Lincolnshire was kept in reserve as part of the 26th Indian Infantry Division when the second Arakan invasion started. With the Japanese counter-invasion beginning to run out of steam, Hoey's regiment was sent forward to the Ngakedauk Pass and the Admin Box area. It found that a particular Japanese hill called Point 315 was causing much trouble and that Hoey and 'B' Company had been designated to neutralise it.

Setting out at night, their advance hidden by the mist that clung to the valley floor, they walked in single file 10 miles to the Japanese position. They took along ten mules that carried mortars and wireless sets. Emerging at dawn, the enemy was taken by surprise as 'B' Company fell upon them. The disturbance alerted the rest of the defenders, who started to lay down a heavy fire and one of the Bren gunners was hit. Hoey grabbed his weapon and, calling to the others to follow, charged up the slope. All the time he was firing from the hip and, despite being hit twice, managed to enter a bunker, killing all the crew. The rest of the company had a hard time keeping up with him but finally the hill was taken. As he ordered his men to fall back, Hoey was killed by a sniper.

The Japanese were driven back from Ngakedauk Pass and the following day called off their offensive in the Arakan.

Hoey was recommended for the Victoria Cross, which was gazetted on 18 May 1944. His VC and MC were sent to Government House, Victoria in British Columbia, where they were presented by the Governor General to his mother. His family had to contend with a double tragedy as Charles's younger brother, Trevor, was killed during the D-Day Landings.

Hoey's VC group is held by the Royal Lincolnshire Regiment Museum.

NAND SINGH VC

Nand Singh was born on 24 September 1914 in the Punjabi village of Bahadur in Patiala state. Like many of his martial race, Singh chose to join the Army when he was old enough. On 24 March 1933, he enrolled in the 1st Sikh Regiment before transferring to the 1/11th Sikhs during the Second World War.

During the early years of the war against the Japanese, the Indian Army saw its reputation tarnished by a series of catastrophic defeats. The 11th and 17th Indian Divisions were largely under-trained and were little match for the Imperial Japanese Army as it swept all before it down the Malay Peninsula before the ripe plum of Singapore fell into its hands. On the grounds that my enemy's enemy is my friend, many of the captured Indian soldiers were recruited into the Indian National Army, which sided with the Japanese with the promise of the overthrow of the British Raj. To their shame, many of the POW guards initially used by the Japanese were Sikhs.

Against the Afrika Korps in North Africa, the Indians acquitted themselves well and the Sikhs were recognised as fine fighting men. With experience, thorough training and improved leadership in the person of Lieutenant General William Slim, the Indian Army developed into a potent unit.

In January 1944, Slim got wind that the Japanese were about to launch an offensive and ordered a counter-offensive in the Arakan. General Frank Messervy and his HQ Staff were forced to withdraw to the Admin Box. The three brigades under his command formed separate defensive boxes, which were encircled by the Japanese, but Allied air superiority enabled them to be supplied by air. After an initial setback, in which Messervy's 7th Indian Division Headquarters was overrun, the 1/11th Sikhs were in the 33rd Brigade Box and, on 18 February, as the Japanese attack ran out of steam, they were able to go on the offensive. It was during this phase that Naik Nand Singh performed his outstanding act of bravery.

In order to open the road to Buthidaung, the 1/11th Sikhs were placed under the command of another 7th Division brigade, the 89th Indian Brigade. On 10 March, the Sikhs made a frontal assault preceded by a 7,000-shell barrage on a 500-yard front. The following day, the 1/11th Sikhs advanced rapidly and captured the most strongly held Japanese position without encountering stiff opposition.

That night, the Japanese counter-attacked. A forty-strong Japanese platoon, armed with medium and light machine-guns and a grenade discharger, infiltrated into the battalion's position covering the main Maungdaw to Buthidaung road. Here it occupied a dominating feature, where it dug foxholes and underground trenches on the precipitous flank of the hill. From here it could prevent any forward movement along the road.

Singh commanded the leading section of the platoon that was ordered to recapture this threatening position at all costs. Under intense machine-gun and rifle fire, he led his section up the very steep knife-edged ridge towards the Japanese position. Despite being wounded in the thigh, he rushed ahead of his men and single-handedly took the first trench with the bayonet.

Under heavy fire from the next enemy trench, Singh crawled forward alone. To his horror, an enemy grenade landed just a yard in front of him and exploded. His efforts to protect himself succeeded, although he sustained a wound to the shoulder and fragments in his face. This only spurred him on to rush the second trench and bayonet its occupants.

As he lay in the trench and took stock of his situation, he realised that all his section was either dead or wounded and that he was isolated. Instead of staying put or retreating, which his wounds alone would have warranted, he dragged himself out of the trench and charged into the third enemy position, again killing all the occupants with his bayonet.

Due to the capture of these three enemy strongpoints, the remainder of Singh's platoon was able to advance and seize the rest of the hill. When the enemy dead were counted it was found that Singh had killed seven Japanese in hand-to-hand combat and, despite painful wounds, through his determination, outstanding dash and magnificent courage he had caused this important position to be retaken.

On 6 June 1944, lost among news of D-Day, *The London Gazette* announced the awarding of the Victoria Cross to Singh. The investiture was a full-blown ceremonial affair held in Delhi on the Maidan between the Red Fort and the River Jumna. The ceremony was presided over by the Viceroy, Lord Wavell, who shared the dais with Lord Mountbatten and General Sir William Slim.

There were four Victoria Crosses bestowed that day; Nand Singh, Kamal Ram (8th Punjab Regiment), Ganju Lama (1/7th Gurkha Rifles) and posthumously to Abdul Hafiz (9th Jats). Honour guards from the recipients' regiments stood to attention on the vast parade ground as the Viceroy pinned the simple bronze cross onto the left breast of each of these outstandingly valiant native soldiers. For these men, there would be no more fighting against the Japanese. However, Singh's fighting days were not yet over.

Weakened by the war and occupied with its own huge programme of domestic recovery, Britain gave India its long awaited independence in August 1947. At the behest of the Muslim leader, Muhammad Ali Jinnah, and in its hurry to be rid of the former Jewel in the Crown, a poorly conceived compromise was reached that would partition the Sub-continent into Hindu and Muslim countries, India and East and

SECOND ARAKAN CAMPAIGN

West Pakistan. This led to the most appalling atrocities committed by both sides. One of the greatest flashpoints was the northern province of Kashmir claimed by Pakistan and India, which is still an unresolved issue even today.

During the winter of 1947, while the rest of the world collectively licked its wounds and concentrated on rebuilding, a vicious war was being fought in the snows of Kashmir at the foothills of the Himalayas. The Indian front-line garrison town of Uri, to the east of the capital Srinagar, and its surrounding roads were under enemy fire from the nearby hills. The Indian Army decided to dislodge the enemy from their threatening positions in these hills and ordered an attack. At 07.00 hours on 12 December, the 1st Sikhs marched out from Uri and steadily advanced into the hills, easily overcoming the Pakistani positions. By noon, they had reached the main enemy strongpoint and met much stiffer opposition, suffering heavy casualties.

Singh, now commissioned to jemadar and platoon commander, had been left out of the morning battle but was allowed to re-join his command in the afternoon.

The citation for a posthumous Maha Vir Chakra (MVC) was published in the *Gazette of India* of 26 January 1950:

> His platoon went into the attack like a band of Troajens [sic] with himself to the fore. The fire was intense and his men were falling left and right of him, yet he pressed on and while doing so picked up a rifle of one of the casualties. His men followed him shouting 'Sat Sri Singh' and closed in on the enemy. He was himself hit in the leg. Nothing daunted he carried on. A fierce and violent hand to hand fighting now ensued. The band of brave stalwarts threw themselves on the enemy in range, shouting war cry after war cry. The leader, Jemadar Nand Singh, was the first to draw blood with his bayonet. Although wounded, he killed five of the enemy. By this fine example his men were now inspired to frenzy and were acting like fiends, bayoneting right and left. The enemy broke and fled, but very few of them could escape.
>
> This brave VCO (VC Officer) had carried out his CO's orders and captured his objective but as he stood there on top of the bunker, a burst of enemy LMG hit him in the chest and killed him on the spot. However, his mission had been completed. The enemy had shown his back and the situation was saved.

How different from the more restrained citations normally published im *The London Gazette*.

On 26 January 1950, the Indian Government established a new award called the Maha Vir Chakra, the second highest award for gallantry against the enemy. In recognition of Singh's exceptional record of outstanding service and bravery, he had been posthumously given the award and became the only recipient of both this and the Victoria Cross. He was also the only Second World War VC recipient who was killed in action in a subsequent war.

Chapter 7

Wingate's VC Chindits

When he commanded the Army in the Middle East and Africa, Archibald Wavell had been impressed by the exploits of Major Orde Wingate. Commissioned in 1923, Wingate joined the Royal Artillery before transferring to the Sudan Defence Force from 1928 to 1933. In 1936, he was assigned to Mandatory Palestine, where he set up a joint British–Israeli counter-insurgency force to fight Arab agitators. Despite being brought up in a strict Plymouth Brethren environment, Wingate became a great supporter of Zionism.

In 1939, he returned to staff duties with Wavell in Cairo at the onset of war. Major Wingate's experience in Sudan prompted Wavell to encourage this unconventional officer to form a group of Sudanese and Ethiopian partisans, known as Gideon's Force, to disrupt the Italian supply lines in Ethiopia and provide intelligence in the East African Campaign of 1940–41.

When Wavell was moved from Africa to India he requested the newly promoted Colonel Wingate for service in Burma. He had in mind a similar long-range penetration group that could operate behind the Japanese lines. Under the command of the eccentric Wingate, the Long-Range Penetration Brigade, better known as the Chindits, would carry out operations behind Japanese lines in Burma. Unlike Gideon's Force, where irregular locals had been used, Wingate chose men of the 13th (The King's) Liverpool Regiment. He told the *Daily Express* war correspondent, Alaric Jacob, that:

> Most of my Chindits are not in their first youth but married men between 28 and 35, who had done coastal defence work and never dreamt they would be shock troops during one of the toughest jobs of this war. If any ordinary man from Liverpool or Manchester, etc., can do this specialised jungle war behind the Jap lines, then any fit

man in the British Army can do likewise and we show ourselves to the world as fighting men second to none – which I believe we are.

The rest of the force was made up of men from the former Bush Warfare School, the newly formed 3rd Battalion, 2nd Gurkha Rifles and the 2nd Battalion Burma Rifles. They were thoroughly trained in the jungles in the western part of India, including being supplied by air. They were given the official title of the 77th Indian Infantry Brigade but were soon known as the Chindits after the mythical Burmese beast that appeared on their cloth badge worn on the sleeve.

The training started in the summer of 1942 and by early 1943 Wingate was satisfied that his men were ready for taking the field against the Japanese. This was not the opinion of many of the Chindits, who felt they were still untrained. An example of this was made when it was pointed out that even though they would have to cross a number of rivers and streams, few of the men could swim. Many working-class Britons who attended the poorly funded state schools never had the opportunity to learn to swim. Although Wingate ordered that all non-swimmers must learn to swim, he did not put an instruction system in place. A young officer later remarked: 'We were badly trained, badly led and the plans over-optimistic.'

Wavell had planned to use the Chindits in an operation conjunction with IV Corps but this was postponed. Wingate persuaded Wavell to let the Chindit part of the operation go ahead to test his theories about a future larger operation. On 8 February 1943, Operation *Longcloth* was under way. Dividing his columns into north and south groups, it was arranged they would meet up in the Indaw area where the railway ran. The Japanese were soon aware of their presence and set up ambushes and pushed the Chindits into a tightening box east of the Irrawaddy River. Apart from some minor destruction of track and bridges, the Chindits were not able to achieve very much.

With mounting pressure from casualties, mostly sickness, and an alerted enemy, Wingate gave the order for his men to scatter in small groups and try and make their way back to India. By the end of April, the last of the straggling Chindits had reached the border. The debit side showed that of the 3,000 men who set off, a third had died in combat, been taken prisoner or died of disease. Of the 2,182 men that made it back to India, 600 were so debilitated from wounds and disease they were withdrawn from active service. The general feeling was summed up by the remark: 'Never have so many marched so far for so little.' The results had been mixed. Lasting disruption of Japanese supply routes had not been achieved but the sense that the Allies were fighting back lifted the spirits. On the positive side, the operation gave a boost to the morale of the Allied troops in India. The press gave the Chindits plenty of glowing publicity, in part because Wingate permitted four members of the press to accompany his southern group as far as the Chindwin River while his men were still fit and healthy.

In his operations report, Wingate was scathing about many officers under his command and skated over his own changes of mind that he had omitted to convey to his officers. In the search for a hero in this so-far disastrous war in the east, this unconventional man could do little wrong. He was championed and supported by the government, senior officers and the press. It was of little surprise that another incursion was soon planned but on a grander scale.

Churchill was sufficiently impressed to take Wingate with him to the Quebec Conference, where he was able to receive the backing from the Americans to mount another long-range penetration operation. Crucially, he was promised full co-operation for air support, mostly in the form of USAAF aircraft and crews. Instead of having to march from the border to their target, his men would be flown to various open sites some 200 miles behind Japanese lines. The sites would be prepared for large-scale landings for transport aircraft and fortified to repel Japanese attacks. The dropping zones were code-named *Piccadilly*, *Broadway* and *Chowringhee*. The latter was quickly abandoned once the drop had been completed. Other bases were established further north: *Blackpool*, *Aberdeen* and *White City*.

The main objectives of the operation were to support the advance on Myitkyina by the American-led Chinese troops and establish a strong position astride the Japanese lines of communication. The other was to impede the anticipated build-up of the Japanese forces for the invasion of India by harassing them in the Mogaung area.

Operation *Thursday* got under way on 5 March 1944. The first wave was glider-borne and a near disaster. As the gliders landed, they hit deep furrows made by teak logs dragged to the river by elephants. Wheels were ripped off and gliders crashed into each other, causing many casualties. Fortunately the gliders carrying the men of the American Airborne Engineer Company landed safely and they were able to clear the wreckage and prepare a landing strip for the 9,000 men arriving over the next seven days.

Among these arrivals were men of the 1st Battalion South Staffordshire Regiment. They would soon to be in close combat with the enemy and where one of their number would be the first Chindit VC.

GEORGE CAIRNS VC

George Cairns was born on 12 December 1913, in Sidcup, Kent, the son of Albert Henry and Rose Sophia. He was educated at Fulham Central School and the Lycee, Kensington, before joining the Bank Belge in the City of London.

On 20 June 1940, Cairns enlisted in the Somerset Light Infantry (Territorial Army) and was soon made up to corporal. Having attended OCTU at Taunton, he was given an emergency commission on 26 July 1941 and joined the 6th Battalion Somerset Light Infantry. He also was married that year to Ena, a girl he had met at the bank. The following year, the battalion was posted to India, arriving there on 29 September 1942.

On 11 November, Cairns transferred to the 1st Battalion South Staffordshire Regiment, which undertook specialist jungle training and became part of the 77th Independent Infantry Brigade under the command of the unconventional Major General Orde Wingate. In 1943, Wingate had led his first Chindit incursion behind Japanese lines in Burma with disappointing results, due in main to the raw recruits that had been assigned to him. Now he had a highly trained force of 9,000 who were to take part in the airborne Operation *Thursday* aimed at cutting enemy lines of communication and generally to create havoc in the Japanese rear.

On 5 March 1944, the 77th Independent Infantry Brigade, of which the 1st Battalion formed part, landed by glider at *Broadway*, west of the Irrawaddy. Between 5 and 10 March, a total of 100 gliders and 600 air supply sorties built up a strong well-equipped force that was then ready to take on the Japanese.

As soon as they landed, Brigadier Mike Calvert ordered the South Staffords to establish a road and rail block across the enemy's line of communication between Mandalay and Myitkyina. To reach the railway, the men had to cross the 3,000ft Gangaw range and ford the Kawkke Chaung. After seven days they reached a little village called Henu, which Calvert decided was the place to block the railway. They had arrived in the dark so when dawn broke they found they were overlooked by the Japanese on a small hillock called Bare or Pagoda Hill. Almost immediately, they came under fire. Calvert called for his men to attack: 'Staffords to the right and Gurkhas to the left.'

The small force was a mixture containing a mortar platoon, machine-gunners and animal handlers. Nonetheless, they fixed bayonets and followed Calvert up the slope. As they reached the summit, the Japanese left their shelter and came hurtling towards them. They clashed head-on in an area some fifty yards square. Calvert later wrote that the action resembled an officers' guest night:

> The air was filled with the sound of steel crashing against steel, the screams and curses of wounded men, the sharp crack of revolvers and rifle shots, the eerie whine of stray bullets and the sickening crunch of breaking bones. Everyone slashed and bashed at the enemy with any weapon that came to hand, yelling and shouting as they did so. In Europe the cold steel part of it would have been restricted to bayonets; out here there was more variety, with Japanese officers wielding their huge swords and the Gurkhas doing sterling work with the *kukri*.

Calvert would have seen one of these sword-wielding officers attack the mortar platoon commander, Lieutenant George Cairns. Cairns was seen at the front of the charge when a Japanese officer came at him with his *katana* and hacked at his left arm. The shock of seeing his arm hanging by a few strips of muscle must have sent a rush of adrenaline through Cairns. He shot the enemy officer, picked up his sword and pitched into the mêlée. Despite his severe injury, exacerbated by two bayonet wounds in his side, he continued to lead his men, slashing left and right with the captured sword, killing several of the enemy.

A fellow officer saw Cairns struggling on the ground with a Japanese until he broke free, grabbed a rifle bayonet and stabbed the soldier repeatedly 'like a mad-man'. Soon after a reaction set in and he collapsed, mortally wounded. The attack successfully dislodged the enemy, who retreated. Calvert stood over Cairns as he whispered: 'Have we done all right, sir?' George Cairns lingered until the following morning before he died. The short and violent battle of Pagoda Hill resulted in twenty-three killed and sixty-four wounded. The Japanese suffered forty-two dead and many more wounded. This newly won area became another Chindit base known as *White City*, named because of the numbers of parachutes dropped and hanging from the surrounding trees.

Calvert and other officers recommended Cairns for the Victoria Cross, which was given to Wingate on 24 March. The Chindit commander was returning to Imphal in an American B-25 Mitchell bomber when it crashed in deep jungle during a violent tropical storm. All on board were killed and Cairn's recommendation was scattered.

Regimental representatives, aware of the recommendation, alerted the War Office. An investigation found that two out of the three officers who had witnessed Cairns' exploit had later been killed in action. The War Office followed the prevailing rule governing the awarding of the VC, which required three officer witnesses, and shelved the matter.

In 1948, Cairn's widow, Ena, contacted her local Member of Parliament and as a result of a BBC broadcast describing her husband's feat, the recommendation was back on the table. With further support from Brigadier Mike Calvert, who witnessed the action, a fresh application was placed before the Awards Committee of the War Office. This time the application was accepted and the award was announced in *The London Gazette* dated 20 May 1949. Cairns' Cross was presented to his widow at Buckingham Palace on 26 July by King George VI, the last Second World War VC to be awarded. His medal is held by the Staffordshire Regimental Museum at Lichfield.

With the enemy alerted, the base at *White City* was strengthened with artillery, mines and thirty-yard deep belts of barbed wire. On 6 April, the Japanese began a five day-long attack and without any pretence of thoughtful strategy, repeatedly hurled themselves at the barbed wire to be killed. One of the defenders recalled:

> There were hundreds of Japanese bodies hanging on the wire ... The Japs were very brave but stupid – they'd attack the same place every night. They came across the Paddy banging and shouting.

By 17 April, even the Japanese recognised they were never going take *White City* and pulled back.

With the death of Wingate, the role of the Chindits changed. Although Brigadier 'Joe' Lentaigne was appointed as his replacement, the feeling was that the drive that Wingate managed to induce had disappeared. Now the role had changed to supporting the Chinese forces in the north under the command of US General Joseph Stilwell, a man who neither liked the British nor understood the role of the Chindits. Relations between the British and General Stilwell's team continued to be poisonous. When Stilwell took command of the Chindits he told Lentaigne that they were 'a bunch of lily-livered Limey popinjays' and he re-rolled them as conventional infantry.

Stilwell could barely contain his gloating when he was able to inform Mountbatten and Slim that his men had captured the all-important town of Myitkyina without the help of the British. He was soon forced to backtrack when it became clear that his Chinese–American force had only captured the airfield. False intelligence led 'Vinegar Joe' to believe that the town was held by just 350 Japanese. When he sent in a Chinese regiment to complete the capture, they were forced to retreat by a much stronger enemy force.

On 30 June Mountbatten told Stilwell to evacuate the 77th and 111th. They were exhausted, sick and been kept in action too long. John Masters requested that his 111th Brigade should be medically assessed. All 2,200 men were examined and only 118 were passed fit for service. Refusing to acknowledge this list, Stilwell ordered the fit men to mount guard on a Chinese artillery battery. After ten days of this nonsense, the 111th finally caught a plane back to India.

MICHAEL ALLMAND VC

Born into a strong Roman Catholic family in Golders Green, North London, on 22 August 1923, Michael Allmand attended Ampleforth College in North Yorkshire. Entering Oxford University in 1941, he studied history and was the founding editor of a literary review journal named *The Wind and the Rain*. He had also started writing a biography of the eighteenth century political philosopher, Edmund Burke, when he received his call-up papers. He joined the Royal Armoured Corps (RAC) before being sent to India to sit for his OCTU at Mhow. Once commissioned in the Indian Armoured Corps (IAC), he was appointed to 6th Duke of Connaught's Own Lancers (Watson's Horse), but never served with them. Instead, he was posted as instructor at the IAC Armoured Car School at Ferozepore.

Tiring of the mundane routine of an instructor, Allmand leapt at the chance of joining the Chindits for Operation *Thursday*. After his jungle training, he was attached to the 3rd Battalion, 6th Gurkha Rifles (3/6GR) and assigned to Brigadier Mike Calvert's 77th Brigade. On 5 March 1944, the regiment was flown in by glider to *Broadway* and, following the same route as the South Staffords, helped establish *White City*. After *White City* was abandoned, 3/6GR was sent north along the railway to Hopin. Here it sent out patrols to locate the Japanese defences. A little later it marched further north to another Chindit-established base called *Blackpool*.

The 77th Brigade, along with the rest of the long-range penetration groups, was exhausted, starving and suffering from malaria and dysentery. Their equipment was falling to pieces. Personal equipment such as their bush hats were green with mildew and even watch straps had rotted away. The last thing they wanted to hear was Stilwell's order to attack the important rail hub, Mogaung.

The 77th began their final 10-mile advance on 6 June 1944 with about 2,000 men. By the time they reached Mogaung, their numbers had been whittled down to just 550, victims in the main from disease. Opposing them were 4,000 Japanese who were well dug in. By necessity, they made their way on a narrow front; the only approach being along a narrow causeway surrounded on either side by monsoon-flooded terrain. On the approach, villages were cleared of small parties of Japanese and by the 10th they were about 400 yards from the Pin Hmi Railway Bridge.

The Japanese were dug in along the banks of the road and in the surrounding jungle. They put up a fierce resistance and it was not until the following day that Temporary Captain Michael Allmand's platoon managed to get within twenty yards of the bridge. Here the Gurkhas were pinned down by heavy and accurate fire. With the attack stalled, Allmand rose and, calling his men to follow, charged the bridge. Hurling grenades into the gun positions and killing three Japanese with his *kukri*, Allmand inspired his men to follow and soon the objective was taken.

On 13th, Allmand took over a company following the death of its commander. He was ordered to take a ridge that was holding up its advance. Leading from the front, Allmand dashed thirty yards ahead through long grass and marshy ground into the teeth of machine-gun fire and single-handedly killed a number of machine-gunners, allowing his men to take the ridge.

On the 23rd, his luck ran out on the final assault on the bridge. Having been withdrawn from the front line and suffering from trench foot, Allmand and his Gurkhas were called upon for a final push on the railway bridge. Although barely able to walk, Allmand moved forward alone through the deep mud and shell holes and attacked a Japanese machine-gun nest with grenades before being wounded. He was carried to safety by Havildar Tibir Gurung but died of his wounds the following day. Later in the same action, a second member of the 3/6GR, Rifleman Tul Bahadur Pun, made a single-handed attack that finally secured the bridge.

Allmand was a few weeks short of his twenty-first birthday when he died, having made three daring charges, each of which was worthy of the Victoria Cross. His citation appeared in *The London Gazette* on 26 October 1944 and his VC presented to his family by King George on 17 July 1945.

A most moving presentation parade was held in Hong Kong on 22 July 1991 when the Allmand family presented Michael's VC group to the Colonel of the Regiment, General Pett. The medal was passed to the Gurkha major and escort, who trooped the medal along the front row of the parade to a specially composed tune, 'Allmand VC'.

TUL BAHADUR PUN VC

Born on 23 March 1923 in the village of Myagdi west of the Nepalese capital, Kathmandu, Tul Bahadur Pun enlisted in 1941. He completed his eight-month recruit training in the Regimental Centre of the 6th Gurkha Rifles at Abbottabad in Northern India before being posted to the 3rd Battalion.

A second operation was proposed for 1944 but this time it would be strongly supported from the air, mostly by the USAAF. The 3rd Battalion 6th Gurkhas formed part of 77 Infantry Brigade under the command of Brigadier Mike Calvert. There followed intensive jungle training in Gwalior, where they were trained in crossing rivers, demolitions and bivouacking. For some reason, Wingate was reluctant to use Indian Army formations and was especially prejudiced against Gurkha officers. He also cited the varied dietary requirements of the different Indian and Gurkha castes and religions. He was, however, overruled by General Wavell.

On 5 March 1944, Rifleman Pun and his comrades landed by glider at their designated box or area, code-named *Broadway*. This turned out to be a poor landing ground and there were many casualties from the crash landings. Calvert got his men to clear the ground to make a strip suitable to take transport aircraft the following day. Over the next week, 600 sorties delivered 9,000 men to the various landing zones. On 27 March, the Japanese attacked *Broadway* and there was plenty of hand-to-hand fighting before the enemy was repulsed. Pun recalls this second Chindit operation:

> Out of 1,800 that landed, about 500 hit logs and the pilots were seriously injured. Mules were used to carry goods. They underwent operations of the throat so they wouldn't bray and give away our position to the enemy.

The Gurkhas, including Pun, had marched over the Gangaw range and taken part in the fight on Pagoda Hill, where George Cairns gained his VC. They then helped establish the *White City* base before moving north to another base on the railway, *Blackpool*. Wingate's successor, Brigadier Lentaigne, ironically a Gurkha officer, ordered Calvert to abandon *Broadway* and *White City* and move north to support another brigade. Because the monsoon had broken, movement in the jungle was extremely difficult and Calvert's command was unable to carry out this order. Now under the command of General Stilwell, the 77 Brigade was ordered to take the key railway town of Mogaung. After an arduous eight-day trek, they reached a bridge over a river leading to the town.

Six unsuccessful attacks were made on the Pin Hmi Railway Bridge before Pun was sent out on a night reconnaissance:

> Making the slightest noise could spell doom. In those days, we had shoes fixed with nails and they made creaking noises, so I wrapped cloth on my feet and inspected the bridge, which had gun-posts on both ends.

The assault on the bridge was launched that night and by dawn it had been taken. Two nights later, Pun's platoon was involved in attacking the railway bridge at Mogaung. Without artillery support, the mission stalled:

> Almost all our infantry was wiped out. Since there was nowhere to take shelter, many were killed. We were pinned down in the open fields. I was leading my platoon and was in the extreme right corner and the section commander was in the middle.
>
> Everyone else was killed but I escaped because I was on the edge. I looked to the right and left and found no trace of anyone, they had all been killed. I was the lone survivor and it was clear I would also be killed. I raised my head and the enemy spotted me.

This concentrated crossfire came from a position known as the Red House and from a strong bunker position about 200 yards to its left:

> I jumped forward twice to reach where the section commander's gun was lying. I picked it up and jumped into the midst of the enemy, firing at all sides until they were all killed.

Pun's citation states that:

> Pun the seized the Bren Gun, and firing from the hip as he went, continued the charge on this heavily bunkered position alone, in the face of the most shattering concentration of automatic fire directed straight at him. With the dawn coming up behind him, he presented a perfect target to the Japanese. He had to move for thirty yards over open ground, ankle deep in mud, through shell holes and over fallen trees ... He killed three and put five more to flight and captured two light machine guns and much ammunition.

Pun then turned his attention to another enemy position:

A little distance away there was a bunker and a circular sentry post. Four enemy soldiers were in the process of loading their guns. When I jumped in among them, they were surprised and couldn't figure out what to do. I pulled the trigger, but had run out of ammo. They were advancing when I threw a grenade into the trench and killed them all.

Pun was isolated, out of ammunition and pinned down by enemy fire:

I was in a dilemma. The bullets I needed were very close, yet I didn't know how to get to them. A British regiment was fighting close by, firing at the enemy posts. In one leap, I got to the ammunition boxes and threw them inside the bunker. From there, I tried to throw hand grenades at the enemy, but they kept bouncing back and exploding behind me, no matter how hard I threw them.

I kept reloading and firing. There was uninterrupted firing from a Japanese soldier on the other side, which destroyed part of my hideout. After six attempts, I hit the enemy and the firing from his side stopped. I raised my head and saw him lying flat on the ground.

I went to the edge of the bunker to take his gun and discovered there was a wire mesh in front of him to protect him from grenades. That is why my grenades were bouncing back.

I took out my *kukri* and cut through the mesh. As I was snatching the gun off the fallen man, two enemy soldiers came up behind me and tried to capture me. I had left my weapon outside and all I had at my disposal was the *kukri*. I beheaded one of them and hit the second on his shoulder – I had to cut him several times before he also died. Suddenly a third enemy appeared but I cut him with my *kukri* too. Others from the trench followed, but I kept slashing them with my *kukri*. When there were too many of them, I took out another grenade and threw it at them. Then it was all quiet.

The Japanese were finally driven out of the town, helped on their way by that most terrifying of weapons, the flame-thrower. The attack on Mogaung had cost the lives of some 800 Gurkhas, including Lieutenant Michael Allmand, who was awarded a posthumous VC for outstanding gallantry. Pun was one of only two men from his platoon to survive the battle. He was praised by his commanding officer, who wrote a recommendation for a gallantry award:

One day I had been assigned to bring the rations, which were carried by mules. When I got to the headquarters, a message had arrived from the War Office. The clerk on duty took me aside and said 'Pun, one of the soldiers from your company has done an excellent job. I have collected the message. In all probability he will get a gallantry award.' He gave me the message and told me to give it to the company. I glanced at it and saw my name on it.

Pun's citation was published in *The London Gazette* on 7 November 1944. He was one of four men of the Chindits to be awarded the Victoria Cross. In a special parade held at the Red Fort, Delhi, on 3 March 1945, he received his Cross from the Viceroy, Field Marshall Lord Wavell.

After Indian Independence in 1947, Pun's regiment was transferred to the British Army, a testament to how high the Gurkhas were regarded. He served in Malaya during the Emergency (1948–60) and Hong Kong. He rose through the ranks until he was promoted to regimental sergeant major. When he retired on 14 May 1959, he was appointed to honorary lieutenant and returned to his home at Myagdi. Always concerned with education, he opened two primary schools in the area.

In 1986, his farm was washed away by floods but a benefit football match played in Kathmandu raised enough funds to re-establish his smallholding. In 2006, it was learned that Pun's health was suffering and that it was necessary to come to Britain for treatment. This was a period when the government of the time had tried to stem immigration with some very insensitive conditions.

This came to the notice of Rod Liddle, who wrote an article in *The Sunday Times* on 27 May 2007 entitled, 'A rape conviction is better than a VC if you want to stay in Britain'. He reported the plight of Pun, whose health was deteriorating and could not afford medical treatment. His only hope was to come to this country but he was denied a visa by the immigration service at the UK embassy in Kathmandu. The reason it gave was breathtaking in its ignorance and insensitivity: 'He (Tul Bahadur Pun VC) had failed to demonstrate that he had strong ties with the UK.' It appeared that an illegal immigrant with criminal intent stood a better chance of entering the UK than a loyal ex-Gurkha soldier who had been awarded the most prestigious award for gallantry the country could bestow.

This started a movement that was strongly supported by the public. There were several people involved in lobbying for the retired Gurkhas' cause and among the most prominent was the actress Joanna Lumley, whose father had been a Gurkha officer present at Mogaung. After months of media pressure the government finally acknowledged that the Gurkhas were a special case. Pun was granted residency and, together with Lachihman Gurung, came to Britain in 2007. He lived in Hounslow and was made a Freeman of the Borough of Hounslow in 2009.

In 2011, he returned to his home village at Myagdi to open a new school but died there on 20 April.

FRANK GERALD BLAKER VC

Frank Gerald Blaker was born in Kasauli, Punjab, India, on 8 May June 1920, the son of Dr Gerald Hugh Blaker (Indian Army Medical Department.) and Nora Mildred Blaker (née Fox). His father served with the Pasteur Institute in Rangoon, Mandalay and Meikteila. When his father retired in 1940, he and his mother moved to Tanganyika. Blaker learned to be independent early through attending boarding schools in Burma and India from 1926 to 1936 before going to England and attending Taunton School in Somerset until 1939. He loved the outdoors and became an enthusiastic Scout, spending his holidays in the countryside. His first taste of Army life came through School Cadets whilst boarding at Taunton and he rose to become a cadet sergeant.

After leaving Taunton School at the end of 1939, Blaker immediately enlisted in the Somerset Light Infantry in early 1940. On gaining his officer's commission in mid-1941, he transferred to the Highland Light Infantry (Glasgow Regiment) and by his own request went out to India to be seconded to the 9th Gurkha Rifles in 1942. He had grown up in Burma and understood the country and its culture.

To his fellow officers Blaker was known as 'Jim', an allusion to the cereal advertising character 'Sunny Jim', because of his cheerful nature. The Gurkhas had trouble with his name and called him 'Blanket Sahib' as they couldn't get their tongues around Blaker. The regiment formed part of the 4th Indian Infantry Brigade of the 26th Indian Division in its abortive first incursion into the Arakan.

Blaker and his platoon did have one of the few successes when he was sent to investigate enemy activity at a village about five miles from Taung Bazaar. Making contact with the Japanese led to a sharp exchange of fire. Finally, the Japanese broke and ran across open ground to take a defensive position on a nearby ridge. Disregarding the fire from two machine-guns, Blaker led his twenty-six men up the slope and forced the enemy to retreat to the south. Following up, the enemy were chased for a further two miles, during which the Gurkhas killed sixteen men and captured three wounded. One of the wounded was an officer who carried valuable intelligence. Blaker's commanding officer, Major Alec Harper M.C., recommended him for an immediate award of a Military Cross for one such action.

During Operation *Thursday*, the 3/9th Gurkas were originally part of Calvert's 77th Brigade. During the siege of *Blackpool*, they were transferred to the depleted 111th Indian Brigade. The 111th was withdrawn on 31 May 1944 and given the task of defending the northern half of Lake Indawgyi as it was not considered fit for further operations. The lake was used by two Sunderland flying boats to carry the wounded and sick back to India. This respite lasted just a week before the brigade was recalled for operations at Taungni.

On 9 July 1944, in the push north towards Myitkyina, three Gurkha columns of 111th Brigade converged to the south of Point 2171, part of high ground some eighteen miles west-south-west of Mogaung so named for the height of its peak. The 4th Gurkhas had bumped into the outlying positions of the Japanese, who were determined to hold this strategic point where the terrain drove the road and rail route close to the high ground on the north side of the valley. Point 2171 dominated the approaches to the town of Taungni, the railway and the valley some 400m below, all of which were crucial to the north–south movement of troops and supplies. Outside this corridor, movement was by foot and pack animal, and then usually with some difficulty.

The lead up to the attack on Hill 2171 took four days, taken up with clearing the Japanese outer defensive posts so that the Gurkhas could form up at the bottom of the slope for a consolidated attack on the final position. The enemy strength was about one company and they were well entrenched in bunkers and foxholes. The only way to the summit was a steep track up the north-west side of the hill.

Two companies of Colonel Harper's 3/9th Gurkhas were chosen to assault the steep, jungle-covered spur that had some preparatory track clearing done leading towards the summit. 'B' company under Major Thorpe would conduct the main attack on the south side of the spur leading up to the hill while 'C' company, under the command of Major Frank Blaker, would carry out a flanking attack. The planned air strike to soften up the heavily entrenched and defended Japanese position was aborted, which left the Gurkhas with little option but to launch a full frontal assault on the position with only mortar fire as a support. Colonel John Masters, who became a highly successful author when he left the Army, wrote of Blaker's VC action:

> By this time the whole brigade was nearly exhausted. Moving and climbing in the jungle was very difficult. It took Jim Blaker an hour and a half to reach the foot of his ridge. Nearly five hours to climb it. Near the top he saw that the crest and northern flank of Hill 2172 were strongly defended by automatics, woodpecker machine guns

and mortars. After sending his message to me, 'ready, very close, ready to go' and waiting for the covering bombardment, Jim ordered the charge.

His leading men came under machine guns firing directly down the ridge. They dived into the dense jungle, tried to crawl up on their hands and knees, Men fell, the advance stopped. Jim went forward alone then, firing his carbine, calling 'Come on 'C' Company. Seven machine gun bullets through the stomach. He sank down, against a tree, turned his head, 'Come on 'C' Company, I'm going to die. Take the position'. The Gurkhas swept on up. Bayonets. *Ayo Gurkhali*, the Gurkhas have come! That night I wrote out the citation for Blaker's Victoria Cross, which was immediately awarded, posthumously.

The rest of the Gurkhas followed and soon all enemy resistance on Hill 2171 was overcome. Another version written soon after also describes the last moments of Blaker's life. Acting Captain Jimmy Sweetman's personal account of standing shoulder-to-shoulder with Blaker provides the vivid detail of that action in a letter he wrote to Blaker's parents on 14 August 1944. Sweetman says:

> The other Company got there first, and we could tell by the firing that they were in rather a tight spot. 'Jim' (as we called Frank) urged us to redouble our efforts and we pushed round onto a ridge which would take us up to the peak. Almost at the top, we ran into heavy machine gun fire and were held up. Jim came up at once and spotted the machine gun that was causing us so much trouble. He fired at it a couple of times and then we saw a grenade fall about two yards in front of us. I dived to the right, Frank to the left and unfortunately he got a wound in the left wrist from the burst.
>
> He got up and calmly went ahead through the thick undergrowth, firing his carbine as he went. When he was within seven yards of the gun, he got to a large bush and was just trying to get round it when he was fatally wounded by a long burst from the gun. But by this time the men were following him and we pressed on and captured the position. Frank then went back towards the route by which we came and got about five hundred yards down the track before he collapsed.
>
> As soon as I could I went back, following him, and came across him lying by the side of the track, with four of our men who had followed him back. I asked him how he was and he said 'There's something in my stomach, Jimmy.' I had a look and found three bullet holes. Then I eased him over and saw that they hadn't come

out. I told him so, and he took it magnificently. I said I'd dress his wounds and give him some morphia. He also had bullets in his chest and right shoulder. But he just said, 'No, they'll do it.' meaning the men. 'You go back and get the hill and contact the other Company.' He knew I'd have to obey him and not see him safely back, but I told the men to carry him carefully and only give him a little water. As I left him he was as calm and serene as he always had been, though he knew he was going to die. (It would have been two weeks before he'd have had a chance to get to a hospital.).'

About 2 pm, Sweetman went back to the Company to finish the attack on the hill. The men with Jim Blaker made him a stretcher from their shirts and started back. Around 4 pm, Frank said to the men: 'Two of you go on and get more help, Havildar Major, you stay here and wait with me.' Soon afterwards he said he was dying.

During his last minutes Blaker told the havildar major (company sergeant major) to give Jimmy Sweetman the names of two men he wished to be recommended for gallantry. Then he said: 'Thank "C" Company for all they've done for me. Tell them I have gone from them but they must go on fighting to the end.' Blaker died at about 16.30 hours.

The havildar major was in tears when he later related Blaker's last moments to Sweetman. When he announced Blaker's death to the platoon commanders they were visibly upset by it despite their war experiences generally having made them very callous. A testament of the high regard Blaker was held by his men was when they went to Sweetman later and asked: 'Will you please write to the Major Sahib's family and tell them that we looked upon him as the most efficient and bravest officer we've ever had.'

The 111th Brigade had attacked and cleared the Japanese outpost positions in the hills west and south-west of Mogaung. For its part it held Hill 2171 for several days while it waited to be relieved. The Japanese kept up an incessant artillery bombardment and counter-attacks. This did not cause any significant casualties but the slow and constant erosion of the brigade's numbers forced Colonel John Masters to order a withdrawal before the relief arrived. A few days later, Point 2171 was retaken when fresh troops from 14th Brigade took over from the exhausted 111th and cleared the surrounding hills, thus enabling the subsequent capture of Taungni to the north-east.

Owing to the slow communication lines with East Africa, Blaker's parents learned of his death through *The London Gazette* in an article on the posthumous award of his Victoria Cross. It was impossible for Dr

Above: Charles Anderson in Malaya (The Malayan Campaign).

Right: Thomas Wilkinson (The Fall of Singapore).

Above: Thomas Wilkinson's VC action on *Li Wo* (The Fall of Singapore).

Below left: Gaje Ghale (The Chin Hills).

Below right: Alec George Horwood (Second Arakan Campaign).

Above left: Nand Singh (Second Arakan Campaign). Above right: Michael Allmand (Wingate's VC Chindits).

Below left: Tul Bahadur Pun (Wingate's VC Chindits). Below right: Frank Gerald Blaker (Wingate's VC Chindits).

Above: The Japanese tanks knocked-out in Ganju Lama's VC action (The Battle of Imphal). (Courtesy of J. Glanfield)

Below left: Agansing Rai (The Battle of Imphal). Below right: John Harman pictured in 1939 (The Siege of Kohima).

Right: Umrao Singh (The Follow-Up – Arakan).

Below: George Knowland's VC action (The Follow-Up – Arakan).

Above left: Bhanbhagta Gurung (The Follow-Up – Arakan). Above right: Bhanbhagta Gurung (The Follow-Up – Arakan) with Gian Singh (Marching South).

Below left: Prakash Singh Chib (Marching South). Below right: Karamjeen Singh Judge (Marching South).

Above left: Lachhiman Gurung (Marching South). Above right: John Newton (Australia's War).

Below left: Sefanaia Sukanaivalu (Australia's War). Below right: Leslie Starcevich (Australia's War).

Above: A group of four VC recipients pictured in 1953. They are Richard Kelliher, Edward Kenna, Reginald Partridge, and Reginald Rattey (all Australia's War).

Below: Robert Gray's VC action (Australia's War).

and Mrs Blaker to travel to receive their son's VC at Buckingham Palace, so the presentation was made to his brother, Hugh, who was serving in the Merchant Navy at the time. The VC and MC were then sent to Blaker's parents in East Africa, where they remain with the family.

After the taking of Hill 2171, the 7th Leicesters fought their way into Taugni and elsewhere other small towns were taken. By the end of August, the last of the Chindits had been evacuated. For five months they had blocked the railway to Myitkyina and suffered one of the hardest campaigns in history. The sour Joe Stilwell barely acknowledged the Chindits' contribution to his opening the Burma Road, stating that British soldiers were 'pig-fuckers'.

Trained to be a purely mobile force, the Chindits often became embroiled in static fighting and most of their time was spent marching rather than fighting. The enormous debt the Chindits owed to the USAAF in keeping them supplied went a long way to obviate the anti-American sentiment generated by Stilwell. The high rate of sickness depleted their efficiency and they were evacuated as a spent force. An attempt was made to resurrect them but they were disbanded in February 1945, much to Mike Calvert's dismay. By this time the well-trained XIVth Army had started its march into Burma and, as Mountbatten wrote, 'the whole Army was Chindit-minded'.

Chapter 8

The Battle of Imphal

Manipur was one of the most remote and quiet regions of India, with few links with the outside world. It was swallowed up by the British Raj in a brief war in 1891 but soon reverted back to its quiet ways. Imphal, its small capital – more a large village than a town – was shaken out of its torpor in 1942 when soldiers of the British Indian Army and 100,000 refugees fleeing from the Japanese in Burma passed through on the way to Dimapur and Silchar. A large refugee camp was built on what became Koirengel airfield and soon after the Japanese Air Force began bombing Imphal. The whole complexion of the area changed. Civilians fled the area to be replaced by the military.

In the months that followed, Imphal became an important supply base and Manipur's infrastructure was developed to accommodate road and air traffic. Bridlepaths became tarmac roads and, on the Imphal plain, airstrips were built and thousands of soldiers from other parts of India and Britain poured in.

Imphal was developed into a substantial Allied logistic base and linked to an even larger base 100 miles away at Dimapur. Manipur had been forcefully promoted to a front-line state and was the only Indian region in which a major battle was fought.

In March 1943, the Japanese command in Burma had been reorganised. The 15th Army under the control of Lieutenant General Renya Mutaguchi occupied the border area facing Manipur. He strongly advocated an invasion of India and was enthusiastically supported by Subhas Chandra Bose, the Nationalist leader and commander of the Indian National Army, and sought to overthrow the British rule by force. The ambitious Mutaguchi was determined to win the decisive victory that would drive out the British from India as well as halting General Stilwell's building of the Ledo Road linking India and China. He was impatient to launch his assault despite the activities of the

THE BATTLE OF IMPHAL

Chindits in disrupting his supply lines. He also had to contend with reservations over the scale of his plans by the senior officers of the Burma Area Army, but they were eventually persuaded.

The British commanders knew that there was to be an invasion and that Imphal and Dimapur would be the targets. Imphal was held by IV Corps, commanded by Lieutenant General Geoffrey Scoones, and part of Bill Slim's XIV Army. The defence of Imphal was widely spread and Mutaguchi's intention was to isolate and destroy these forward outpost divisions.

It had initially worked in the Arakan, where the Japanese had counter-attacked the XV Corps invasion in February. They had deployed their usual tactic of successfully encircling the Allies in the Battle of the Admin Box. What they had not taken into account was that the Allies were resupplied from the air and able to resist the Japanese, whose own supply lines were disrupted. Hunger and shortage of ammunition had caused the Japanese to withdraw but Mutaguchi dismissed these concerns, claiming that within a short time he would occupy Imphal with its vast stores and landing strips.

Scoones and Slim decided to withdraw their outpost divisions to the Imphal plain and so further extend the enemy's supply line. The 20th Division under the command of General Gracey occupied Tamu near the Chindwin in the malaria bed known as Kabaw Valley. He was opposed to making any retreat but by 25 March 1944 he complied and withdrew to the Shenam Saddle in the hills south-east of the Imphal plain.

The 17th Division had a torrid retreat from its base at Tiddim. When its commander, General 'Punch' Cowan, received his orders to withdraw on 12 March, he proposed to move on the 14th. As he lay awake at 3 am that night, he decided to go that day instead; a fortunate decision as the Japanese were moving faster than was anticipated. Leaving Tiddim in flames, the 17th took with it 4,000 mules and 2,000 vehicles. Pursued and harried by the Japanese, the division fought several skirmishes at roadblocks the enemy had thrown up. The delays in overcoming these blocks enabled the Japanese to encircle the 17th.

General Scoones then ordered his reserve 23rd Division from Imphal to drive the Japanese from the Tiddim–Imphal Road. With the division supported by light tanks, the Japanese were driven off, enabling the 17th to reach their new defensive position at Bishenpur south of Imphal.

Lord Mountbatten ordered that the 5th Indian Division be flown in from the Arakan and eleven days later it was in position north of Imphal. It was here that the first of five Imphal VCs was won.

ABDUL HAFIZ VC

Rao Abdul Hafiz Khan was born on 4 September 1915 in the village of Kalanpur in the Rhotak District of Punjab. His parents were Nur Mohammed and Hamidan and he later married Jigri Begum. On his nineteenth birthday (4 September 1934) he enlisted in the Indian Army and joined the 3rd Battalion, 9th Jat Regiment. The Jat battalions were separated by a variety of religions; two companies of Hindu Jats, one company of Musulman Rajputs and one of Punjabi Muslims.

After basic training, Hafiz was posted to the Landi Kotal Brigade on the North West Frontier and served in the Bara Fort in the Khyber Pass. Recruits who served in the Landi Kotal were regarded as experienced and tough enough to be sent to overseas fronts that opened with the coming of the Second World War: Africa, Italy and Burma.

At the end of 1943 the Indian 5th Infantry Division, in which the 3/9 Jats served with the 9th Indian Infantry Brigade, was taking part in the Burma Campaign. Sent to the second invasion of the Arakan, the 5th Division played a major part in the defeat of the Japanese 55th Division in what was the first victory against the Japanese for two years. From the Arakan, the 5th Division was airlifted to the central front and took part in the sprawling battle of Imphal.

Now promoted to Jemadar, Hafiz's regiment was advancing along the Litan Road in the Nungshigum area to the north-east of Imphal. The 3-mile-long Nungshigum Ridge that dominated the road and the Imphal plain was fought over between the Jats and the Japanese 51st Regiment. On 6 April 1944 the Jats reached the summit after an arduous climb up the steep flanks, but before they had time to set up a defensive position, the Japanese counter-attacked causing heavy casualties.

It was during this part of the battle that Hafiz performed the exploit that earned him a VC. His citation, which appeared in *The London Gazette* dated 27 July 1944, is detailed and reflects the regiment's War Diary:

> In Burma, in the early hours of the 6th April 1944, in the hills 10 miles North of Imphal, the enemy had attacked a standing patrol of 4 men and occupied a prominent feature overlooking a Company position. At first light a patrol was sent out and contacted the enemy, reporting that they thought approximately 40 enemy were in the position. It was not known if they had dug in during the hours of darkness.
>
> The Company Commander ordered Jemadar Abdul Hafiz to attack the enemy, with two sections from his platoon, at 0930 hours.

An artillery concentration was put down on the feature and Jemadar Abdul Hafiz led the attack. The attack was up a completely bare slope with no cover, and was very steep near the crest. Prior to the attack, Jemadar Abdul Hafiz assembled his sections and told them they were invincible, and all the enemy on the hill would be killed or put to flight. He so inspired his men that from the start the attack proceeded with great dash. When a few yards below the crest the enemy opened fire with machine-guns and threw grenades. Jemadar Abdul Hafiz sustained severe casualties, but immediately ordered an assault, which he personally led, at the same time shouting the Mohammedan battle cry. The assault went in without hesitation and with great dash up the last few yards of the hill, which was very steep.

On reaching the crest Jemadar Abdul Hafiz was wounded in the leg, but seeing a machine-gun firing from the flank, which had already caused several casualties, he immediately went towards it and, seizing the barrel, pushed it upwards, whilst another man killed the gunner. Jemadar Abdul Hafiz then took a Bren gun from a wounded man and advanced against the enemy, firing as he advanced, and killing several of the enemy. So fierce was the attack, and all his men so inspired by the determination of Jemadar Abdul Hafiz to kill all enemy in sight at whatever cost, that the enemy, who were still in considerable numbers of the position, ran away down the opposite slope of the hill [later called Runaway Hill] Regardless of machine-gun fire which was now being fired at him from another feature a few hundred yards away, he pursued the enemy, firing at them as they retired. Jemadar Abdul Hafiz was badly wounded in the chest from this machine-gun fire and collapsed holding the Bren gun and attempting to fire at the retreating enemy, shouting at the same time 'Re-organise on the position and I will give covering fire.' He died shortly afterwards.

Inspiring leadership and great bravery was displayed by Jemadar Abdul Hafiz in spite of having been twice wounded, once mortally. So encouraged were his men that the position was captured, casualties inflicted on the enemy to an extent several times the size of his own party, and the enemy arms recovered on the position, which included 2 Lewis machine-guns, 2 grenade dischargers and 2 officer's swords.

The complete disregard for his own safety and his determination to capture and hold the position at all costs was an example to all ranks, which it would be difficult to equal.

THE FORGOTTEN VCs

The attacks in and around Nungshigum Ridge continued until 13 April, when the feature was finally captured. The only known image of Hafiz shows a wild-eyed soldier with a bristling moustache; just the look he would have worn in his charge up the Nungshigum Ridge.

Hafiz was laid to rest in the Indian Army War Cemetery, Manipur. His VC was presented to his widow on 24 October 1944 by Lord Wavell at a ceremony outside the walls of the Red Fort, Delhi. His medal group is now on display in the Lord Ashcroft VC Gallery at the Imperial War Museum, London.

HANSON VICTOR TURNER VC
Hanson Victor Turner was born in Andover, Hampshire on 17 July 1910 to James Herbert and Alice Turner. He was young when the family moved to Halifax, Yorkshire, where he joined the 6th Halifax Company of the Boy's Brigade. He married Edith Rothery and lived at Woodhall Crescent, Copley. Before he was called up at the beginning of the Second World War, he worked as a bus conductor.

In June 1940, he enlisted in the Duke of Wellington's Regiment and was soon on his way to India. When the 1/West Yorkshire Regiment was sent to Rangoon as the Japanese began their invasion, they were involved in the terrible retreat to India. Crossing the border into Assam, they were in a poor state and in dire need of reinforcements. Turner was one of the many to be transferred from his regiment to bring the West Yorks up to strength.

The regiment was attached to the 17th Division and fought at Imphal in some of the heaviest action around the area of Bishenpur, Moirang and the Silchar Track. Major General Nobuo Tanaka, newly commanding the 33rd Japanese Division, exalted his men to greater efforts to take Imphal but privately noted that they looked dreadful; emaciated and unkempt. On 7 June, despite their condition, he urged them to mount a strong attack on the Allied position just north of Ningthoukhong. This was held by the men of the West Yorks, who had been involved in the Burma conflict from day one.

Taking the brunt of the attack was a weak platoon of twenty men, of which Acting Sergeant Turner was one of the section commanders. In pouring rain, the enemy made a night attack by creeping up close to the defences and using grenades against the platoon. This was very effective as three of the four machine-guns were put out of action and the platoon was forced to give ground.

Turner at once reorganised his party and withdrew forty yards. All the time they were under concentrated fire and this fire was kept up for two hours on Turner's dwindling party. Despite this, the enemy achieved no further success in this sector and were repelled in all their attacks. It became clear that the Japanese were trying another tack and attempting to outflank the position. Turner took the initiative and decided that a strong counter-attack would thwart the enemy's plans.

Leaving his men in their positions, he went forward alone armed with all the hand grenades he could carry and attacked the enemy single-handed. Hurling grenades with devastating effect, he disrupted the attack. When his supply was exhausted he went back for more grenades and returned to the offensive again. During all this time the enemy were keeping up intense small arms and grenade fire.

In all, Turner made five journeys to obtain further supplies of grenades. On the sixth occasion, while throwing a grenade among a party of the enemy, he was killed. His superb leadership and gallantry in the early stages of the attack was undoubtedly instrumental in preventing the enemy plan from succeeding. The next morning, after the enemy had retreated, the number of enemy dead found was ample evidence of the effect of his grenade throwing.

His fearless bravery in protecting the men in his platoon was rewarded with the awarding of the posthumous VC and his citation appeared in *The London Gazette* dated 14 August 1944. There was no presentation of his VC, so it must be assumed that it was posted to his family. In 1985, it was purchased by Calderdale District Council for £17,280 and is now on loan to the Duke of Wellington Regimental Museum in the Bankfield Museum, Halifax.

GANJU LAMA VC

Ganju Lama was born on 22 July 1922 (some accounts state it was 1924), in the village of Sangmo in South Sikkim to a Bhutia father, Kinchuk Shangdepa, who was the village headman. He was named Gayamcho, which later became corrupted to Ganju. His mother died when he was two and his childhood was spent helping his father look after their livestock and cutting wood. His elder brother had run away from home to join the Assam Rifles and when he visited their home, Lama was greatly impressed by the uniform and his brother's smart appearance.

When he reached twenty, Lama trekked over the mountains to Darjeeling and enlisted in the Gurkha Rifles. Although not Nepalese, the Gurkhas were prepared to accept any likely-looking recruit who closely resembled the Gurkha. As Lama lived near the Nepalese border, he was accepted. A British officer took his details and misinterpreted his name as Ganju, and so it remained for the rest of his life. He was enlisted in 1942 and joined the 1st Battalion, 7th Gurkha Rifles.

After basic training, he joined 180 recruits in six months' jungle training before being sent by train and road to Kohima. He then made the long journey to Tiddim, where he joined his regiment with the 17th Division. He joined 'B' Company under the command of Major Roy Gribble and became his batman. Gribble recalled that on the first day Lama came into his dugout at 04.00 hours carrying a mess tin of tea. He did not bother to say 'Good morning' or 'Sir'; he just said 'Get up!' Gribble took to him instantly.

It was not long before Lama had his first experience of warfare when 1/7th Gurkha was involved in a fight with the Japanese at Kennedy Peak. Despite firing many rounds, Lama was unable to claim a kill. A few days later he was quietly searching the bamboo jungle for wild fowl, when he spotted a Japanese soldier and was able to draw his first blood.

Lama was appointed the man in charge of his platoon's Projectile, Infantry, Anti Tank weapon, more commonly referred to as just PIAT. This was a dubious honour as it was heavy, bulky to carry and usually needed two men to cock it. It also had a fearsome kick if fired from the shoulder. The PIAT, despite its drawbacks, was quite an effective weapon and extensively used against, not only armour, but also enemy strongpoints and bunkers. Six Victoria Crosses were awarded to members of the British and Commonwealth armed forces for actions using the PIAT. Besides Lama, they were CSM Stanley Hollis, Fusilier Frank Jefferson, Major Robert Cain, Private Alvin Smith and Captain John Brunt.

Following the order to retire to Imphal, the 17th Division was under almost constant attack from the Japanese. At one of the roadblocks, the Japanese used tanks to try and destroy the column. Now was Lama's first opportunity to use his PIAT and he managed to destroy two tanks and put the rest to flight. For this action, he was awarded the Military Medal.

With the assistance of the 23rd Division, which broke the Japanese encirclement, the 17th reached its new defensive position at the village of Bishenpur on the Tiddim–Imphal Road. In mid-May the 17th was detailed to clear the area north and south of the Silchar Track with its 32nd Infantry Brigade while the 63rd Infantry Brigade advanced south down the Tiddim–Imphal Road towards Ningthoukhong. The 1/7th Gurkha and 2/5th Gurkha of the 48th Infantry Brigade were given the task of making a wide left flank movement around Loktak Lake and approaching Ningthoukhong from the south. The 63rd Brigade ran into problems that left 48th Brigade in danger of being surrounded so the 1/7th and 2/5th were ordered to take Moirang on the south bank of

THE BATTLE OF IMPHAL

Loktak Lake and establish a roadblock. On 25 May, the 48th was ordered to continue its withdrawal northwards and establish another roadblock at Ningthoukhong with the assistance of 1st West Yorkshire Regiment and a troop of medium tanks.

As the brigade withdrew from Moirang it came under fierce attack until it reached the village of Ningthoukhong. All efforts to take the village from elements of the 33rd Japanese Division failed and the brigade bypassed it and linked up with the 63rd further up the road at Potsangbam, just south of Bishenpur.

By June, the XIVth Army had stemmed the efforts of the Japanese 15th Army to capture Imphal. Mutaguchi's soldiers were now feeling the effects of an over-extended supply line that was being constantly harried by the Allied air force. Their general's boast that they only needed food for ten days before they could feast on the supplies at Imphal rang hollow. The Japanese, however, were not yet on the run and were still able to mount aggressive attacks.

On the morning of 12 June, they launched a major attack with tanks just north of Ningthoukhong. Facing this assault was the 2nd Battalion, 5th Gurkha Rifles. An intense artillery barrage was followed by a tank and infantry attack. Lama's 'B' Company was ordered to counter-attack to relieve the pressure on its fellow countrymen. Their efforts faltered in the face of the armoured attack. Picking up his heavy PIAT and a supply of projectiles, Lama went forward. It was highly dangerous for the tanks were advancing over an open field and had a clear view of their enemy. They spotted Lama and fired on him, breaking his wrist and wounding him in the leg and both hands. Undeterred, he crawled through the slick mud, dragging his PIAT and ammunition and bleeding profusely. When he was thirty yards from the first tank, he set up his weapon, knelt and fired. He scored a direct hit and saw the tank burst into flames.

Despite his painful wounds, he managed to reload and fire at the second tank and destroy it. By this time, the surviving crew of the first tank had crawled out of their burning vehicles and were attempting to escape. With one finger almost severed and his hand slippery with blood, Lama pulled the pins from his grenades and killed or wounded the last of the tank crews.

Now out of ammunition, he managed to crawl back to get some more. Ignoring pleas to get medical treatment, he returned to take out the third tank but was beaten to it when it was destroyed by an anti-tank gun. This enabled the Gurkhas to move forward and beat off the attack. Now faint from loss of blood, Lama allowed himself to be taken to the regimental aid post. His wounds were so severe that he spent twenty-two months in hospital. He had recovered enough to attend his own investiture of the Victoria Cross and Military Medal at the Red Fort, Delhi on 24 October 1944. Sitting in a wheelchair, he was presented his medals by the Viceroy Lord Wavell, in the presence of Admiral Lord Louis Mountbatten, General Bill Slim and members of his family.

When India declared its independence in 1947, Lama elected to remain in the Indian Army. He joined a new Gurkha regiment, the 11th, made up of men from the 7th and 10th who chose to continue their service with the Indian Army rather than with the British Army. During the 1960s, a large swelling appeared on his leg and when it burst, a Japanese bullet came out. Lama was promoted to subadar major and appointed ADC to India's president in 1965. On his retirement, the ADC appointment was extended for life. He returned home and became a successful farmer.

Lama died at his home on 30 June 2000. His impressive VC group is on display at the Gurkha Museum, Winchester.

NETRABAHADUR THAPA VC

Netrabahadur Thapa was born on 8 January 1916 in Rahu Village in the Lamjung district of Nepal. When he was eighteen he was recruited into the 5th Gurkha Rifles and after basic training, joined the 2nd Battalion. In 1940 having been promoted to naik, he joined the recruit training staff at the Regimental Depot at Abbottabad. Due to the large number of casualties the regiment suffered during the retreat from Burma in 1942, he and his colleague, Gaje Ghale, were sent to join the 17th Division in the Chin Hills.

The order to withdraw to Imphal was not met with universal approval, but the 17th did retreat up the Tiddim–Imphal Road, meeting strong opposition most of the way. Finally it reached the Imphal plain and in early June the Gurkhas were assigned to the Bishenpur area by Loktak Lake, astride the all-important highway to Imphal just 16 miles away. The 50,000 defenders of IV Corps now faced 90,000 Japanese of the 15th, 31st and 33rd Divisions, but had the advantage of being frequently supplied by air. The Japanese knew they had to capture Imphal before more reinforcements arrived and the monsoon season started.

Running west out of Bishenpur was the Silchar Track, along which there were isolated defensive boxes and British artillery. During late May there had been fierce clashes resulting in many Japanese casualties. The Japanese senior officers, including the increasingly frustrated General Mutaguchi, demanded more attacks. Mutaguchi was so confident of sweeping aside the Allies that he had brought along twenty geisha girls to install in Imphal and could not comprehend the lack of progress. To add to his woes, the monsoon started, slowing any advance to a crawl.

On the morning of 25 June, orders were received for the 2/5th Gurkhas to relieve the piquets occupying the hills overlooking the Silchar Track. The War Diary records that the march in the pouring rain march from Bishenpur to a hill named Evans Knob took six hours. The feature was occupied by 'D' Company, while 'A' Platoon, with two 3in mortars, moved further on to a feature called BP Piquet. Another platoon commanded by Thapa, along with two sections from 'C' Company, moved 400 yards still further to a small isolated hill named Mortar Bluff Piquet. This position was devoid of cover and overlooked by the higher Water Piquet, which had been taken by the Japanese. It was now essential that Mortar Bluff Piquet was held by Thapa's small command.

Less than an hour after relieving the piquet, Thapa's small force came under fire from 75mm and 37mm guns on Water Piquet. This was followed by an attack by a company of the enemy, which was beaten off. Thapa called up for covering artillery fire and made preparations for the next onslaught, which was not long in coming. Under cover of darkness and in torrential rain, the enemy moved through the jungle and attacked from a new direction. At a crucial moment, two of the Gurkhas' machine-guns jammed and the enemy forced an entrance, killing twelve of the sixteen men in the section. Thapa grabbed some grenades, went forward and drove the Japanese back. He then reported his dire situation and requested reinforcements and ammunition. Meanwhile, he moved among his men with words of encouragement.

At 04.00 hours a section of eight men with ammunition arrived but were greeted by a hail of enemy fire, which rendered them all casualties. Thapa managed to retrieve the ammunition and prepared to take the attack to his enemy. As he closed with the Japanese, he was shot in the mouth and killed by a grenade. When his body was found later that day, he had his *kukri* in his hand and a dead Japanese with a cleft skull by his side. He had defended his position for eight hours against overwhelming odds before being killed. By 04.15 hours, Mortar Bluff had been overrun and occupied by the enemy.

Thapa was to be one of three men of 5th Gurkha Rifles to receive the Victoria Cross within a year of the fighting on the Burma border. His VC was presented to in a special parade to the 5th Gurkhas at Nowshera in northern India on 23 January 1945. Lord Wavell presented Thapa's posthumous VC to a pre-teenaged girl named Nainasara Magarni, who had been betrothed to him.

AGANSING RAI VC

Agansing Rai was born on 24 April 1920 in Amsara Village in the Okhaldunga District of Nepal. He was recruited into the 5th Gurkha Rifles in 1941 and on completion of his training joined the 2nd Battalion. He was sent to join the famous 17th Indian Infantry, the 'Black Cat' Division, in the Chin Hills. He was part of the retreat down the Tiddim–Imphal Road and involved in much of the considerable fighting as the unit fought its way back to Bishenpur.

During May and June 1944, the Bishenpur–Silchar Track had seen some heavy fighting and on 25 June Subadur Netrabahadur Thapa had died winning the Victoria Cross for gallantry on Mortar Bluff Piquet, which the Japanese had occupied along with Water Piquet 200 yards away. Both positions were mutually self-supporting. Major General Nobuo Tanaka sent 151st Regiment from 53rd Division to secure the Silchar Track and felt that the tide was turning in his favour. The occupation of these two positions put the 17th Division position in danger at Bishenpur and the possibility of driving on to Imphal was a distinct possibility.

On the morning of the 26th, 'C' Company was ordered to BP Piquet, a small hill south of Mortar Bluff. Here it was shelled by the Japanese 75mm from the jungle close to Water Piquet and took some heavy casualties.. Under cover of the Royal Artillery, Naik Agansing Rai's 'C' Company moved to within eighty yards of Mortar Bluff. The ground over which they moved was completely bare and covered by heavy and accurate fire from machine-guns and the 37mm on Water Piquet.

Rai realised that any delay would lead to more casualties. Calling his section to follow, he charged up the slippery slope firing his Thompson machine-gun. Closing in on the enemy machine-gun, he killed three of the four-man crew. His section followed, driving off the rest of the enemy, who were terrified of the *kukri*-wielding men.

Almost immediately, the Gurkhas came under fire from the 37mm gun and from another strongpoint on Water Piquet. Once again Rai did not hesitate and rallied his section in another charge to silence the 37mm, firing from the jungle behind Water Piquet. Half his men were killed in the charge but Rai reached the gun and killed three of the five crew, leaving the remaining two to be dealt with by his men.

Withdrawing to Mortar Bluff, Rai collected the rest of the platoon, rearmed and rushed once again to Water Piquet with bursts from his Tommy gun. Reaching the strongpoint bunker, he threw in his grenade and fired his gun until all the occupants were killed. The remaining Japanese fled into the jungle, leaving Mortar and Water Piquets in the hands of the Gurkhas.

These extraordinary series of charges in the face of machine-gun fire, which secured these two vital positions, practically won the final battle for Imphal. Rai's award of the Victoria Cross was a forgone conclusion and was gazetted on 5 October 1944. He was presented with his Cross by the Viceroy, Lord Wavell at a special ceremony at Nowshera on 23 January 1945.

Along with Gaje Ghale VC, Rai took part in the controversial Victory Parade in London on 8 June 1946. All the Allies took part in the parade except the Polish servicemen, of whom some 200,000 served under the British High Command. It was controversial because the newly elected Labour government chose to recognise the Soviet-backed Polish government and not the men who had fought alongside the British.

Rai returned to serve with the 2/5th Gurkhas in the Army of Occupation in Japan and promoted to Subadar. After Indian independence he chose to remain with the regiment in India and served as a peacekeeper with the United Nations in the Congo in 1962–63. On retirement from the Army he was granted the honorary rank of lieutenant. After a battle with cancer, he died in Kathmandu in May 2000. His medals are on display in the Lord Ashcroft Gallery.

Chapter 9

The Siege of Kohima

Kohima was the administrative centre of Nagaland in the furthermost north-eastern part of India. It lay forty-two miles from Dimapur and eighty-five miles from Imphal, and its strategic value to the Japanese was that the Dimapur–Imphal road ran along a north–south ridge through the settlement. The deputy commissioner lived in a bungalow at sharp bend in the road, with gardens, a tennis court and clubhouse. North of the ridge lay the large, straggling Naga village and two churches.

Under the plan Operation *U-Go*, Lieutenant General Mutaguchi sought to take Imphal but needed a clear road to sweep on to Dimapur. He detached Lieutenant General Kotoku Sato's 31st Division of 15,000 men to block the road at Kohima and, when Imphal had fallen, to push on and take Dimapur. Sato had a more realistic view than Mutaguchi, whom he regarded as a 'blockhead'. The poor lines of supply made the probability of starvation a more likely outcome for his men.

Starting out on 15 March 1944, the 31st Division crossed the Chindwin River near Homalin and moved north along jungle trails to the border. He detached the left wing of his formation, which consisted of the 58th Regiment. They ran into the Indian troops of the 50th Indian Parachute Brigade covering the northern approaches to Imphal and were embroiled in a battle that lasted six days. This delayed the occupation of Kohima by a week.

Lieutenant General Bill Slim belatedly realised that the Japanese had sent a whole division to take Kohima. He asked for more troops and most of the 5th Indian Infantry Division was hurriedly flown from the Arakan to bolster the defences at Imphal. The 161st Indian Infantry Brigade was detached and sent to Dimapur but upon arrival was ordered to travel to Kohima. A confusion of conflicting orders delayed the 161st until it was decided to send the 4th Battalion Royal West Kent

Regiment (RWK) ahead to relieve the Assam Rifles. On 5 April, it arrived just as Sato's command blocked the road behind them, so encircling the small garrison. The remainder of the 161st Brigade, the 4/7 Rajput and 1/1 Punjab Regiments supported by artillery, were placed 2 miles west of Kohima at Jotsoma. The 4/RWK and the green troops of the Assam Rifles and Assam Regiment were positioned in a series of trenches along the Kohima Ridge consisting of features such as Garrison Hill, Jail Hill, Field Supply Depot (FSD) and Detail Issue Hill (DIS).

The defenders were totally outnumbered and the first Japanese attack on the evening of 5–6 April made significant inroads into the ridge. By the 7th, the Rajputs had made their way in by jungle tracks from Jotsoma, which greatly helped the defence. The defenders now numbered 2,500, of which about 1,000 were non-combatants. Facing them were 12,000 men of the 31st Division.

On 8th, the Japanese launched a series of attacks into the north-east defences around the district commissioner's bungalow and by the 9th the British and the Indians had been forced back to the tennis court. Sato's troops had also cut the tracks from Jotsoma, further isolating the defenders. Increasing pressure on DIS and FSD and mortar attacks on the DC's bungalow and tennis court saw some of the grimmest hand-to-hand fighting. They were saved by the remarkably accurate fire from the Royal Artillery positioned on Jotsoma ridge, all the more amazing given the closeness of the fighting. The Japanese then turned their attention on the positions on Jotsoma but the British and Indians were able to repel these attacks.

The 14 April saw a turning point in the siege. While the Japanese continued to shell and fire on the defenders, they did not mount any infantry attacks. The 4/RWK's War Diary records the night of 13–14 April:

> At the FSD the Rajputs were forced from their trenches by direct hits from the 75mm guns opposite, so that A Coy at Kukri Piquet position had to send one platoon forward to save the front positions … The Japs made a heavy rush attack at B Coy from the DC bungalow, and succeeded in penetrating into a shed on a small but important hillock when a Bren jammed. The platoon commander, Lt. King, restored the situation by driving them out with grenades, but not before the Bren gunner himself picked up a shovel and cracked at his assailants with it.
>
> Early morning brought a further attack on B Coy, supported by grenade discharge bombs, but it was repulsed with many casualties

to the enemy. Air supply drop of water very successful. Enemy mortar activity continued throughout the day, interspersed with smoke bombs, which was taken to mean that his stock of captured ammunition was running low. This assumption was correct.

The British 2nd Division had travelled some 2,000 miles from Belgaum in the far west of India to Dimapur and set about in the relief of Kohima. On 15 April, the 2nd broke though the Japanese roadblock to relieve the 161st Brigade at Jotsoma. When word reached the men besieged at Kohima they knew that the lifting of the siege was inevitable and morale soared. On the evening of 16–17 April, knowing that reinforcements were on the way, the Japanese were spurred to launch a final deadly attack on the positions on FSD. The British and Indians sustained heavy casualties, which forced them to withdraw from FSD to the Garrison Hill positions.

The defensive position had shrunk further with the defenders hemmed in from the south, north and east. On the morning of the 18th, the British artillery opened up from the west, heralding the arrival of elements of the 2nd British Division, 161st Brigade and the tanks from XXXIII Corps, who pushed the Japanese from their positions. The road between Dimapur and Kohima had been opened and the siege was lifted.

JOHN HARMAN VC

John Pennington Harman was born in Beckenham, Kent, on 20 July 1914. He was the first child of Martin Coles Harman and his wife Amy Ruth (nèe Bodger). There followed three more additions; Albion, Ruth and Diana. The family lived at Deans Place in Chaldon near Caterham, Surrey. At an early age, John was sent to the Clifton Preparatory School in Bristol, which he hated. He was particularly distressed by the sounds from the nearby zoo, which perhaps represented, for him, unwelcome captivity and restraint, even in his tender years. Twice he ran away from school, until his parents brought him back to the new family home at Heathfield in Sussex. There he was in his element, for he loved the countryside and wildlife.

In 1925, he was sent to board at the progressive school, Bedales, near Petersfield, Hampshire. Here he found more freedom and thrived on the liberal time he was allowed out of doors. He built a tree house, was allowed to keep various pets and followed his own interests whenever possible. His individualism was understood and tolerated by the staff and pupils and he was well liked. Classroom study was irksome to him and he lacked concentration in things that did not interest him. It was hardly surprising that he did not take the School Certificate before leaving Bedales at seventeen.

John's father, Martin Coles Harman, had been born in 1885, one of six sons and five daughters. Educated at Whitgift School, Croydon, he left and developed a talent as an entrepreneur and financier, although he was in no way hard-nosed. Like John, he was a lover of the countryside and encouraged his rather problematical son to pursue his enthusiasm for nature. In 1925, Martin put into practice his passion for remote natural beauty when he bought Lundy from the Christie family for £15,000. The island, which is 3 miles long by ½ mile wide, lies off the North Devon coast in the Bristol Channel and is a wildlife haven.

John and Albion accompanied their father to spend Christmas on the island at the elegant Millcombe House. John in particular explored the island endlessly, observing the huge bird colonies and seals that swam offshore. He was naturally inventive and some of his ideas were ingenious, such as a fence for keeping the deer out of the crops.

Lundy was a huge challenge and had to be self-sufficient. Crops were sown and sheep introduced. Felix Gade, employed by Martin as Lundy's manager, wrote in his memoirs, *My Life on Lundy*:

> John seemed to feel that it only needed a stroke of genius for him to be provided with a fortune, without grinding work!

The family were devastated by a double blow. In 1931, Harman's mother died at the early age of forty-seven. This had followed the loss of the family fortune in the Great Depression. Martin was bankrupted, but he had had the foresight to put Lundy in trust, which gave the children a base during this distressing period.

John Harman spent the next few years travelling in Australia, New Zealand, South Africa and Spain. He tried lumberjacking, gold prospecting and sheep farming. Harman was always able to live rough if necessary and would explore any natural place he found himself in. When he returned to England, Harman set himself up as a bee-keeper, a lifelong interest he shared with his father. Unfortunately, no occupation provided him with satisfaction for long. This restlessness meant that whatever he wanted to do especially well he always found a stumbling block that discouraged him, which lead to its abandonment. The outdoor life had suited him and he developed into a tall, well-built youth, something that would later cause problems when he joined the Army.

In 1935, he applied to the Air Ministry for a short service commission but, when the letter came back requesting details of his maths qualification, he had to give up any hope of joining the RAF. He did, however, have lessons with a tutor and acquired a civil pilot's licence to fly at Heston.

Another flush of enthusiasm occurred when a Spanish metal diviner was engaged to do a mineral survey on Lundy. Harman was fully convinced by this man that there was buried treasure somewhere on the island. Sadly, none was found.

Harman was called up on the 29 November 1941 and joined the Household Cavalry. It became obvious from the start that military life did not suit him, as can be gleaned from his comments in letters to his family:

> I have now completed three weeks training: drill comes easier with physical improvement. Life is just bloody hell – dirty, noisy, crude and inefficient. I heartily wish I had never joined up. There is no time to do anything after set tasks are done – except clean equipment for the following day.

On 1 January 1942, he was complaining:

> I scrubbed floors instead of going on 'road walk', which would have crippled my feet completely. My feet seem all broken up inside. I loathe having to wear boots and stamp my feet a hundred times a day in a way quite unsuited to my bone structures. I guess there are men who are not suited to this kind of life and I am one of them. I learn almost nothing each day.

Harman continued to criticise Army clothing and equipment, which he described as 'crude and inefficient'. He replaced the blankets with his Icelandic sleeping bag:

> The total weight of the soldier's equipment is out of all proportion to its value!

He was moved to Pirbright Camp for training in the Guards Armoured Training Wing and wrote, 'I can hardly constrain a desire to desert and damn the consequences'. He followed this on 7 April 1942 with, 'I wonder if I can refrain from running away from the army to a life of solitude?'

Harman managed not to yield to this temptation even at its most powerful. On 8 April 1942, he wrote to his father:

> I have given the matter of taking a commission a lot of thought and there is no doubt that if I was an officer, I would be able to resume the life I was used to, to some extent. On the other hand, I am constitutionally so unsoldierly that I am filled with doubts about the whole thing. What I would like to know is just where I really belong in the Army (if I am unable to be anywhere else now). Does the status of Gentleman entitle a man to be an officer with the King's Commission 'though he is not of the soldier-type? I think not ... well! I suppose it all depends on me; and if I am to get a commission I had better get a move on and brace up.

He complained of being bored to distraction, which was followed the next day with:

> Begrudge every minute I spend working in the army and I hate Gunnery above everything. When I think of being free to enjoy the countryside in this wonderful sunny weather I can hardly bear this dismal existence etc, etc.

To his obvious delight, on 26 May, Harman was granted a month's agriculture leave to assist work on Lundy and he immediately undertook the planting of 5,000 cabbage plants. Six days later, in patchy fog, a Whitley bomber crashed into the top of the cliff on the west side of the island, just south of Pilots Quay. Harman quickly arrived on the scene and, with help, made fast the fuselage of the plane with ropes. He then crawled out along to the tail, which was suspended over the cliff precipice, and managed to drag the rear gunner clear. Unfortunately, it was found that Sergeant O.A. Jones had been killed on impact. The rest of the crew had perished when the burning mass of the cockpit had plummeted on to the rocks below. Harman returned later to the site to collect ammunition and recover the bodies of the aircrew until he deemed it too dangerous to continue.

Harman returned to duty and his liturgy of complaints continued. July 1942:

> I find barrack-room conditions very crude and painful. Even if I were an officer, my hatred of soldiering would prevent me from being any use.

Evidently, the Household Cavalry agreed with Harman, for it gave up trying to make a soldier of him and transferred him out of the regiment.

In September, Harman was sent to a drafting station near Worcester to become a private in the Worcestershire Regiment, which prompted another change of mind: 'I shall apply for a commission as soon as I can.'

Harman's stay with his new regiment was brief for, on 3 December 1942, he was transferred to the Royal Fusiliers at Kenley. On 28 January 1943, the 20th Battalion Royal Fusiliers was on its way to India, which it reached on 22 March. Harman's brother, Albion, was already in India serving as an officer in the Madras Sappers and Miners but they never met up.

On 14 August 1943, Harman wrote of his dislike of the tropical sun:

> Nevertheless, four years in NZ stand me in good stead and if we ever have to fight in the Burmese jungles it will be right up my street. Frankly, I would sooner hear the noises of the jungle that the ceaseless clattering and yapping of the barrack-rooms; and eating food almost entirely out of tins gets me down. In the jungle, a man may 'spit' a snake over a fire and eat it all himself and make a decent cup of tea.

On 20 January, Harman sent a letter to his Aunt Beryl, in which he prophetically and poignantly wrote:

> I think the European War will be over in March soon and followed by the Japanese War. How thankful I shall be if I survive, there are so many big things that I want to do; and I am in my 30th year, too. Life is so short!
>
> In my youth I constantly heard War stories and reminiscences of 14–18. I will always remember them: but now another chapter of History is almost done and people will spend another twenty years swapping yarns and recounting the different stages of this terrible war. I think there is much to be said for the Llama monks who shut themselves away in the lonely peaks of the Himalayas to keep away from the strife and temptations of this world. Were it not for my own hearty share of the good things in life, my family, and my sworn oath, I should have gone thither long ago.
>
> If only I get back to England! The things I am going to do!! I think I shall do! I had my fortune told (I will live to be 72 and begat four children and everything will be hunky dory). It only cost me half a crown in Durban, South Africa, but I really think that woman was a genuine clairvoyant and it gives one a lot of confidence. In any case, whatever happens is God's will and I am satisfied to take what comes.

Just before Christmas, Harman was part of a draft transferred to the 4th Battalion, The Royal West Kent Regiment (RWK), for the invasion of Burma. He was put into the newly formed 'D' Company under the command of Major Carey. They were able to have just one week's training as a company before being moved into the line.

The advance south through the Arakan province was most dangerous. The mountainous and rugged terrain heavily favoured the Japanese defenders. Every position had to be wrested from the Japanese in fierce, mostly hand-to-hand, fighting.

For three months, the regiment was continually engaged in the fighting and none more so than 'D' Company. Harman appears to have relished this release from the daily drudgery he had endured for the past two years. He was recognised as having a fine fighting spirit, always volunteering for patrols and often going out on his own for several hours to return claiming to have killed several Japanese.

In a letter dated 18 February 1944, he describes the birds and animals he spotted during these private excursions, which were probably more to do with enjoying some privacy than engaging the enemy. On 22 March, the 4/RWKs were relieved by the South Wales Borderers before they could complete the capture of the two strategically vital road tunnels along the Maunglaw–Buthidaung Road.

They were sent north with the 5th Indian Division to the Naga Hills. A huge Japanese Army was threatening to invade India by way of this remote region on the Burma–China border and the British rushed in all available forces to counter this threat. On 5 April, the 4/RWK took up position at the vital road junction at Kohima. It replaced the inexperienced Assam Rifles, who had at least provided trenches and dugouts. The battalion arrived under fire from the surrounding hills and within a short time, it was surrounded by the Japanese 31st Division. So began the epic Siege of Kohima.

Harman had impressed his superiors during the Arakan fighting and been promoted to lance corporal. He immediately showed his contempt for the enemy by taking little notice of the snipers and his self-confidence encouraged his comrades. It may well have been at this time that he told his company commander, Major Donald Easten, of the prediction he had received that he would live until he was at least seventy. According to his youngest sister, Harman had an open mind regarding the spiritual and was quite taken with the mysteries of unexplained phenomena.

The perimeter that the 4/RWK was defending was small and the Japanese had closed to within yards. The defence was concentrated around the district commissioner's bungalow and surrounding area and, because of the terracing of the slopes, the fighting was at platoon and section level. The 4th Battalion was a Territorial regiment and the men all came from the Tonbridge area. They all recalled that the close proximity of the Japanese meant they could smell them if they attempted to creep up to the wire. One Bren gunner had a narrow escape. In a night-time attack by the Japanese, he fired off a magazine and quickly replaced it. He continued to fire but after a few rounds the Bren stopped. He quickly changed another magazine and the gun fired perfectly. When it was light, he picked up the faulty magazine and found that a Japanese bullet had hit the magazine square on about where his eye would have been.

The Japanese attack began in earnest on the night of the 6th and was repulsed. The following morning, 'D' Coy put in a counter-attack, in which some seventy of the enemy were killed. Harman was in the thick of it and managed to capture a wounded Japanese officer. He was certainly a one-off who would infiltrate the Japanese lines and kill any enemy he came upon. He also told some of his comrades that if they were short of rice he knew where the Japanese kept a supply. Quietly creeping through the enemy's lines, he returned with a bag. He got on well with his fellow soldiers, who thought he was a bit bored with life but nevertheless a very brave man. He was one of three or four men who dashed into the nearby bakery and killed the Japanese who had taken shelter in the six ovens.

The next day, Harman performed the first of his outstanding acts of gallantry. During the night, the Japanese had established a machine-gun nest, which gave them a commanding field of fire. The terracing on Detail Issue Hill made direct fire impossible, so without orders, Harman crawled out of his position, slowly ran forward and, gathering momentum, he flung himself down at the very mouth of the bunker. He then took a four-second grenade, pulled the clip, counted to three and threw it through the slit. The two crewmen were killed and Harman returned with the machine-gun.

Major Donald Easten later recalled that Harman was a very big man and half his uniform did not fit him. Harman wrote home to say that the British Army had not got a pair of boots of his size. His father, Martin, must have had some influence because a message came direct from Churchill demanding that Harman should be issued with the correct-sized boots.

On the 9th, five Japanese with machine-guns and automatics pushed 'C' Company out of its forward trenches on a nearby ridge that overlooked the whole British position. Again without orders, Harman instructed a comrade on a Bren gun to give him covering fire as he dashed down the slope. Pausing, he aimed his rifle and shot one of the Japanese. He then moved on and shot another. By this time he was under automatic fire from the remaining three.

Fixing his bayonet, Harman crossed the valley floor and dashed up the slope toward the Japanese position, ignoring the heavy incoming fire. By some miracle, he reached the post unscathed. Leaping down on the enemy, Harman bayoneted all three and held up the machine-gun, to the cheers of his comrades, before flinging it away among the trees.

He then made his way back half running, half stumbling. Urged on by his comrades, Harman was obviously so exhausted by his uphill charge that he didn't take precautions or use cover. As he approached the safety of his own lines, a burst of machine-gun fire hit him in his side, mortally wounding him. A comrade pulled him to cover and his last words were: 'I got the lot. It was worth it.' Five minutes later, he died and was buried on the spot.

For this action and that of the previous day, Harman was recommended for the Victoria Cross.

The siege was raised on the 20th, but the fighting went on in the area for a further two months before the Japanese withdrew. In this epic battle, about 500 Kentish Territorials together with Indian troops had held at bay some 13,000 highly trained and experienced Japanese. This was the high water point of the Japanese invasion. From that point, they were in retreat.

Lord Mountbatten made the point in a speech when he said, 'The Battle of Kohima will probably go down as the greatest battle in history. It was in effect the Battle of Burma.'

Harman's Victoria Cross was gazetted on 22nd June 1944 and his father received it from the King at a Buckingham Palace investiture.

He is buried in the Kohima War Cemetery, sited on Garrison Hill. Part of the cemetery encompasses the tennis court that featured so prominently in the battle and is marked out in metal lines. In June 1949, a memorial to Harman was unveiled on Lundy in a disused granite quarry, now called VC Quarry.

On 13 August 1952, Martin Harman gave his son's Cross to the Royal West Kent Regiment and the complete group can now be viewed at the Regimental Museum in Maidstone, Kent. Martin had also previously installed another symbolic memorial. He had purchased a seven-acre field at Chaldon, which he later called 'Six Brothers Field'. He decided there should be link between his two homes and ordered that six granite boulders from Lundy should be placed in the field to commemorate the six brothers. This meadow is now owned by the National Trust and is home to the Chaldon Cricket Club.

With the siege lifted and the Dimapur–Kohima road opened, the 2nd Division and men from XXXIII Corps were able to go on the counter-attack. Although the siege was over, Sato's 31st Division still occupied the surrounding hills and had closed the Imphal–Kohima road. Major General John Grover, GOC 2nd Division, ordered the 4th Infantry Brigade, made up of men from the Royal Scots, Lancashire Fusiliers and 2/Royal Norfolk regiments, to destroy the Japanese to the south of GPT Ridge and in the Aradura region.

The terrain and climate made this a difficult task, which was explained by Lieutenant Horner of the 2/Royal Norfolks:

> The physical hammering one takes is difficult to understand. The heat, humidity, altitude (Kohima was at 5,000 feet above sea level), and the slope of almost every foot of ground combine to knock hell out of the stoutest constitution. You gasp for air which doesn't seem to come, you drag your legs upwards till they seem reduced to the strength of matchsticks, you wipe the sweat out of your eyes … So you stop, horrified to be prodded by the man behind you or cursed by an officer in front.

It was during this phase in the fighting that a Royal Norfolk officer was awarded the Victoria Cross.

JOHN RANDLE VC

John Niel Randle was born in Benares, India, on 22 December 1917, the son of Dr Niel Randle and his wife Edith (née Whitby). The family moved back to Radlett, Hertfordshire, and John commenced his education at the Dragon School, Oxford, where he befriended Leonard Cheshire. He passed his exams, which gained entrance to Marlborough College. He then qualified to read Law at Merton College, Oxford, and renewed his friendship with Cheshire, a fellow law student.

Leonard Cheshire recalled in his book, *The Face of Victory*:

> I had heard of people charging their enemy and carrying on to their objective in spite of being mortally wounded; in fact Jack Randle, with whose help I had climbed back into college in the early hours of the morning so often, had done exactly that and been awarded a posthumous VC for doing that. But I had never heard or dreamt of

this, a man already dead yet deliberately threading his way through a series of obstacles.

Coincidentally, Randle joined the family of another Victoria Cross recipient when he married Mavis Manser of Radlett. Her brother, Leslie Manser, also born in India, joined the RAF, and was killed on 31 May 1942 while remaining at the controls of his stricken plane to allow his crew to parachute to safety.

Jack Randle, as he was commonly named, was due to take up a position in the Bombay Training Company and to sail to Burma when the war broke out. After some months training with the East Surrey Regiment, Randle was commissioned in May 1940 as a 2nd Lieutenant in the Royal Norfolk Regiment. The unit was part of the 2nd Division sent to India in April 1942 but, instead of being involved on the Burma front it was sent for specialist training. Much of the following two years was spent trying to keep the peace from the many protests for Indian independence.

With the crucial battles at Imphal and Kohima, the 2nd Division was sent to Dimapur and then acted as the relief of the siege of Kohima. The 4th Infantry Brigade, made up of men from the Royal Scots, Lancashire Fusiliers and 2/Royal Norfolk regiments, was sent in a wide flanking movement to attack the Japanese, who had control of the road to the south of GPT Ridge and in the Aradura region.

The brigade left Khonoma, skirting Mount Pulebadze, and headed for the Aradura spur. The approach through mountainous jungle was debilitating, made even worse by the onset of the monsoon. The men reached the fringe of the spur on 4 May and after a fight with the Japanese, in which Randle was wounded by grenade splinters in the knee, the Norfolks finally reached and dug in on top of GPT (General Purpose Transport) Ridge. Despite his painful wound, Randle went forward and collected all the wounded men who were lying outside the perimeter. In an interview after the war, Captain Samuel Horner, described the objectives before them:

> Jack Randle was wounded in the leg quite nastily, he was limping about and he'd got it bandaged up, but he wasn't going to be evacuated, especially as his company commander was knocked out ... a plan was made because it was quite clear that on the left front was a bunker, a big one. It had been overrun (by the Norfolks) but they couldn't hold it because all these bunkers were covered by each other. They were very clever, the Japs. They'd put a chain of bunkers

and each one would cover the next one, so if you captured one you'd get shot to pieces by the next one.

After an abortive attack that resulted in many casualties, it was decided that this large bunker, now named Norfolk Bunker, just had to be taken. Captain Horner spoke of the daring reconnaissance undertaken by Captain Jack Randle and a few of his platoon commanders:

> Jack was just given his orders, not in any very great detail. One of his platoon commanders was in fact (Company) Sergeant Major Fitt because officers, you see, were dwindling all the time and platoons hadn't got platoon commanders any more. And at last light, as it was getting dark, Jack Randle went out. His leg wasn't improving things but he managed it all right. He went out with Fitt ... They had to crawl very carefully so that they could get a good view of Norfolk Bunker and also a view of a bunker, but further back, which was covering it. Jack Randle detailed Fitt to pay special attention to that, for his platoon to attack that bunker, which was critical to the whole thing. At the same time he would deal with the attack on Norfolk Bunker. It was a very, very brilliantly done reconnaissance, just as all reconnaissance should be before a battle.

Just before dawn, the two platoons lined up and began to advance up the hill. CSM Bert Fitt later recalled:

> It was sloping, fairly steep, open ground, the trees had all been shelled and all their branches had been knocked off. There was very little cover ... We moved forward, we got about halfway, and when we got to the bottom of the hill, Captain Randle had already been hit. Then he was hit again, in the upper part of his body, and I shouted at him to go down and leave it to me, because you see he had already lost blood. 'No. You take that left-hand bunker; I'll take the right-hand one.'
> I didn't see his wounds but he was hit at least twice more before we ever got to the bottom of the hill and he staggered twice. And when he staggered, that told me he had been hit fairly heavily ... there were two light machine-gun posts and they were carving up the company terrible. We'd been under fire all the while ... I went straight in and got this bunker. The Japanese didn't realise that I was coming up the slope underneath them, as I moved so quickly. I managed to push a grenade in through the slit and after four seconds it went off. I knew that anybody inside the bunker was

either dead or knocked out. I immediately spun right because I thought I could get to where Captain Randle was before anything happened.

As I turned, I saw Captain Randle at the other bunker's entrance. He had a grenade he was going to release into the bunker. I just stood there. I couldn't do a thing to save him. If he could have held out for about three minutes I would have got on top of the bunker and knocked it out without getting hurt. But unfortunately he had been hit again at point blank range.

As he was going down, he threw his grenade into the bunker and he sealed off the bunker's entrance with his own body so that nobody could shoot out of it. But he got the occupants, killed them. It was the main gun position and I am certain that's why he went for it. He knew that if he didn't knock it out, it would be lights out for the rest of us. It was a quite deliberate act to block the opening of the bunker to save the remainder of the men.

Randle had been mortally wounded and knew he was dying. He still had sufficient adrenalin pumping through his body to complete his task.

Bert Fitt was then pinned down by a machine-gun that he could not see. Hurling a few grenades, he got lucky when one bounced though the slit and killed the crew. The platoon continued its attack until GPT Ridge was finally taken but with heavy casualties.

CSM Fitt told his commander, Colonel Scott, exactly what had happened and that Randle should get the VC. This was put in motion and Randle's citation appeared in *The London Gazette* on 12 December 1944. His medal was presented to his widow and is now on loan at the Imperial War Museum next to the VC of his friend, Leonard Cheshire.

The 2nd Division continued to push back Sato's starving but still fanatical troops. The Japanese were still in the mood to put up a stiff resistance and prolonged the battle for a further three weeks. The 5th Infantry made a right flank attack on the Naga village while the 6th Brigade undertook the task of clearing the centre; FSD Hill and Jail Hill. Major Boshell, of the 1/Royal Berkshire Regiment, later recalled:

To begin with I took over an area overlooking the Tennis Court ... The lie of the land made it impossible to move by day because of Japanese snipers. We were in Kohima for three weeks. We were attacked every single night ... They came in waves; it was like a pigeon shoot. Most nights they overran part of the battalion position, so we had to mount counter-attacks. Water was short and restricted to about one pint per man per day. So we stopped shaving. Air supply was the key, but the steep terrain and narrow ridges meant that some of the drops went to the Japs. My company went into Kohima over 100 strong and came out with about sixty.

By 13 May, many of the Japanese positions had been taken. The monsoon had broken and the horror of close-combat fighting was compounded by the torrents of rain estimated at 4 inches per day. The battlefield turned to glutinous mud, flooding foxholes and trenches and rotting the troops' clothing. Men's flesh became wrinkled with the constant soaking and intestinal sickness was endemic.

Step by step, hill by hill the British slowly pushed the Japanese back into the surrounding jungle. With little in the way of supplies, General Sato informed his commander that he was withdrawing. Mutaguchi could not accept the failure of his campaign, which he was convinced he would win. All threats of a court martial did not deter Sato as pulled back the remnants of his 31st Division towards the Chindwin River. The fighting at Kohima had lasted sixty-four days and had cost the British and Indian troops some 4,000 casualties. The Japanese losses were about double that figure. It would take a further fifteen days to open the road to Imphal but on 22 June it was and so formally ended the sieges at Imphal and Kohima.

Chapter 10

The Follow-Up – Arakan

After Kohima and Imphal, General Slim noted that 'the advantages of pressing the beaten enemy were so immense that I called on the troops and air forces supporting them for the impossible – and I got it'.

One of the hardest military operations is to hang on the heels of a defeated enemy because he withdraws so swiftly and given time can form another formidable defensive position that can stall any advance.

Slim's strategy was to drive the Japanese from the mountain barrier, across the Chindwin River and on to the plain above Mandalay. Here he hoped to force a battle before the Japanese could re-form. The Japanese commander, General Kimura, had counted on the XIVth Army being halted by the monsoon. However, despite the torrential rain, it did not deter the Allies in their pursuit. As Kimura drew back his shattered divisions, abandoning many of his guns in the glutinous mud, the XIVth dogged him with unrelenting blows. The Allied planes had a virtually free hand at bombing and strafing the retreating Japanese Army. The nearest Japanese fighters had been pulled back to Rangoon and their heavy bombers had withdrawn to Bangkok.

On the Tiddim Road from Imphal the Japanese contested every foot: hairpin bends and narrowing ledges were mined, booby-trapped or covered by mortar fire. The 5th Indian Division was tasked with opening the Tiddim Road and beyond. Progress was slow as the division contended with these obstacles the Japanese had put in its way. To break the deadlock, Major General Warren ordered the 123rd Brigade to make a wide flanking movement to emerge to the rear of Tongzang, causing the Japanese to pull back to Tiddim. Once Tiddim was fairly easily taken, the next target was Kennedy Peak and the subsidiary hills between.

It was during the attack on one of these heights, Salium Vum that a posthumous VC was awarded to a subadar of the 2/1st Punjab Regiment.

RAM SARUP SINGH VC

Born on 12 April 1919, Ram Sarup Singh was brought up in Kheri-Talwana Village in Patiala State, India. He joined the 2nd Battalion, 1st Punjab Regiment based in Jhelum, which was a mixed race regiment with separate companies for Punjabi and Hazara Muslims, Rajputs and Sikhs. It was regarded as a crack unit and Field Marshal Claude Auchinleck served with it during the First World War. In 1937 the regiment was honoured when King George VI was appointed its colonel-in-chief.

After taking part in the 5th Indian Division's invasion of the Arakan in March 1944, the 2/1st Punjab Regiment was sent to Imphal and was involved in the operations in the Lintan–Ukhrul Road area at the end of April. As the Japanese started to pull back, Field-Marshal Slim ordered his XIV Army to launch an offensive to chase the Japanese out of Burma. The 5th Indian Division's progress on Tiddim was frequently delayed by the Japanese, who set ambushes at nearly every corner of the road, which had become a morass. To break this deadlock, 123rd Brigade, consisting of 2/Suffolks, 2/1 Punjabs, 3/2 Punjabs, 1/17 Dogras and 3/9 Gurkhas, was ordered to retrace its steps, cross the Manipur river at a narrow point and make a 80-mile detour through thick jungle.

When it emerged at Tongzang, a Chin district centre on the Tiddim road, it took the Japanese completely by surprise, killing many and capturing eleven artillery pieces trained on the Manipur river crossing. With the Japanese in retreat, 123rd Brigade advanced on Tiddim and the heavily defended positions to its front.

Once again, the 2/1 Punjabs made another wide flanking movement, which brought them 8 miles beyond Tiddim and caught the Japanese unawares. It took a further two weeks before Tiddim was taken. While the Japanese continued to starve and be denied supplies, the 5th Indian Division was constantly being supplied by air drops that enabled them to keep up a continuous pressure on the enemy.

From its position eight miles east of Tiddim, the 2/1st Punjab could see the 8,000ft high conical mass of Kennedy Peak, the next objective. To attack it the unit had to overcome the Japanese on the heights of Salium Vum, which guarded the ridge that led to Kennedy Peak. In this preliminary phase of the attack on Kennedy Peak, 2/1st Punjab was tasked with the capture of Salium Vum.

On 25 October, 'A' and 'C' Companies launched a diversionary attack from the north-east. At the same time, 'D' Company sent two platoons to make an assault from a different direction, which took the Japanese by surprise. Before the advance began, Subadar Ram Sarup Singh shook hands with his commander, saying: 'Sahib, either the Japs or myself today.' The Japanese had turned this feature into a natural fortress and every approach was covered by machine-guns sited in bunkers. The aggressive charge unnerved the Japanese, who quit the main bunker, suffering casualties as they fled.

Singh was wounded in the legs but made no fuss as he organised his platoon. The Japanese made a counter-attack from the front and flanks and rained grenades on the platoon, calling on it to surrender. Singh collected a few men and surprised the Japanese by taking the fight to them. In the melee that followed, he managed to bayonet two more Japs but was simultaneously hit in the leg and chest by a burst of fire. The sudden attack by Singh platoon caused the Japanese to pull back.

As he lay dying he told his men: 'I am dying but you carry on and finish the devils.' His commanding presence on Salium Vum directly led to the capture of Kennedy Peak.

His citation was published on 8 February 1945 and the VC was presented to his widow by Viceroy Lord Wavell on 1 April 1945 at the Red Fort, Delhi. His medal group is displayed at Lord Ashcroft's Gallery at the Imperial War Museum.

Worthy of note is the performance of 2nd Battalion, 1st Punjab Regiment, which received more gallantry awards than any other unit in the Indian Army during the Second World War.

Slim had been advised that he could expect no more reinforcements from Europe. The main thrust against the retreating Japanese was in central Burma and he ordered three divisions from XV Corps in the Arakan Peninsular, where they were containing the Japanese 28th Army between the Irrawaddy River and the Bay of Bengal. This left Lieutenant General Philip Christison with two Indian and two West African divisions with which to clear the Arakan.

The success of the Second Arakan invasion had continued until June 1944. With the onset of the monsoon, the Indian Army withdrew to a line encompassing Maungdaw, the Tunnels and Goppe Pass. Here it remained until October until the monsoon ended.

The Indian 25th Division held Maunglaw and the western side of the Mayu Range area. At least it had made plans to ride out the seven rain-drenched months with reasonable shelters and a strict anti-malaria regime. The Japanese did not have the same facilities or medicines and consequently were in a poor state once the monsoon ended in late October.

The Japanese 28th Army commanded by Lieutenant General Shozo Sakuri defended the coastal region down to the lower Irrawaddy valley.

The XV Corp's first objective was Akyab Island with its airfield and port at the tip of the Mayu Peninsular.

Before the XV Corps began its final advance to take the whole coastal region down to Rangoon, a series of softening up raids were launched. Prominent among these was the action of the all-India 51st Indian Brigade made up of men from 2/2nd Punjab, 8/19th Hyderabad and 16/10th Baluch Regiments. It was the outstanding act of gallantry by a member of the last mentioned that resulted in the award of the Victoria Cross.

BHANDARI RAM VC

Bhandari Ram was born on 24 July 1919 at Pargna Gugeda village in Himachal Pradesh, India. He worked as a farmer before enlisting in the Indian Army in 1941 and soon obtained the Army First Class Education Certificate. He was posted to the 16th Battalion, 10th Baluch Regiment, which comprised of a mix of two-thirds Muslim and one third Dogra Hindu Brahmin. His regiment saw action in the Second Invasion of the Arakan and, with the breaking of the monsoon, held the line to the east of the Mayu Range.

Although he had not gained promotion, Sepoy Bhandari Ram was a keen and resourceful soldier, something he needed when he took part in an attack on one of the hills in East Mayu. By 1944, through the efforts of India's Commander-in-Chief Claude Auchinleck, there were now Indian regiments that were entirely officered by Indians including their battalion commanders. The 10th's outgoing British commanding officer, Lieutenant Colonel John Fairley, was on the point of being transferred to make way for Lieutenant Colonel L.P. 'Bogey' Sen. Under the temporary command of Major Mohammed Usman, Fairley's last order was to take a hill just north of Razabil. The junior Indian officer Zarawar Chand Bakshi was to lead the Dogra section of the battalion but, as it was not up to full strength, it called on some non-combatants, including men employed in the officers' mess. One of these was Sepoy Bhandari Ram.

The objective was a strongly held bunker position that could only be reached by a steep slope and a narrow sheer-sided ridge. Led by Bakshi, the platoon advanced to within fifty yards of the crest when it came under heavy fire from the machine-gun nest blocking their way. Ram was badly wounded in the leg and shoulder and lay with three of his dead comrades in front of the machine-gun nest. The rest of the company pulled back in the face of what seemed an impossible objective.

The blood-splattered Ram feigned death as the Japanese came out to check on the four dead bodies and returned to their trench. Mustering his strength, Ram slowly crawled towards the enemy but was spotted and the Japanese hurled grenades at him, further wounding him in the face and chest. In extreme pain, he pulled himself towards the trench and when he was about 5 yards away he pulled the pin from a grenade and lobbed it into the trench. Following up, he found the three-man gun crew dead. As other Japanese soldiers came rushing out of their positions towards him, he turned the machine-gun on them and killed all four.

The rest of the platoon then surged across the ridge and captured the hill. Ram was found bleeding profusely, more dead than alive. He asked: 'Is the enemy position taken?' When assured it was he added: 'Then I can die now, my duty is done.' But he survived.

After hospitalisation, he was able to return to his regiment. His platoon commander, Zarawar Bakshi, recommended him for the Victoria Cross, which was endorsed by Major Usman. This passed to the new CO, Lieutenant Colonel L.P. 'Bogey' Sen, who forwarded Ram's name, but altered the award to the lesser Indian Order of Merit (IOM). Usman felt this was unfair as he had been commander and insisted his opinion be taken into account. In the end, Usman went to the brigade commander, Brigadier Kopdandera Thimayya, who agreed that Ram should receive the Cross.

The London Gazette published the citation of 8 February 1945 and on 3 March 1945 he received the Victoria Cross from Viceroy Lord Wavell at the Red Fort, Delhi. After the 16th Battalion was disbanded in 1946, Ram returned to the regimental centre. The partition in 1947 brought a tremendous upheaval to the continent, one of which was the splitting up of the regiments. Since it had been recruited in Baluchistan, which went to Pakistan, it was clear that for the Hindu minority there could be no future. With other Hindus from the 10th Baluch, Ram was transferred to the 8th Battalion, The Dogra Regiment, in the new Indian Army in February 1948. He subsequently fought in the wars over Kashmir, often against his former colleagues.

Ram was promoted to subadar major in 1964. When he retired in November 1969, he was appointed honorary captain. He was also awarded the Param Vishishi Seva Medal and Tamar Patra by the President of India. In retirement he farmed in the Bilaspur district until he was forced to stop through ill health. He was a frequent and popular visitor to London for the bi-annual reunions of the Victoria Cross and George Cross Association. At the age of eighty-two, he died on 19 May 2002 and was survived by his wife and five children.

Following the successful raids in November, the XV Corps resumed the advance on Akyab Island for the third year in succession. The 25th Indian Division reached Foul Point and Rathedaung and the tip of the Mayu Peninsular. All the time it was supplied by landing craft from Chittagong and Cox's Bazaar, which were now able to land on the beaches. Starved of supplies and reinforcements, the Japanese 28th Army evacuated Akyab Island on 31 December 1944 without a fight. The 3rd Commando Brigade carried out an unopposed landing and secured the all-important airfield. The RAF was now able to bring forward its aircraft to give close support to the rapidly advancing XV Corps.

Further east, the 82nd (West African) Division cleared the Kalapanzin River valley before crossing the mountain range into the Kaladan River valley. The 81st (West African) Division advanced down the Kaladan River and met up with the 82nd Division at Myohaung near the mouth of the river, thus cutting the supply line to the Japanese troops in the Mayu Peninsular.

It was during the manoeuvrings of the 81st (West African) Division, that another Victoria Cross was won, this time by an Indian artilleryman.

UMRAO SINGH VC

On 21 November 1920, Umrao Singh was born into a Hindu Jat (Yadev) family in Paira, a small village in Jhaijar district in Rhohtak, Punjab. His family raised cattle, for which the Yadev caste was known. After attending the local school, Singh joined the Indian Army on 20 November 1939 as a gunner in the Royal Indian Artillery. He saw early service in service in Africa, which qualified him for the Africa Star war medal. In June 1942, he was promoted to havildar and joined the 33rd Battery, 30th Mountain Regiment, which was sent to the Burma Front.

The 30th Mountain Regiment had spent the monsoon season with the 25th Indian Division around the Maungdaw–Buthidaung area. By the end of October it was transferred with the 32nd and 33rd Batteries to the 81st (West African) Division. After three weeks marching, they reached their new command in the Kaladan Valley on 21 November. Although the 81st was only 60 miles from the coast, it was shut off by a range of 2,000ft mountains and a barrier of solid bamboo forests. The Africans managed to hack and level several airstrips so that they could be supplied by the Dakotas of Transport Command and remain in contact with the rest of XV Corps. Being on the eastern-most flank, the 81st was subjected to almost constant nightly shelling from the Japanese 28th Army.

Singh was No.1 on a 3.7-inch howitzer, which was designed to be dismantled and carried on pack mules. He was with his gun in advance of the 8th Gold Coast Regiment when it came under fire from the Japanese 75mm guns and mortars, which lasted for eighty minutes. Under cover of this bombardment, the Japanese launched a two-company attack on the battery.

Using a Bren gun, Umrao fired over the gun-shield while his crew fought off the attack with rifles. A second wave killed all but Singh and two other gunners, who managed to fend off the attack. Now almost out of ammunition, Singh's two companions fired off their few rounds. Singh, who had been wounded by a grenade, grabbed the only weapon available; a gun-bearer (a heavy iron rod used to move the tail of the howitzer). In a frenzy of hand-to-hand fighting, he led his men until they were overwhelmed. He was seen to lay out three Japanese before falling under a rain of blows to the head, which rendered him unconscious.

Six hours later, after a counter-attack, he was found alive but unconscious by his gun. He was almost unrecognisable from his head injury but the evidence of his outstanding defence of his gun was the ten dead Japanese that lay dead around him. Even more satisfying was that his gun was back in action later that day.

Singh was recommended for the Victoria Cross, which was gazetted on 31 May 1945. His companion in the fight, Surat Singh, received the Indian Distinguished Service Medal (IDSM). Singh travelled to London with two other Indian recipients, Gian Singh and Bhanbhagte Gurung, to receive his Cross from King George VI on 16 October 1945. He was the only Other Rank artillerymen to receive the VC in the Second World War.

He was promoted to subadar major and retired from the British Indian Army in 1946. The following year he re-joined the Indian Army following its independence and served until his retirement in 1965 when he was made honorary captain. He retired to farm a two-acre smallholding he had inherited from his father and found life hard. His Indian Army pension was £14 per month but he would not be tempted to sell his Victoria Cross, which would have made him a rich man. Instead it was during his visit to London for the 50th anniversary of VE Day in 1995 that he caught the attention of the newspapers and managed to obtain justice for his fellow VCs.

Having been turned away for not having a pass for the VIP Enclosure in Hyde Park, his VC was recognised by the organiser and admitted. Later, as he was leaving Hyde Park and waiting to cross the road, a car pulled to a halt and its passenger got out. It was Michael Heseltine, the

UK's Deputy Prime Minister, who introduced himself. Singh expressed his thanks for being invited, to which Heseltine replied:

> It is we British who must thank you and the Indian Armed Forces for the contribution made during the First and Second World Wars.

When he was told that his car was causing a traffic jam, Heseltine insisted that Singh should cross the road first, and waited until he had done so.

Singh also met with the Prime Minister, John Major, and took the opportunity to point out that the current VC pension was inadequate. Major took this on board and announced to the Tory Party Conference that year that the pension was to be raised from £100 per annum, set after the Second World War, to £1,300. The pension was later raised to £10,000 by the former Chancellor, George Osborne.

Singh was able to give up his subsistence existence and live a more comfortable life. On 21 November 2005, Umrao Singh died after a prolonged illness at the Army Research and Referral Hospital in New Delhi.

After the unopposed occupation of Akyab Island, the 25th Division was joined by 1 and 2 Commando and 42 (Royal Marine) Commando in clearing the coastal region of the Arakan. Moving south of Akyab Island, the 53rd Brigade took the port of Pauktaw on 9 January 1945 and made a diversionary operation towards Minbya. The 53th Brigade consisted of 9/York and Lancaster Regiment, 17/5th Mahratta Light Infantry and 4/18th Royal Garhwal Rifles. It was joined by the Divisional HQ Battalion, the 7/16th Punjab Regiment, which was given a independent brief to carry out fighting patrols and ambushes to annoy the Japanese.

Moving upriver, the 7/16th Punjab encountered Japanese resistance around the village of Kyeyebyin. The enemy had established a mountain stronghold about two miles south of Minbay that was covering the Japanese withdrawal. After three days of fighting patrols, 'D' Company had established itself in Kyeyebyin and was reinforced by another platoon. On the night of 18 January, the Japanese attacked but largely due to the selfless efforts of a lance naik they were defeated.

SHER SHAH VC

Sher Shah was born on 14 February 1917 in Chakrala Village near Mianwali in what was the North West Frontier. He was from the Awan tribe, one of the famed 'martial races' favoured by the British Indian

Army. It is still the most heavily recruited tribe in the modern day Pakistan Army. Little is known of Sher Shah except that he was enlisted into the Punjab Regiment at Multan and later promoted to lance naik.

Shah was a member of a platoon from 'D' Company, which was occupying Kyeyebyin, when about 150 enemy, who outnumbered them three to one, began their attack on 18 January. The enemy were supported by a 75mm gun, a 4-inch mortar and two machine-guns. The action is well-described in Shah's citation dated 8 May 1945, which reads:

> In Burma on the night 19th–20th January [sic] 1945, at Kyeyebyin Kaladan, Lance-Naik Sher Shah commanded the left forward section of his platoon.
>
> At 1930 hours a Japanese platoon attacked his post. Realising that overwhelming numbers would probably destroy his section, he, by himself, stalked the enemy from their rear and broke up the attack by firing into their midst. He killed the Platoon Commander and six other Japanese and, after their withdrawal, crawled back to his section post.
>
> At 0015 the Japanese, who were now reinforced with a Company, started to form up for another attack. He heard their officers giving orders, and bayonets being fixed prior to the assault. Again he left his section post and, in spite of Japanese covering fire from small arms and mortars, crawled forward and saw Japanese officers and men groups together. He fired into this group and they again broke up and started to withdraw in disorder.
>
> Whilst on his way back for the second time, he was hit by a mortar bomb, which shattered his right leg. He regained his position and, propping himself against the side of the trench, continued firing and encouraging his men. When asked if he was hurt, he replied that it was only slight. Some time afterwards it was discovered that his right leg was missing.
>
> The Japanese again started forming up for another attack. In spite of his severe wounds and considerable loss of blood, and very heavy Japanese supporting fire, Lance-Naik Sher Shah again left his section post and crawled forward, firing into their midst at point blank range. He continued firing until for the third time, the Japanese attack was broken up, and until he was shot through the head, from which he subsequently died.
>
> Twenty-three dead and four wounded Japanese, including an officer, were found in daylight, immediately in front of his position.

> His initiative and indomitable courage throughout this very critical situation undoubtedly averted the over-running of his platoon, and was the deciding factor in defeating the Japanese attacks. His supreme sacrifice, disregard for danger and selfless devotion to duty, were an inspiration to all his comrades throughout the Battalion.

His Victoria Cross was presented to his widow, Mehr Bhari, on 19 December 1945 by the Viceroy Lord Wavell at the Red Fort, Delhi. His medal was sold at auction for £85,000 in London in 2002.

The 25th Indian Division and the 3rd Commando Brigade made amphibious landings further south to catch the 28th Army in a pincer movement. On 12 January 1945, No.42 (Royal Marine) Commandos landed on the south-eastern face of the Myebon Peninsular. Over the next few days the commandos and a brigade from 25th Division drove the Japanese out of the coastal area, thus denying them the use of the many waterways to land supplies. With support from the tanks of the 19th Indian Lancers, the 3rd Commando Brigade cleared several Japanese hilltop strongpoints.

On 18 January, 3rd Commando Brigade leapfrogged to the next objective – Kangaw, which was the only remaining escape route for the Japanese 28th Army. Picking its way through the maze of *chaungs* and mangrove swamps, the mixed flotilla of landing craft, river barges, lighters, motor launches and other vessels slipped into Dainngbon Chaung on the morning of 22 January. Without the customary fanfare of artillery or aerial strafing, the commandoes waded quietly ashore undetected by the Japanese.

Each unit was given a different objective. No.42 (Royal Marine) Commando was responsible for the beachhead, while No.44 (Royal Marine) Commando's objective were two valleys code-named *Milford* and *Pinner*. The latter encountered only slight enemy resistance, but this did not last long. The Japanese reaction was to pound the British positions with four days of shelling. Given the paucity of Japanese artillery, this was unprecedented in the Burma Campaign. In an act of desperation and with little to lose, the Japanese fired off their remaining stocks of artillery ammunition. In the end it came to nought as the Indian 51st Brigade, supported by a troop of Sherman tanks from the 19th Lancers, passed through the defending commandos and drove off the Japanese.

Fighting, mostly hand-to-hand, continued until the Japanese were pushed out of Kangaw and the surrounding area. With the 82nd (West

African) Division fighting its way west towards Kangaw, the Japanese 28th Army was forced to scatter into smaller groups to try and escape the trap. It left behind thousands of dead and most of its heavy equipment.

When the troops had waded ashore on 22 January, No.1 Commando was given the task of securing and defending Hill 170, (a 700-yard long, 300-yard wide and 1,000ft high feature) which was the lynchpin of the occupation around the village of Kangaw. It was here that a posthumous Victoria Cross was awarded to a young Commando officer.

GEORGE KNOWLAND VC

George Arthur Knowland was born in Catford in south-east London on 16 August 1922 and, after the death of his mother when he was eleven, he spent some time in care at an orphanage. He had a younger sister, Brenda, and a brother who died when he was three. Although they lived in different children's homes, his sister remembers how he kept in touch and made sure she was doing well at school, even though he was only a teenager himself.

On his mother's death in 1933, he lived for a while with his father in Greenfield Road, Croydon, and attended the local school, Elmwood Junior School. He also joined the Scouts in Croydon. It would appear that his father was unable to cope with raising his children and George was sent to the Methodist School of Fellowship of St Christopher. Here he won a scholarship to a technical school. He joined the Church Lads Brigade in Chiswick, which gave him a taste for Army life.

As soon as he was old enough, he enlisted in the Army in 1940 and the following year joined the Royal Norfolk Regiment as a private. When the opportunity to volunteer for a newly formed front-line unit, he joined No.3 Commando. After rigorous training, he was sent with his regiment to take part in the Sicily and Italian Campaign.

In 1943, he took part in Operation *Devon*, the amphibious landing by British commandos at the port of Termoli in the Adriatic coast. In the early hours of 3 October, No.3 Commando, along with No.40 Royal Marine and the Special Raiding Squadron, landed behind German lines north of the Bifurno River. Their approach was so well disguised that they penetrated to the port before the Germans were aware. A brisk close-quarter fight with the German paratroopers of 1 *Fallschirmjäger* Division saw the British capture the town by breakfast time. So complete was the surprise that German vehicles and motorcyclists still drove into the Commando ambush until noon.

Once they realised Termoli had been taken by the British, the Germans sent in the infantry supported by tanks from the 16 Panzer

Division. The commandos were reinforced by men of the 78th Division and managed to hold off repeated attacks until 6 October. By that time they had been linked up with the British Eighth Army and the enemy was in full retreat. The operation had been an outstanding success. The Germans had been forced to leave their natural line along the Bifurno River and abandon the important lateral road to Naples. The downside was the costly casualty rate to the commandos.

George Knowland had distinguished himself during this daring operation and was promoted to sergeant. He was also persuaded to apply for a commission. On his return to England for officer training, he married Ruby Weston. In January, he was sent to join No.1 Commando in the Burma Campaign and assigned to 4 Troop as a section leader. 3 Commando Brigade, of which No.1 Army Commando was a part along with No.5 Army Commando and 44 and 42 RM Commando, was given the task of assaulting the Arakan Peninsular at Myebon. Here it was to take and hold the dominant features of the southern Chin Hills. If the brigade could achieve this, it would cut off the supply and escape routes of the enemy and secure the bridgehead.

The commanding officer of No.1 Commando was Lieutenant Colonel K.R.T. Trevor, who wrote an account of the battle of Hill 170:

> This is about No.1 Commandos operations in Burma … The task was to drive the Japanese 28th Army out of the Arykan. General Christison proposed to use 3 Commando Brigade which composed of No.1 and No.5 Army Commandos and No.42 and 44 Royal Marine Commandos on assaults from the sea to support 25 and 26 Indian Divisions.
>
> On the night of 19/20th January, the Combined Operations Pilotage Party (COPP) were able to select beaches up the Daingbon Chaung for landing to attack Kangow. The Japanese 54 Division under Myazaki were thought to be concentrated around Kangaw, which was a small village. They also had 111 Group of about 5,000 men and a matzo detachment in reserve at Kaladan. The plan was on 22 January 1945, for 74 Indian Infantry Brigade, which had the 2/Oxford and Bucks, 14/10th Baluchis and 3/2nd Gurkhas with some tanks of 19th Lancers, to strike for Kangaw. At the same time, 3 Commando Brigade were to come by water to land near Kangaw in order to try and turn the Japanese left flank. For 1 Commando it meant a five mile approach up the Daingbon Chaung which was about 25/35 yards wide and flanked by overhanging mangrove trees growing in swamps on either side.

Our objective was Hill 170, with a code-name *Brighton*. It was about 800/1000 yards long north to south; a wooded feature over 160 ft high at the highest point, way in the middle of a flat paddy field with steep sides. The plan was for No.1 Commando to lead the assault supported by No.5 Commando to seize the hill and 42 Commando were to hold the banks of the Chaung at the beachhead … One of the advantages that No.1 Commando had over the other units was that we had brought from North Africa when we were with the Americans, Garand self-loading rifles with a bore of .3 inch with which they were armed. These rifles give a very high rate of fire, we also had the normal British .303 LMG, 3inch mortars and American Thompson Sub-machine guns. We decided not to wear steel helmets but would wear our green berets … No.1 were able to capture Hill 170 without much opposition but at night there was a strong counter-attack which was beaten off.

No.1 Commando dug in on Hill 170, about half a mile from the village of Kangaw. Lieutenant Knowland's No.4 Troop defended the most northerly end. It was the start of what was to become an epic battle lasting ten days. Finally, the Japanese commander concentrated his numerically superior force of 300 against the surviving twenty-four men of 4 Troop in a last attempt to drive the commandos from the hill. An estimated 700 shells landed on the hill on that last day of the battle. In a day of continuous fighting, much of it hand to hand, the commandos repulsed and counter-attacked the waves of fanatical Japanese. Prominent among the defenders was the newcomer, Knowland, whose energy and bravery acted as an inspiration to his comrades. This made him a particular target and he drew heavy incoming fire, but miraculously he was unscathed.

In an effort to keep the enemy at bay, Knowland used just about everything he could lay his hands on; grenades, rifle, light machine-gun and even a 2-inch mortar, which he fired from the hip against a tree stump. This use of a mortar was both difficult and dangerous, as the recoil would have been considerable. At a moment when the Japanese were only about ten yards away, Knowland grabbed a Tommy gun from a casualty and, standing up in full view, sprayed the attackers until they fell back. At this moment of victory, he was mortally wounded. The crucial ground, however, was never lost and the critical position secured until reinforcements arrived.

When 3 Commando Brigade second in command, Brigadier Peter Young, arrived, he noted that:

Almost the first of our dead I saw was Knowland. He lay on his back, one knee slightly raised, with a peaceful smiling look on his face, his head uncovered.

Around the forward positions occupied by 4 Troop lay 340 enemy dead and a further 2,300 dead around the whole of Hill 170. Knowland's outstanding bravery was noted and he was recommended for the Victoria Cross. His citation appeared on 12 April 1945:

> In Burma on January 31, 1945, near Kangaw, Lieutenant Knowland was commanding the forward platoon of a troop positioned on the extreme north of a hill, which was subject to very heavy and repeated enemy attacks throughout the whole day. Before the first attack started Lt Knowland's platoon were heavily mortared and machine gunned, yet he moved about among his men keeping them alert and encouraging them, though under fire himself at the time.
>
> When the enemy, some 300 strong in all, made their first assault they concentrated their efforts on his platoon of twenty four men, but in spite of the ferocity of the attack, he moved about from trench to trench distributing ammunition, and firing his rifle and throwing grenades at the enemy, often from completely exposed positions.
>
> Later when the crew of one of his forward Bren guns had all been wounded, he sent back to troop HQ for another crew and ran forward to man the gun himself until the crew arrived.
>
> The enemy was less than ten yards away from him in dead ground down the hill, so, in order to get a better field of fire, he stood on top of the trench firing the light machine gun from the hip and successfully kept them at a distance until a medical orderly had dressed the wounded men behind him.
>
> The new Bren team became casualties on the way up, and Lt Knowland continued to fire the gun until another team arrived.
>
> Later when a fresh attack came in he took over a 2inch mortar whose team had been ordered to the forward trenches to replace casualties, and in spite of heavy fire and the closeness of the enemy he stood up firing the weapon from the hip and killing six of the enemy with his first bomb. When all bombs were expended he went back through heavy grenade mortar and machine gun fire to get more, which he fired in the same way in front of his platoon in the open. When those bombs were finished he went back to his own trench and continued to fire his rifle at the enemy. Being hard pressed and with the enemy closing in on him from only 10 yards away he had no time to recharge his magazine. Snatching up a

tommy gun of a casualty he sprayed the enemy and was mortally wounded stemming this assault, though not before he had killed and wounded many of the enemy.

Such was the inspiration of his magnificent heroism, that, though fourteen out of twenty four of his platoon became casualties at an early stage, and six of his positions were overrun by the enemy, his men held on through twelve hours of continuous and fierce fighting until reinforcements arrived. If this northern end of the hill had fallen, the rest of the position would have been endangered, the beach head dominated by the enemy and other units inland cut off from supplies.

It was little surprise that No.1 Commando was honoured with many gallantry awards, of which Knowland's was the highest. In addition, there were two MCs, two DCMs and thirteen MMs. Knowland's Victoria Cross was presented to his widow, Ruby, by King George VI on 9 April 1946. She handed it on to George's father, now a publican. For many years it was proudly displayed in his Spreadeagle Inn in Finsbury, London, but, in 1958, it was stolen and has never been seen again.

Knowland's body was buried at Taukkyan War Cemetery, twenty miles north of Rangoon. On 9 May 1995, a brass plaque was unveiled by the late Captain Philip Gardner VC to the eight VC recipients, including Knowland, from the London Borough of Lewisham. On 31 January 2002, Knowland was further honoured by his old school in Croydon and a handsome plaque was placed in the hall at Elmwood Junior School and unveiled by Countess Mountbatten.

Subsequently, the Commando Association contacted the school's head teacher, Heather Jones, and together formulated an annual award to be given on 31 January, to mark the anniversary of Knowland's death. The George Knowland Certificate of Merit will now be presented to the Elmwood pupil who exhibits the lieutenant's example of selflessness.

The 25th Indian Division continued its advance down the Arakan and, after the capture of Myebon and Kangaw, launched a sea-borne attack on 15 February against Ru-Ywa, about 25 miles south of Myebon. After it was taken, the 74th Indian Infantry Brigade was ordered to capture Tamandu, which was heavily defended as the Japanese thought they would be the target rather than Ru-Ywa. Despite this, Tamandu soon fell. The next objective was the enemy communications centre at An. The road to An was dominated by steep, jungle-covered hills, the most prominent being code-named *Snowdon* and *Snowdon East*, both of which were heavily defended.

The 3/2nd Gurkhas were ordered to clear and occupy the two *Snowdon* positions to make the An–Tamandu road safe for traffic. This they did with little opposition but in the early hours of 5 March, the Japanese put in a strong counter-attack and recaptured *Snowdon East*.

It was thanks to a rifleman of the Gurkha Rifles that the position was retaken that same morning, resulting in the award of the Victoria Cross.

BHANUBHAKTA GURUNG VC

Bhanubhakta Gurung was born in September 1921 at Phalbu, in western Nepal. He was recruited into the old Indian Army soon after the outbreak of the Second World War and joined the 3rd Battalion of the 2nd Gurkhas in 1940.

Bhanubhakta was a Gurung, one of the two main tribes from which the second (King Edward VII's Own) Gurkha Rifles (the Sirmoor Rifles) enlisted its men. Soon after promotion to lance naik (lance corporal), he first saw action with the legendary Brigadier Orde Wingate's Chindit expedition into Upper Burma in March 1943. He was with Wingate's No.4 Column, which crossed the Chindwin on a deep penetration march behind the Japanese lines. Despite causing much damage and proving that the British could go on the offensive, Gurung's battalion suffered many casualties and had to be withdrawn. A period of training replacements and refitting, in which Gurung was promoted to naik, found the battalion prepared for the invasion of Burma in March 1944.

The XIVth Army was making a drive toward Mandalay in central Burma, and the task of the 25th Division (of which the 2nd Gurkhas were part) was to engage in diversionary action along the coastal sector of Arakan. In the costly but successful fighting for a feature known as the 'Tiger', Gurung did well commanding a rifle section but then he was reduced to rifleman for an offence that was subsequently found not to have been his fault.

His platoon commander, a Gurkha officer, sent him with his section to establish a picquet position on what turned out to be the wrong hill. When reports that the intended hill had not been secured reached the battalion commander, he was furious. Gurung was charged with neglect of duty, despite following his officer's order. The platoon commander remained silent and Gurung was reduced to the ranks and transferred to another company under a cloud.

In a subsequent action when a fellow rifleman was badly wounded, Gurung carried him on his back for 3 miles over difficult jungle tracks to his base. The action for which he was awarded the Victoria Cross followed the 25th Indian Division's landings in February 1945 at Ru-Ywa in an operation designed to divert Japanese attention away from General

THE FOLLOW-UP – ARAKAN

Slim's main offensive towards Mandalay. The 25th Division's advance through the An Pass was fiercely opposed by part of the Japanese 54th Division, which was holding a series of hill positions, including one code-named *Snowdon* to the east of the village of Tamandu.

Capturing the area was essential to the progress of the British reaching and crossing the Irrawaddy. The dominant feature was *Snowdon*, to the east of which was another high hill known as *Snowdon East*. No enemy was encountered on either hill and by the evening of 4 March, 'A' Company was in position at both points.

During the night the Japanese attacked *Snowdon East* in overwhelming strength, killing half the Gurkhas on it; the remainder, completely out of ammunition, managed to cut their way through to their comrades on *Snowdon*. The following day 'B' Company, with which Gurung was serving, was ordered to retake *Snowdon East* regardless of cost. Gurung's citation recorded that:

> On approaching the objective, one of the sections of the company was forced to the ground by a very heavy light-machine-gun, grenade and mortar fire, and owing to the severity of this fire was unable to move in any direction.
>
> While thus pinned down, the section also came under accurate fire from a sniper in a tree some 75 yards to the south. As this sniper was inflicting casualties on the section, Rifleman Bhanbhagta [sic] Gurung stood up and, while fully exposed to heavy fire, calmly killed the enemy sniper with his rifle, thus saving his section from suffering further casualties.

Gurung then began to run for the top of the hill, yelling for his comrades to follow him. Though the casualties were heavy, the section ploughed forward until within 20 yards of their objective, when the Gurkhas were again halted by exceptionally heavy fire. Without waiting for any orders, Gurung dashed forward alone and attacked the first enemy foxhole. Throwing two grenades, which killed the two occupants of the trench, he immediately rushed on to the next enemy foxhole and killed the two Japanese in it with his bayonet.

All this time he was under continuous light machine-gun fire from a bunker on the north tip of the objective, and two further foxholes were still bringing fire to bear upon the section. Gurung dashed forward and cleared these trenches with bayonet and grenades.

He then turned his attention to the machine-gun bunker, and realising it would hold up not only his own platoon, which was not behind him, but also another platoon that was advancing from the west.

He ran forward a fifth time and leapt on to the roof of the bunker from where, his hand grenades being finished, he flung two No.72 smoke grenades into the bunker's slit. Two Japanese rushed out of the bunker partially blinded by the smoke and with their clothes aflame with phosphorous. Gurung promptly killed them both with his *kukri*.

One Japanese soldier remained inside, holding up 4 Platoon's advance with the machine-gun. Gurung crawled in and, prevented by the cramped space from using his bayonet or *kukri*, beat the gunner's brains out with a rock. The enemy troops who had been driven off were collecting for a counter-attack beneath the north end of the objective. Gurung ordered the nearest Bren gunner and two riflemen to take up positions in the captured bunker with him, from where they repelled the enemy counter-attack.

Gurung's citation concluded that he had

> showed outstanding bravery and a complete disregard for his own safety. His courageous clearing of five enemy positions single-handed was in itself decisive in capturing the objective and his inspiring example to the rest of the Company contributed to the speedy consolidation of the success.

The cost had been high as Gurung's company lost half its men dead or wounded. As a result of this engagement, his regiment gained the Battle Honour *Tamandu*.

It was said that Gurung's unfair loss of rank played a part in his determination to prove that he had been unjustly treated, but in fact he was a reasonable man and not one to bear a grudge. On 16 October 1945, along with Gian Singh and Umrao Singh, Gurung received his Cross from King George VI at Buckingham Palace.

After the war his company commander tried to persuade Gurung to continue serving but he had a frail widowed mother and a young wife at home, so he decided to leave. When he quit the regiment in January 1946 he had already regained his former rank of naik and had been given the honorary rank of havildar (sergeant).

In the years after the war he visited his regiment in Malaya, Hong Kong and in Britain, and was always greeted as an honoured guest. In addition to his VC, he was also awarded the Star of Nepal, 3rd class. His medal group is with the 1/Royal Gurkha Rifles. In 2000, the Gurkha training company block at Catterick was named after him. His three sons also served in the 2nd Gurkhas.

Gurung suffered from asthma for many years and for the last four years of his life was housebound at his youngest son's house at Gorkha.

He died there on 1 March 2006 aged eighty-six. His company commander (later Colonel D.F. Neil) described him as:

> A smiling, hard-swearing and indomitable soldier who in a battalion of brave men was one of the bravest.

While the fierce fighting continued around Kangaw, an Anglo–Indian force landed further south at the 60-mile-long Ramree Island with the intention of occupying and establishing forward airbases. The landing area of this large island was bombarded by the battleship HMS *Queen Elizabeth* and the cruiser HMS *Phoebe*, supported by bombers and fighters from the RAF's 224 Group. An hour later, the Indian 71st Brigade landed unopposed. It was found that the Japanese had withdrawn to form a defence in depth to the south and centre of the island.

As the 26th Indian Division pushed back the first line of defence, about 900 Japanese troops fell back to their second line. This involved them having to make their way through a ten-mile-wide swamp. By this time the Japanese soldiers were in a poor state. Lack of food and water, wounds, tropical diseases, snakes and poisonous insects added to their misery. Something even more terrifying awaited them in the gloomy swamp – the saltwater crocodile. Calls for them to surrender were ignored as they tried to cross this dangerous swamp. The blood from the many wounded attracted these fearsome reptiles, which tore into the tattered remnants of the Japanese garrison. Witnesses reported hearing screams, gunfire and sounds of animal attack.

When the British Indian forces flanked the swamp they found and captured just twenty survivors. A rumour quickly gained momentum that the Japanese had been killed by the crocodiles and few had survived. The *Guinness Book of Records* added credence to this story by publishing the event as 'The Greatest Disaster Suffered from Animals'. It is more likely that the scale of the attacks was much smaller according to animal experts, who state that Ramree Island's ecology simply could not sustain a large crocodile population. An estimated 500 Japanese troops are thought to have escaped undetected to help mount a determined resistance.

With the major Japanese bases secured by the end of February, XV Corps was able to release some of its units. Although the Arakan region was considered conquered by the Allies, there were still pockets of Japanese resistance. The *Manchester Guardian*'s leaderwriter, Ian Colquhoun, wrote that he was enjoying the sight of units of the British 2nd Division diving and swimming in the Myitinge River. When he remarked on this peaceful scene to the Adjutant of the 2/Berkshires, he retorted:

> Peaceful, hell! About six hundred yards away there are some mad Japanese. They have a gun, and they insist on firing it, although they know we are going to get them any moment now. They're a bloody nuisance, but they won't go away.

The occupation of Ramree Island opened the way to take Taungup to the south. Using landing craft, a brigade of the 26th Indian Division was thwarted by the lack of beaches and a coastline shrouded in mangrove jungle. It was decided to reconnoitre the area further south and find a more suitable landing area. A patrol was sent to gather information about the enemy's disposition and numbers. It was led by the last VC of the Arakan campaign.

CLAUD RAYMOND VC

Claud Raymond was born on 2 October 1923 at Mottistone on the Isle of Wight to Lieutenant Colonel Maurice Raymond and his wife Margaret (née Brown). The family moved to Belgrave Road, Seaford in East Sussex, and Claud was sent to board at Wellington College. He passed his entrance exams and attended Trinity Hall, Cambridge. Although he had the appearance of a quiet, studious boy he had a rebellious streak in him and often got into scrapes. According to a fellow student at Cambridge, he was one of the 'night climbers' who scaled the spire of King's College Chapel. He was a strong personality and seemed destined to great things. Having qualified, Raymond left and was commissioned in the Royal Engineers on 2 May 1943, attaining lieutenant in April 1944.

Among his talents was his ingenuity, which was rewarded when he was assigned to join a unit called D Force – the D stood for Deception. It was based on R Force, which used its unusual skills in Europe after D-Day. D Force was to try replication in Burma. Among the deceptions used were fireworks and compressed air that fooled the Japanese in pouring fire into areas that were unoccupied. After being designated 303rd Indian Brigade, the D Force was revived in the summer of 1944 and amalgamated with 4 and 5 Light Scout Car companies to form Observation Companies. The unit's title gave nothing away as it was a sound deception unit equipped with amplifier systems known as Poplin. It used the soundtracks of battle noises, including the movement of tanks and other vehicles, to give the impression of a large force being built up. The renamed D Force, Intelligence Corps (India) was commanded by Peter Fleming, the author, explorer and brother of James Bond creator, Ian Fleming.

Three squadrons of D Force were operating along the Arakan coast, one of which was Raymond's 58 Squadron. An example of D Force's deception tactics was during the advance on Ramree Island. In early February, 71st Brigade had been held up at a *chaung* as it attempted to outflank the Japanese position. Calling upon D Force and its use of noisy sound effects fooled the enemy into believing they occupied the far bank and triggered their retirement.

The next objective was for the 26th Indian Division to land its troops and advance on Taungup, about fifteen miles south of Ramree Island. A reconnaissance found that there were no beaches and the coast was lined with mangrove swaps, making landing impossible. The men of 58 Troop were tasked with reconnoitring further south to try and find a suitable landing place and obtain information of the Japanese dispositions.

Landing about fifteen miles south of Taungup, on a slim island at the mouth of Thinganet Chaung, 58 Troop found footprints on the beach, which led to a small party of Japanese. After a brief skirmish, the enemy ran away – 58 Troop then moved north about seven miles to Thinganet Island, which was free of Japanese. On 22 March, Raymond was ordered to take a patrol and advance on Taungup. Re-embarking on its assault craft, Raymond's team went up the Thinganet Chaung until it came upon a bamboo and wire boom across the *chaung*. As the men destroyed it, they saw a Japanese soldier running away to alert his comrades.

The patrol found a place to land and, moving on, it learned from local villagers that the enemy were dug in a few miles to the north-east. As the men neared the village of Talaku, they came under heavy fire from the slopes of a jungle covered hill. With three men giving covering fire, Raymond led the rest of the patrol in a charge uphill. As he began to climb, Raymond was hit in the shoulder. Ignoring this wound, he advanced, firing his rifle from the hip. He had only gone a few yards before a grenade was thrown and burst close to his face, badly wounding him. Picking himself up, he again advanced, only to be hit a third time in the wrist by an explosive bullet.

In spite of the painful wounds and the loss of blood, he led his men into the enemy position, killing two defenders and wounding another. The rest of the Japanese fled into the jungle. The position was strongly fortified with foxholes and small bunkers and would have been difficult to take but for Raymond's decision to immediately go on the attack.

Several of the patrol was wounded but Raymond insisted they were treated before him. He began walking back to his landing craft but after a mile he collapsed and had to be carried. Despite this, he gave the thumbs up to his wounded companions to keep up their spirits. On being taken on board, Raymond succumbed to his terrible wounds. It was something of a miracle that, although mortally wounded, he was able to continue to fight until the enemy were driven off. It was inevitable that he would be awarded a posthumous Victoria Cross, which was gazetted on 28 June 1945 and presented to his family at Buckingham Palace on 12 February 1946.

Claud Raymond's award was the last VC on the Arakan. The campaign had been a success. Although it was regarded as a diversionary advance, with the main thrust coming from IV and XXXIII Corps in the centre, the men of XV Corps in the Arakan took control of the coastal ports and airfields. They had also tied up the 28th Japanese Army by hemming them in from west of the Irrawaddy River and using their water-borne assaults to leapfrog behind their defences. Starved of support and supplies, the 28th fragmented, with some units holding out until the end of the war, impotent and withering on the vine. Crucially, they were unable to join the rest of the Japanese Army in defending Mandalay and Meiktila in central Burma, which had become the main objective of both sides.

Chapter 11

Marching South

General Slim had taken the bold decision to pursue and fight through the impending monsoon. With XV Corps tying up the Japanese 26th Army in Arakan, Slim followed two routes to the Chindwin River via the mountain road through Tiddim and Kennedy Peak and the other down the malarial Kabaw Valley. The object was Burma's second city of Mandalay. Slim planned to force a battle near the town of Shwebo, north of Mandalay, but the new Japanese commander, General Hyotaro Kimura, withdrew east across the Irrawaddy, where he expected to confront the full force of the XIVth Army. Acting on this intelligence, Slim altered his plans and sent IV Corps from Kalemyo on his right flank to move south and east to take the Japanese main administrative centre at Meiktila, south of Mandalay. He consequently altered the name of the operation from Capital to Extended Capital.

At the same time, the 19th Indian Division and the 2nd British Division continued to clear the Shwebo Plain of the Japanese rearguard. The 20th Indian Division advancing from Kalewa took the Chindwin river port of Monywa west of Mandalay after a hard battle.

With General Kimura's 15th Division committed to the north and east of Mandalay, Slim's ruse of screening the advance on Meiktila was paying off. It was vital for IV Corps to seize the area around Pakokku to establish a bridgehead over the Irrawaddy. The area was well defended by the Japanese 214th Regiment. Instead, the brigades of IV Corps crossed further downstream at Pagan and Nyaungu, where they met opposition from the Indian National Army. After exchanging fire, the INA surrendered.

The way was now open for the 17th Indian Division and the 255th Indian Tank Brigade to advance on Meiktila, eighty-two miles away. Coincidentally, the Japanese were holding a high-level staff meeting in

Meiktila to discuss a counter-attack north of the Irrawaddy and were surprised that the Allies were on the way to take their nerve centre. They still ignored their own intelligence, who informed them that 2,000 vehicles were moving on Meiktila. Assuming this was a mistake, the Japanese staff crossed out one of the zeros.

It was during this period that the Japanese made their desperate last-ditch stand in the decisive Battle of central Burma, in which another five Victoria Crosses were awarded.

PRAKASH SINGH CHIB VC

Prakash Singh Chib was born to Udham Singh and his wife, Giano, on 1 April 1913 in Kana Chak Village, Kathua, in the northern state of Jumma and Kashmir. He enlisted as a boy soldier into the 13th Frontier Rifles, formerly the Punjab Infantry. With the outbreak of war, his regiment was assigned to the 100th Indian Infantry Brigade and part of the 20th Indian Division. The 20th was raised in Bangalore in 1942 and commanded by Major General Douglas Gracey. It was formed to fight in the jungle and went through extensive training in Ceylon before joining the Burma Campaign in 1943.

The 100th Indian Infantry Brigade was made up of 2/Border Regiment, 4/10th Gurkha Regiment and 14/13th Frontier Force Rifles. The 20th Indian Division was sent to the Central Front with its headquarters at Tamu at the head of the Kabaw Valley, one of the most malarial regions of Burma. From there it carried out patrols and ambushes until it was recalled to help defend the strategically important Imphal from the anticipated onslaught of the Japanese 15th Army under the fanatical control of Lieutenant General Renya Mutaguchi.

The 20th made a fighting retreat through the rugged Chin Hills until it reached the Imphal plain, where it was given the task of defending the saddle of hills above the Shenam Pass on the Tamu–Palel Road. This was a vital position for it directly led to the all-important three airfields clustered around Palel to the east of Loktak Lake. These saw the almost constant arrival and departure of transport aircraft bringing in supplies and transporting the wounded back to a base hospital.

The Japanese assault was relentless and included a brigade of the Indian National Army, the majority of whom were either captured or killed. The 13th Frontier Rifles was operating from its base at Sugunu on the Manipur River a little way to the west of the Shenam Saddle. From there it created havoc among the Japanese by operating what it called 'Tiger Patrols', which, armed with grenades and automatic weapons, infiltrated the enemy lines and ambushed Japanese columns on their lines of communication.

MARCHING SOUTH

With the defeat of the Japanese 15th Army, the 20th Division was rested and prepared for the follow-up operation to chase the Japanese out of Burma. General Slim placed the 20th on the XIVth Army's right flank as it advanced on Mandalay. The division first had to cross the Chindwin River in early December 1944 and advanced south. Now it was out of the mountains and on to the flat country but it was still coming upon enemy strongpoints that had to be overcome.

On 22 January 1945, Monywa to the west of Mandalay was captured. Three weeks later, on 12–13 February, the 13th Frontier Rifles crossed to the west bank of the Irrawaddy River and helped establish a bridgehead. Although the crossing was unopposed, the Japanese soon began a series of fierce counter-attacks that lasted five days, during which time a VC was gained by Jemadar Prakash Singh; a testament to how desperate was the fighting.

The bridgehead was extended and 13th Frontier Rifles moved south west to Kanlan Ywathit. Confronted by twelve Japanese battalions, it was unable to advance any further. Singh's posthumous citation published in *The London Gazette* on 1 May 1945 vividly describes his actions:

> At Kanlan Ywathit in Burma on the night of 16th-17th February 1945, Jemadar Prakash Singh, 13th Frontier Force Rifles, was in command of a platoon of a rifle Company occupying a Company-defended locality.
>
> At about 23.00 hours the Japanese, in great strength and supported by artillery, mortars, medium machine guns and, subsequently, flame throwers, initiated a series of fierce attacks on the position. The main weight of the attack was directed against Jemadar Prakash Singh's platoon locality.
>
> At about 23.00 hours, Jemadar Prakash Singh was severely wounded in both ankles by machine gun fire and was unable to walk in his sector. His Company Commander, on being informed of this, ordered Jemadar Prakash Singh to be relieved and brought into a trench besides Company Headquarters, from where he kept shouting encouragement to all his men. A short time afterwards, owing to his relief having been wounded, Jemadar Prakash Singh crawled forward, dragging himself on hands and knees, to his platoon sector and again took over command.
>
> At 00.15 hours when his Company Commander visited the platoon area, Jemadar Prakash Singh was found propped up by his batman – who had also been wounded, firing his platoon 2-inch mortar, the crew of which had been killed, shouting encouragement

to his men and directing fire of his platoon. Having expended all the available 2-inch mortar ammunition, Jemadar Prakash Singh then crawled around the position collecting ammunition from the dead and wounded. The ammunition he distributed himself.

As one complete section of his platoon had become casualties, Jemadar Prakash Singh, took over their Bren gun and held the Section's sector of the perimeter single-handed until reinforcements were rushed up by the Company Commander. He fired his gun at this stage from a position completely in the open as he was unable to stand up in a trench. He was again wounded in both legs, above the knees, by a burst of machine gun fire.

In spite of intense pain and the loss of blood from his wounds, Jemadar Prakash Singh continued firing his Bren gun and dragging himself from place to place only by the use of his hands, as his legs were now smashed and completely useless. At the same time he continued to encourage and direct his men, regrouping the remnants of his platoon around him so that they successfully held up a fierce Japanese charge which was launched against them.

At 01.45 hours, Jemadar Prakash Singh was wounded for the third time in the right leg and was so weak from loss of blood that he was unable to move. Bleeding profusely and lying on his right side with his face towards the enemy, he continued to direct the action of his men, encouraging them to stay their ground. Although it was obvious that he was dying, Jemadar Prakash Singh shouted out the Dogra War Cry (*Jawala Mata Ki Jai – Victory to Goddess Jawala*) which was immediately taken up by the rest of the Company engaged in hand-to-hand fighting within the perimeter of his locality. His example and leadership at this period so inspired the Company that the enemy was finally driven out from the position.

At 02.30 hours Jemadar Prakash Singh was wounded a fourth time, this time in the chest, by a Japanese grenade. He died a few minutes later after telling his Company Commander not to worry about him for he could easily look after himself.

Throughout the period of intense hand-to-hand fighting and heavy machine gun and grenade fire from 23.00 hours until the time of his death at 02.30 hours, Jemadar Prakash Singh conducted himself with conspicuous bravery and complete disregard of his severe wounds, and there is no doubt that his ceaseless encouragement of his platoon, his inspired leadership and outstanding devotion to duty, though himself mortally wounded, played an outstanding part in finally repelling the Japanese with heavy casualties.

His posthumous Victoria Cross was presented to his next of kin by Viceroy Lord Wavell at the Red Fort, Delhi on 19 December 1945. A statue of Singh has been built in the village of Nud, Tehsil Akhoor, in Jammu by the Chib community. An annually charity is held each February in his memory to raise funds for distribution to war widows.

Major General 'Punch' Cowan, commanding the 17th Division, advanced on Meiktila and ensured that all roads leading to the town were blocked to deny reinforcements being sent from Mandalay. The task of occupying and holding the road between Kamye and Myingyan was given to the 33rd Indian Brigade of the 7th Division.

GIAN SINGH VC

Gian Singh was born on 5 October 1920 in Shapur Village in the district of Nawanshahz in east Punjab. On his seventeenth birthday he enlisted in the Indian Army and joined the 4th Battalion, 15th Punjab Regiment. The composition of the new regiment was Punjabi Muslims, Sikhs and Jats. The regimental badge was symbolic, comprising of a Muslim crescent entwined with a Sikh quoit, surrounded by a wreath and surmounted by a Tudor crown and the regimental title in a scroll.

In August 1943, the regiment was incorporated into the 33rd Indian Infantry Brigade of the 7th Indian Division. By September 1944, Singh had been promoted to naik in charge of a section in 'A' Company. In the advance on Meiktila, 17th Division was ordered north-west to capture the small Irrawaddy port of Myingyan. The brigade divided into two with Column 'B' consisting of 4/15th Punjab, 139th Field Artillery and a troop of 16th Light Cavalry moved to block any enemy attempt to escape from the advance of Column 'A'.

The 33rd began its advance on 24 February and met stiff opposition, but it reached Sinewa Chaung by 2 March. The enemy position and strength was established after a reconnaissance patrol and 'C' and 'D' Companies made a right flanking movement, with 'A' Company leading the frontal attack with the 16th Light Cavalry tanks. The initial assault pushed the enemy back into a nearby village where Singh performed his outstanding acts of gallantry.

The approach to Myingyan was across a flat, dry sandy plain and the enemy had ample warning due to the clouds of dust thrown up by the accompanying tanks. Dry gullies and deep ravines lay across the approach and hampered the tanks of 16th Light Cavalry.

Singh was in command of his section, which was leading the way towards the village along a road bordered by hedges of cacti. The Japanese were well dug in the surrounding bush and opened fire at close range. Realising that his section was a sitting duck for the enemy artillery and machine-guns, Singh ordered his Bren gunner to give him cover while he rushed at the nearest foxhole just 20 yards away. Firing his Tommy gun, he quickly killed the enemy before turning his attention to the next foxhole. As he charged he was hit in the arm but this did not stop him from pulling the pin of a grenade and killing four of the enemy. Undeterred, he carried on his one-man attack and took another strongpoint with grenades.

He spotted a cleverly hidden anti-tank gun and rushed it, killing the crew with his machine-gun and grenades. Calling on his men, he led them down the road, clearing enemy positions along both sides. The village was taken from the rear by 'C' and 'D' companies. Singh was ordered to go to the regimental aid post but requested permission to see the action completed. Only then did he have his wound treated.

Singh was recommended for the Victoria Cross which was published on 22 May 1945. Despite his wound, he insisted that he remain with the regiment in its drive for Rangoon. He even managed to receive a mentioned in despatches for this final action. He was flown to London and, on 16 October 1945, received his VC from the King at Buckingham Palace alongside Umrao Rao and Bhanubhakta Gurung.

With the partition of India in 1947, he was drafted to the 11th Sikh Regiment in the new Indian Army. His fighting days were not over when his regiment fought off a Chinese incursion in the Himalayas in 1962. He also fought the Pakistanis in Kashmir, for which he received the Indian Military Cross. When he finally retired he farmed in the Punjab until his death on 6 October 1996 at the age of eighty-one.

The Indian 7th Division was engaged in several fierce battles in the bridgehead at Pakokku on the Irrawaddy. The 17th Division was forced to temporarily call off its attack on Myingyan to help reinforce the 7th Division in its push on Taungtha en route to capture Meiktala. They left 4/15th Punjab to hold its position to the south of Myingyan.

KARAMJEEN SINGH JUDGE VC

Karamjeen Singh Judge was born on 25 May 1923 in the city of Kapurthala, in Punjab, where his father was chief of police. As a student at Lahore College he was a member of the Indian National Congress Party and seemed destined to become involved in politics. He cut short his studies to join the Indian Army and enrolled for Officer Training School at Bangalore. On completion, he was commissioned as an infantry subaltern at Ambala and transferred to the 39th Indian

Division, formerly the 1st Burma Infantry Division, which was rerolled as a training division.

On completion of his training, Singh joined the 4th Battalion, 15th Punjab Regiment as part of 33rd Brigade, 17th Division. The 33rd was given the job of clearing the forest around the Nyaunga bridgehead on the Irrawaddy. From there it joined the attack on the river port of Myingyan. Having advanced and overcome the Japanese outer defences, it was called to help the 7th Division at Pakokku. It left behind the 4/15th Punjab to hold the captured position to the south of Myingyan and it was later reinforced on 16 March by 4/1st Gurkhas and the Sherman tanks of the Royal Armoured Corps.

On 18 March, the 33rd advanced steadily until it was just outside the town. Despite repeated attacks by the Japanese defenders, Lieutenant Karamjeet Singh's Jat ('C') Company was ordered to launch an attack on the Cotton Mill area. Confronting them were numerous bunkers amid the broken ground and an estimated 200 artillery shells rained down on the attackers as they advanced.

Singh's platoon bore the brunt as it was the leading unit. He had confided with his company commander, Major Johnny Whitmarsh-Knight, of his desire for glory; something he was soon to achieve, as his posthumous citation describes:

> Except for the first two hours of this operation, Lieutenant Karamjeet Singh Judge's platoon was leading the attack and up to the last minute he dominated the entire battlefield by his numerous and successive acts of superb gallantry.
>
> Time and again the infantry were held up by medium and small arms fire from bunkers not seen by the tanks. On every such occasion Lieutenant Karamjeet Singh Judge, without hesitation and with complete disregard for his own personal safety, coolly went forward under heavy fire to recall the tanks by means of the house telephone. Cover around the tanks was non-existent, but Lieutenant Karamjeet Singh Judge remained completely regardless not only of the heavy small arms fire directed at him, but also of the extremely heavy shelling directed at the tanks. Lieutenant Karamjeet Singh Judge succeeded in recalling the tanks to deal with the bunkers, which he personally indicated to the tanks, thus allowing the infantry to advance.
>
> In every case Lieutenant Karamjeet Singh Judge personally led the infantry in charges against the bunkers and was invariably first to arrive. In this way ten bunkers were eliminated by this brilliant and courageous officer.

THE FORGOTTEN VCs

On one occasion, while he was going into the attack, two Japanese suddenly rushed at him from a small nullah with fixed bayonets. At a distance of only 10 yards he killed both.

About fifteen minutes before the battle finished, a last nest of three bunkers was located, which was very difficult for the tanks to approach. An enemy light machine gun was firing from one of them and holding up the advance of the infantry. Undaunted, Lieutenant Karamjeet Singh Judge directed one tank to within 20 yards of the above bunker at great personal risk and then threw a smoke grenade as a means of indication. After some minutes of fire, , Lieutenant Karamjeet Singh Judge, using the house phone again, asked the tank commander to cease fire while he went in with a few men to mop up. He then went forward and got within 10 yards of the bunker, when the enemy light machine gun opened fire again, mortally wounding Lieutenant Karamjeet Singh Judge in the chest. By this time, however, the remaining men of the section were able to storm this strongpoint, and so complete a long and arduous task.

During the battle, Lieutenant Karamjeet Singh Judge showed an example of cool and calculated bravery. In three previous and similar actions this young officer proved himself an outstanding leader of matchless courage. In this, his last action, Lieutenant Karamjeet Singh Judge gave a superb example of inspiring leadership and outstanding courage.

On 19 December 1945, Viceroy Lord Wavell presented his Victoria Cross to his next of kin in a ceremony at the Red Fort, Delhi.

The 63rd Indian Infantry Brigade of the 17th Indian Division had crossed the Irrawaddy between 10 and 20 February and started the 82-mile advance of Meiktila. The brigade could now be carried by motor transport and, along with the 255th Indian Tank Brigade, advanced quickly. Supplied as it advanced, the brigade captured Mahlaing on 26 February and the airstrip at Thabutkon, thirteen miles north-west of Meiktila, which enabled it to be resupplied by air. Three days later the 63rd set up a roadblock south-west of the town to prevent Japanese reinforcements reaching the 4,000-strong garrison. The other brigades of the 17th Indian Division surrounded the Meiktila and began to pound the defences with artillery and call in airstrikes.

On 1 March, Major General D.T. 'Punch' Cowan the division's commander, was joined by Lieutenant General Frank Messervy of IV Corps and the XIVth Army's commander, General Bill Slim, for what was hoped to be the last major battle in central Burma. It took four days of desperate fighting before Meiktila fell. Lacking anti-tank guns, some of the Japanese defenders improvised with another example of self-sacrifice when they crouched in trenches clutching 550lb aircraft bombs. As the tanks crossed the trenches, they had orders to strike the detonators and destroy the enemy armour. The Allies were wise to this and most such defenders were shot before they could inflict any damage.

It was during this period of the advance that a singular example of outstanding bravery was performed by an acting naik of the 10th Baluch Regiment, resulting in the awarding of the Victoria Cross.

FAZAL DIN VC

Fazal Din was a strict Muslim who was born into the Arian tribe of farmers in the Punjab. He was born and raised in Hussainpur Village in the Hoshiapur District on 1 July 1921 and joined the Indian Army at the outbreak of the Second World War. Many Arians enrolled and Muslims accounted for one third of the Indian Army. Din joined the 7th Battalion, 10th Baluch Regiment, which was raised in 1940. The regiment boasted the first Muslim to gain the Victoria Cross, which was awarded to Khudadad Khan during the First World War.

Din had been involved in most of the Burma Campaign with the Black Cats (17th Indian Division), He had tasted defeat in the retreat from Burma in 1942 and been heavily involved in the fighting around Imphal. On 2 March, his regiment was entering the outskirts of Meiktila and encountering stiff resistance. Now as acting naik, Din led his section in an attack on what was termed the Red House, where it found itself flanked by three bunkers on one side and the Red House and another bunker on the other side.

Pinned down by machine-gun fire, the section took cover. Din summed up the situation and, calling for his men to follow, he charged the neatest bunker and silenced it with grenades. He then went on to attack the other bunkers. As he did so, six Japanese led by two officers rushed from the Red House wielding their *shi-gunto* swords and taking the section by surprise. The section's Bren gunner managed to loose off a couple of shots and killed one of the officers but was unable to change his magazine and the second officer slashed and killed him. As Din rushed to the gunner's assistance, the Japanese officer plunged his weapon in Din's chest with such force that the end protruded from his back. As the officer withdrew his sword, Din, infused with adrenaline, wrestled it from his grasp and killed the officer. Mortally wounded, he turned on another enemy soldier and killed him.

He saw one of his men struggling with another Japanese and, using the officer's sword, killed him. Waving his sword aloft, he urged on his men. Still carrying the enemy's weapon, he staggered to the Platoon HQ to make a report and collapsed.

By the time he was carried to the regimental aid post, he had died. His action had been witnessed by the whole platoon, which inspired by Din's action, surged on and carried the position, inflicting fifty-five Japanese killed.

The award of a Victoria Cross was a forgone conclusion and Din's citation was published in *The London Gazette* on 24 May 1945. His VC was presented to his wife, Sardaw Din, on 19 December 1945 by Lord Wavell at the Red Fort, Delhi.

Post-independence saw the 10th Baluch regiment broken up with the Dogra members transferring to India and the rest to the Pakistan Army. The regiment became the Baluch Regiment. Unfortunately, a silver centrepiece depicting Din's exploit and the sword he captured from the Japanese officer were lost.

Din's VC medal group is now on display in the Lord Ashcroft Gallery at the Imperial War Museum, London.

WILLIAM BASIL WESTON VC
William Basil Weston was born in the small north Lancashire market town of Ulverston on 3 January 1924. He was the son of William Arthur Weston, an outfitter, and his wife Rose. He attended St Mary RC Primary School before going to Ulverston Grammar School. He left in 1942, was immediately called up and was sent to the Infantry Training Centre at Richmond, Yorkshire.

On 29 April 1943, Weston was posted to 2nd Battalion, The Green Howards Regiment, serving in Pershawa in the North West Frontier Province of India. After a year as a private, he applied for officer training and, three weeks after his twentieth birthday, he was commissioned. His regiment was sent to join the 4th India Division and spent four months with his battalion in the Arakan patrolling and laying ambushes. A request from the 17th Division for young officers to replace those who had been killed or wounded during the Imphal battle led to Weston volunteering for a transfer to 1st Battalion, The West Yorkshire Regiment of the 48th Brigade at Imphal.

Lieutenant Weston had just one month with his new command of 11 Platoon, 'B' Company, which had little battle experience. They crossed the Irrawaddy and, taking advantage of the motorised transport, travelled nearly 400 miles to take part in the attack on Meiktila on 28 January. The 48th Brigade was tasked with advancing from the northeast of the town. The West Yorks was held in reserve and watched as the 1/7th Gurkhas with support from the 255 Tank Brigade pushed the

Japanese defenders back south through the town. Coincidentally, this action was also observed by Bill Slim.

Upon nightfall, Major General Cowan withdrew his tanks for fear the Japanese would move in to destroy them. By the end of 2 March, 63rd Brigade had cleared the east and west areas of the town, which left the southern part still defended by the fanatical and desperate defenders.

On 3 March, The West Yorks were ordered to clear south-east Meiktila. By 10.15 hours, 'B' Company, supported by the Sherman tanks of the 9th Royal Deccan Horse, had cleared the town southwards to the railway line. With only 800 yards to the shore of the southern lake, Nos. 10 and 11 platoons of 'B' Company were ordered to clear the area by dusk. The Japanese were desperate to hang on to the only remaining part of the town until reinforcements arrived. Bunkers were fashioned from the ruined buildings, with snipers everywhere. As the advance progressed so the opposition increased and the two sides met in hand-to-hand fighting with knives and bayonets.

Weston led his 'green' 11 Platoon from one position to another, displaying disdain for the incoming fire. For more than four hours he inspired his men to follow him, despite the unpredictable actions of the enemy. A case in point was described by the platoon sergeant:

> The Japs rushed out, and one of their warrant officers tried to cut the tank in two with his sword. We pushed forward to the lake. The Japs by then appeared to have had enough of it and about 50 of them jumped into the water to try and swim across. The tanks lined up with our platoon and we all opened fire. Any enemy who escaped were caught by fire from 'A' Company, who had arrived at the other side of the lake. Then a shot rang out from a bunker behind us …

The shot came from a large well-protected bunker to the rear of the platoon. With nightfall approaching, Weston focused his attention on this final enemy strongpoint and called on three of the Sherman tanks to direct their fire on the bunker. When the fire stopped, he led his men across an open area to destroy this final enemy position. At the entrance to the bunker he was shot and fell forward. His men paused and watched as he pulled the pin from a grenade and rolled it forward into the bunker. The explosion that followed killed all the Japanese inside but also killed Weston.

Weston's sacrifice was the final act in the capture of Meiktila. He was recommended for the Victoria Cross and his citation was published in *The London Gazette* on 15 May 1945. His Cross was presented on 18 December 1945 to his older brother, Dennis, and his aunt Esther

Hathaway at Buckingham Palace by the King. He is commemorated in his home town of Ulverston with a magnificent stained glass window in St Mary's RC Church, where he served as an altar boy.

After four days of fighting, Meiktila fell. But the fighting was not yet over. The Japanese were hastening to reinforce the town but were dismayed to learn this important position was in the hands of the Allies. General Cowan ordered that the 17th Division make ready to repel the approaching 12,000 Japanese and organised his brigades into defensive sectors surrounded by barriers of barbed wire. The 17th Division could muster 15,000 men, 100 tanks and seventy guns and was reinforced by the arrival of 9th Brigade, 5th Indian Division.

On 12 March, the anticipated arrival of the depleted Japanese 18th Division began their assault from the north and west, which were repelled. In order to disrupt the Japanese tactics of mass attacks Cowan ordered brigade strength offensive sweeps supported by tanks on the enemy before they could concentrate their troops. This had the effect of causing the Japanese to counter-attack piecemeal and to be slaughtered as they reached the concertinaed wire.

Unable to sustain such losses, the Japanese made one more determined effort of a breakthrough on the night of 22 March before withdrawing east to Thazi and joining the other remnants of the Japanese Army as they sought to reorganise in the Shan Hills. By the end of March the area around Mandalay had been had been cleared. General Slim could now concentrate in getting to Rangoon before the monsoon broke.

In order to prevent those Japanese forces from crossing the Irrawaddy from west to east, XXXIII Corps detailed the 89th Indian Infantry Brigade of the 7th Indian Division to cross the Irrawaddy and prevent the enemy using the Taungup to Prome road. A sizable Japanese force had been bypassed at Taungup on the Arakan coast and was likely to join others as they made for Prome on the Irrawaddy to link up with their comrades in the hills of Pegu Yomas.

After a series of desperate confrontations, the Japanese retreated towards the Taungdaw Valley. 'B' and 'C' Companies of the 4th/8th Gurkhas were sent to block this route to Taungdaw. In a three-day battle, in which the Gurkhas were entirely surrounded, the last VC of the Burma Campaign was won.

LACHHIMAN GURUNG VC
Lachhiman Gurung was born on 30 December 1917 at Dahakhani Village in the Chitwan district of Western Nepal. He enlisted on 30

December 1940 and was one of the 100,000 Gurkhas who volunteered at the beginning of Second World War. Due to the need for increased manpower, he was accepted despite being just less than 5ft tall, a statistic that would have meant his rejection in peacetime. Having passed his recruit training, Gurung was posted to 4th Battalion, 8th Gurkha Rifles in Burma.

The battalion was engaged in the recapture of Ukhrul near Imphal in July 1944 during General Slim's drive towards the River Chindwin. In May 1945, the 89th Indian Infantry Brigade in 7th Indian Division, 33rd Corps advanced south along the Irrawaddy River to Prome. The object was to occupy the east bank and keep the Japanese 28th Army bottled up on the west bank, while General Masservy's 4th Corps fought its way south to capture Rangoon.

The 4/8th Gurkhas were given the task of preventing the Japanese from crossing the Irrawaddy and were ordered north to hold an important route that elements of the Japanese Army would have to use to reach the Irrawaddy. On 11 May, 'B' and 'C' Company's, commanded by Captain Peter Myers, were ordered to hold an important position astride a track on the west side of the river near the village of Taungdaw. This position was in the path of the enemy's retreat and vital to their withdrawal. Rifleman Lachhiman's 9th Platoon, 'C' Company was in the most forward position, 100 yards ahead of the main company, which dominated the track and so bore the brunt of the desperate Japanese attempts to clear the trail.

At 01.20 hours on the morning of 13 May, at least 200 Japanese attacked 'C' Company's position, where Lachhiman was at the foremost point. Before they advanced, the Japanese hurled dozens of grenades from close range. One grenade fell on the lip of Gurung's trench and he immediately threw it back. Another fell in to his trench and he managed to toss this back before it exploded. A third grenade landed just in front of his trench and he reached out to throw it back when it exploded in his hand, blowing off parts of his fingers, shattering his right arm and severely wounding him in the face, body and right leg. His two comrades were also severely wounded and lay helpless in the bottom of the trench.

The enemy, screaming and shouting, now formed up shoulder-to-shoulder and attempted to rush Lachhiman's post by sheer weight of numbers. Despite his appalling wounds, Lachhiman picked up his rifle and fired and loaded the weapon with his left hand. By keeping up a steady rate of fire, he was able to hold off repeated fanatical attacks.

For four hours, the severely wounded Gurkha remained alone at his post, firing at point-blank range to keep at bay the determined and desperate Japanese. His comrades could hear him yelling: 'Come and fight a Gurkha!' Come daybreak and the enemy had retreated, leaving eighty-seven dead in the area around the companies. Captain Myers dressed the wounds of all the men he could reach, including the much wounded Gurung. When he was relieved, thirty-one dead Japanese were counted in front of his position. Had the enemy succeeded in overrunning his post, the whole of the reverse slope position would have been completely dominated and turned.

The fight to deny the Japanese their escape route continued for three days and two nights and, despite being cut off, 'B' and 'C' companies managed to smash every Japanese attack.

In spite of his terrible wounds and the delay in reaching a hospital, Gurung survived with the loss of an eye and the lower part of his right arm. His tenacity in holding his position while suffering grievous wounds was soon recognised and he was gazetted the Victoria Cross on 27 July. His outstanding action was not typical of a Gurkha VC action, in that he did not charge in to attack but calmly and single-handedly held off repeated enemy attacks.

Gurung later said:

> I had to fight because there was no other way. I felt I was going to die anyway, so I might as well die standing on my feet. All I knew was that I had to go on and hold them back.

On 19 December 1945, he was presented with his Cross by Field Marshall Lord Wavell at the Red Fort, Delhi, the last VC of the Burma Campaign and the last to a Gurkha in the Second World War. His elderly and infirm father, Partiman Gurung, was carried for eleven days from his village in Nepal to be present at the Red Fort to see him decorated.

Gurung continued to serve in the 8th Gurkha Rifles and retired in 1947 as honorary havildar. He returned to his isolated home with its two-and-a-half-acre subsistence farm. Despite his disabling wounds, he continued to plough his land until infirmity made it impossible for him to continue.

The remoteness of his village caused him great hardship as he had to collect his Army pension each month from Bharatpur, some twenty-two miles away. This entailed a walk of twelve miles before he could catch a bus in order to reach Bharatpur. Through the efforts of three former British comrades from the war, funds were raised by a public appeal and Lachhiman was provided with a new house near the Gurkha Welfare Centre at Chitwan.

In 2008, Lachhiman came to England to live in Hounslow, where he was honoured as a Freeman of the Borough. Together with his friend Tul Bahadur Pun VC, he became active in the campaign to allow Gurkhas to settle in Britain which, after much pressure on the Government, they succeeded in doing. He attended the bi-annual meeting of the Victoria Cross and George Cross Association and his last public engagement was at the Cenotaph for Remembrance Day. He died a month later on 12 December 2010 and was buried in Chiswick New Cemetery.

The war in Europe had been won but still the Japanese refused to surrender, although the outcome was self-evident. An army of 30,000 troops were trapped in central Burma with no hope of being supplied or receiving reinforcements. This refusal to surrender, this mindset to fight to the last man – causing huge fatalities to the Allies – was finally settled in August 1945 with the dropping of the two atomic bombs on Hiroshima and Nagasaki.

Chapter 12

Australia's War

Following the British defeat in Burma and Malaya, the Australians looked to America as an ally in the Pacific. This came at a fortuitous time for America for it needed a friendly base from which to fight back against the Japanese. Honolulu and the American West Coast were too far away to conduct an offensive but Australia, with its dock facilities on its east coast, made an ideal base.

Another reason was five-star General Douglas MacArthur, who had served as Chief of Staff of the United States Army during the 1930s. When the Philippines gained semi-independence in 1935, the new government requested that MacArthur should supervise the creation of the Philippine Army and be its commander. With Roosevelt's approval, MacArthur accepted the assignment. On 26 July 1941, the President recalled MacArthur to active duty with the US Army by appointing him commander of the US Army Forces in the Far East.

When the Japanese Army invaded the islands, the poorly equipped US/Philippine Army retreated in the face of a superior force, which had mastery of the skies and seas. As the Japanese were on the point of victory, Roosevelt ordered MacArthur to relocate to Australia. He left his HQ at Corregidor and flew to Terowie in South Australia. It was here that he made his famous speech in which he said: 'I came through and I shall return.' Washington asked him to amend his promise to 'we shall return', which he blatantly ignored. This egotistical reaction was soon to be evident in MacArthur's dealings with the Australians.

Australia regarded the string of islands only fifty miles from the tip of Arnhem Land as a fortress or barrier against any threat from mainland Asia and Japan, so it took on the role of administrator of the Territory of Papua. Although Japan had no plans to occupy Australia, it certainly was serious in its bombing campaign; in nineteen months it attacked Darwin and other targets in northern Australia almost 100 times.

With the Japanese advancing virtually everywhere, Australia became the main base of operations and supply for the US Army in the Pacific. There was no suggestion that America was there to defend Australia from a Japanese invasion. MacArthur's obsession was to retake the Philippines with American troops and to limit the role of the Australian forces. In March 1942, there were 25,000 US troops in Australia. By September 1943 that had risen to 120,000.

From the Japanese perspective, Papua New Guinea held no particular strategic or economic significance and was not even considered part of its Greater East Asia Co-Prosperity Sphere. The Japanese Navy, however, was concerned for its main base in the South Pacific; Truk Lagoon was considered the most formidable of all Japanese strongholds and was regarded as Japan's Pearl Harbor. It was within range of allied bombers operating out of Rabaul at the eastern tip of the island of New Britain off the coast of New Guinea. Rabaul was also seen as an important naval base and, along with Truk and the Marianas, a block to the ships of the US Navy.

While the Malaya and Philippine operations were occupying the Allies, the Japanese occupied Rabaul on 23 January 1942. Despite this, the Japanese did not envisage Papua New Guinea being drawn into the conflict. This changed the following day, when it was attacked by three waves of aircraft flown from airfields at Salamaua and Lae on the east coast of New Guinea. Once again, the Japanese felt compelled to invade New Guinea and it occupied the airfields on 7 March.

It was only another three days before Salamaua and Lae were attacked by aircraft from the US carriers *Lexington* and *Yorktown* and bombers from Port Moresby, the Papuan capital on the south side of the island. The raids caused great damage and a rethinking. There seemed little alternative for the Japanese but to occupy Port Moresby.

In what became known as the Battle of the Coral Sea fought during 4–8 May 1942, the Japanese received a battering and were forced to withdraw to its bases. General MacArthur prepared to establish a base at Buna on the north coast of Papua but the Japanese occupied it before the plan was put into action. Prepared to do the unexpected, the Japanese advanced inland along a track that led to the airfield at Kokoda. From there the track led over the jungle-covered Owen Stanley Mountain Range and down to Port Moresby.

On 28–29 July, a company-sized force of Australian soldiers attempted to defend Kokoda against the advance elements of the Japanese. In a short firefight the Australians were almost encircled and forced to retreat. Reinforcements arrived and Kokoda was briefly retaken before the Australians were forced back to Isurava. This heralded the start of the most significant four-month campaign fought by the Australians in the Second World War. More than 600 Australians were killed and about 1,680 wounded in the narrow confines of the increasingly muddy Kokoda Trail. During a crucial phase of the battle, a Victoria Cross was posthumously awarded.

BRUCE KINGSBURY VC

Bruce Kingsbury, son of Philip Blencowe and Florence Annie Kingsbury, was born on 8 January 1918 near Armadale, Melbourne, Victoria. At the conclusion of his schooling, he was awarded a scholarship to the Melbourne Technical College. After two years, he emerged qualified to work in the printing industry, but instead he chose to work in his father's real estate business in the Melbourne suburb of Preston.

Not happy in this work and missing the company of his friend, Alan Avery, he worked as a caretaker for three months on a property at Natya in the Mallee District of Victoria, near where Alan was working on a farm. With the outbreak of war, and against his parents' wishes, he enlisted in the AIF on 29 May 1940 at the Preston recruiting centre. Coincidentally, Alan had enlisted on the same day. Three days after enlistment, Kingsbury was posted to the 2/2nd Pioneers, but in June, after meeting Alan at the Puckapunyal Training Camp, he gained permission to transfer to the 2/14th Battalion.

On 19 October, the 2/14th left Sydney on HMT *Aquitania* bound for the Middle East. Arriving in Palestine, the men received further training before being moved to Mersa Matruh, 186 miles from the Libyan port of Tobruk. Having dug in, they almost immediately experienced their first air raids.

Early in June 1941, the 2/14th began its first campaign, the invasion of Lebanon, where it fought its first battle, not against the Germans as it had expected, but against the Vichy French Foreign Legion. It was in this campaign that one of Australia's most celebrated heroes, Sir Roden Cutler, performed his VC exploit. Following the defeat of the Vichy French, the 2/14th was given leave in Beirut, before it took up its new position near Tripoli.

With the Fall of Singapore, most of the AIF units were recalled to Australia. On 30 January 1942 the 2/14th embarked on board *Île-de-France*, the 84,000-ton former transatlantic liner, bound for Bombay to meet the threat of a Japanese invasion. From Bombay, the unit transferred to *The City of Paris* for Australia, where it disembarked in Adelaide and entered a period of training.

On 5 August 1942, the battalion embarked aboard the American Liberty ship *James Fenimore Cooper*. Its destination was Port Moresby, the main town in New Guinea, from which all the civilians had been evacuated. The 49th Australian Militia Battalion had moved in, where it was joined by the 39th and 53rd Battalions. These young militiamen welcomed the arrival of the well-trained and experienced men of the 2/14th and 2/16th AIF Battalions from the battles in the Middle East.

The Japanese had taken the Gona–Buna area in the north on the 21 July and had made Port Moresby their target. The mountainous terrain between was covered by impenetrable jungle and the only overland route to take Port Moresby was the Kokoda Trail. Burdened by 40kg packs, the men of the 2/14th and 2/16th were sent up the narrow muddy track to reinforce the men who had been forced back from Kokoda. The 2/14th reached Isurava on 26 August to relieve the 39th and retake Kokoda.

The Japanese commander, Major General Tomitaro Horii, flushed with the successes his troops had had at Guam, Rabaul and Salamaua, was poised to overrun the 300 remaining men of the 39th and advance to Port Moresby.

Instead he was confronted by twelve rifle platoons of the 2/14th, which formed a solid defence around Isurava. They soon came under fire from Horii's artillery that continued throughout the night. Early on the morning of 28 August, Horii released the full strength of his offensive. The Japanese planned the total destruction of the Australian forces at Isurava by a double envelopment with three battalions of their 144 Regiment. The Australian centre in front of Isurava would be attacked and pinned while a second Japanese battalion would move along the eastern side of the gorge against the Australian right flank and the third Japanese battalion would move around the Australian left. The slopes were rugged and covered by jungle, which was difficult but not impossible terrain for the Japanese to adopt their standard outflanking tactics.

The Japanese frontal attack to pin down the Australians began on 27 August but was unsuccessful and required reinforcements from one of the flanking battalions. The Japanese attacked in waves and some succeeded in breaching the Australian lines, despite desperate hand-to-hand fighting by the defenders.

On the 29th, due to the death of their lieutenant and the subsequent serious wounding of their sergeant, the mantle of command fell to Lindsay 'Teddy' Bear, who was acting as Bren gunner. When 'Teddy' was forced to withdraw with multiple wounds, Bruce Kingsbury took over the Bren gun and found himself fighting side-by-side with his friend Alan Avery, who was armed with a Tommy gun.

While Kingsbury was checking the Bren gun, the Japanese made a further attack. He immediately stood and raced toward the enemy, shouting, 'Follow me! We can turn them back'! He rushed forward firing his Bren gun from the hip through terrific machine-gun fire and succeeded in clearing a path through the enemy. Continuing to sweep the enemy positions with his fire, he inflicted considerable casualties on the Japanese. Inspired by his action, his men followed him and they succeeded in slowly forcing the enemy back to their lines.

With the Japanese retreating into the shelter of the jungle, Kingsbury stood relieved for the moment that the fighting was over. A single shot rang out from the top of a 4m-high rock; a Japanese sniper had fired a single shot, which killed Kingsbury. Despite the efforts of Avery, who carried his old friend back to the regimental aid post, Kingsbury was dead. He was laid to rest in the Kokoda War Cemetery.

Kingsbury's initiative and superb courage made possible the recapture of the lost ground, which undoubtedly saved battalion headquarters, as well as causing heavy casualties among the enemy. Japanese records after the war showed that Kingsbury saved his battalion headquarters by helping to wipe out most of a Japanese headquarters and killing the company commander of the Japanese 1st Company, 1st Battalion 144 Regiment.

His Victoria Cross was the first gained on territory administered by the Australian Commonwealth. It was also the first one awarded in the South West Pacific Area. Kingsbury, along with Avery, Lindsay 'Teddy' Bear, Edward Silver, J. Whitechurch, Harry 'Jarmbe' Saunders, B.G. Wilson, D. O'Connor, F.J. Parsons, Neil Gordon and E.R. Jobe, were members of Section Seven of the 9th Platoon, in the 2/14th Battalion, which was later described as the most highly decorated section in Australian and British military history. Between them, these eleven original members of Section Seven were awarded a Victoria Cross, a Distinguished Conduct Medal and four Military Medals.

Breaking contact with the enemy is a most difficult operation. At Isurava it was only partially successful. The Japanese attacks caused the dispersion of the defenders into the surrounding thick jungle. Most managed to find their way back but 2/14th lost its commander, Colonel Keys, who was captured and later executed.

Although the Battle of Isurava was a Japanese victory, Major Horii failed in his main aim of completely destroying the Australian defenders. The resulting casualties favoured the Australians, who lost ninety-nine killed and 111 wounded; the Japanese lost 140 killed and 231 wounded.

There has never been anything but praise for the actions of Kingsbury but the Kokoda campaign was beset by a number of controversies, including the sacking of the Australian commander at Isurava, Brigadier Arnold Potts DSO MC, and the commander of the New Guinea Force, the popular General Sydney Rowell.

War correspondents Chester Wilmot, of the Australian Broadcasting Corporation, Osmar White, of the *Melbourne Sun*, and photographer Damien Parer were sent to cover the fighting and soon became aware of the terrible conditions in which the soldiers had to fight. The campaign lasted four months and was fought in thick jungle and appalling terrain. The Kokoda Trail soon turned into a hilly morass churned up by many feet. The correspondents struggled along with the 21st Brigade as it was forced back by a stronger Japanese force. The Japanese managed to get within 30 miles of Port Moresby but exhaustion and lack of ammunition forced them to retreat.

It had been a close-run thing, but the ill-equipped Australians had managed to prevent the all-important capital from being captured. Wilmot and White, full of admiration for the troops, were highly critical of the failings of the Australian military command. White exposed the Australians' inadequate jungle training and the failure to provide the soldiers with proper equipment, and he campaigned to have the army adopt green camouflaged campaign uniforms. When Wilmot tried to broadcast their views, they were heavily censored. Later, many of their suggestions were implemented.

When Wilmot and his companions reached Port Moresby, they found that General Blamey had taken over and dismissed the commander of the New Guinea Force, General Sydney Rowell, for protesting too vehemently. Wilmot, who disliked Blamey, immediately took Rowell's side, even appealing to Prime Minister Curtin about what he saw as an unjustified sacking. When his representations failed, Blamey had Wilmot's accreditation removed and there were even rumours that Blamey tried to have Wilmot conscripted into the Army. There was a history between Wilmot and Blamey. In October 1939, Wilmot reported that Blamey was taking bribes from a laundry contractor at Puckapunyal Army Base in Victoria and temporally had his accreditation terminated.

Between 14 and 16 September, another attempt failed to stop the Japanese at Ioribaiwa Ridge. The Australians then withdrew to Imita

Ridge, a well-defended position where the fully supplied Australian defenders had superior numbers and artillery support for the only time in the Owen Stanley Range. For the Japanese it was their Torres Vedras and without assaulting the Australian position they began withdrawing back along the Kokoda Trail, closely followed by the Australians.

The Japanese had planned a sea-borne landing at Milne Bay on the southern tip of Papua to work in conjunction with the Kokoda Trail advance. They were not aware of the Australians movements and when they landed at Milne Bay on 25 August they were surprised to encounter two Australian brigades. The outnumbered Japanese, without air or naval support and lacking supplies, suffered heavy casualties. On 7 September the Japanese evacuated their surviving troops by sea. The battle was the first in the Pacific campaign in which Allied troops decisively defeated Japanese land forces.

During the fighting another posthumous VC was awarded to a member of the 2/9th Infantry Battalion.

JOHN FRENCH VC

John Alexander French was born in the rural Queensland township of Crows Nest, approximately 120km west of Brisbane, on 15 July 1914, the fourth of five children to Albert and Lucy French. French's primary education was completed at the Crows Nest State School, and he later successfully sat for the State Scholarship and went to Toowoomba State High School and Technical College.

French returned to Crows Nest, where he was apprenticed to his father as a hairdresser until 1939. With the outbreak of war, John and two of his brothers enlisted but tragically by the end of the war, only one returned home.

At the age of twenty-five, French volunteered on 22 October 1939 and was posted to the 2/9th Battalion, which became part of the 18th Brigade. After several months of intensive training, the battalion embarked on the *Mauritania* and sailed for Britain via Cape Town. When it reached the the Irish Sea, the battalion witnessed the first reality of war when it saw two oil tankers ablaze after being torpedoed by German U-boats the previous day.

Following its arrival in Scotland, the 2/9th was moved to the south of England as part of a mobile strike force to counter any German invasion. Just five months later it once again took a long sea voyage; this time to North Africa via Cape Town. Arriving in Alexandria in January 1941, the battalion trained for desert fighting.

The 2/9th experienced its first battle when it was ordered to capture the Italian fort of Giarabub, 120 miles south of Tobruk. The attack was a success and the battalion flag was hoisted over the fort. The 2/9th was then embarked on the steamer *Thurland Castle*, for a one-and-a-half day voyage to take up position at the much-attacked port of Tobruk, which at the time was under threat from the German Afrika Korps.

The 2/9th took up a defensive position at Fort Philestrino, which commanded the road to Tobruk harbour. No use was made of the fort and instead the unit took up positions in slit trenches and ordered to hold the position at all costs. It wasn't long before the Germans introduced the unit to the Stuka dive-bomber, along with heavy artillery and machine-gun fire. After the siege, the Australians were relieved by the South Africans and the 2/9th was on its way to a new base at Lattakia in Syria.

In spite of strong opposition from Winston Churchill, Australian Prime Minister John Curtin ordered the return of the 6th and 7th Divisions of the 2nd AIF to Australia to help defend the country against the threat of a Japanese invasion. Arriving in Australia, the 2/9th was given seven days' home leave before training resumed again. In early August 1942 the 18th Brigade moved to Papua New Guinea.

Milne Bay was now a key strategic point with a deep natural harbour at the eastern tip of Papua. With aircraft based at Milne Bay the allies were able to attack the Japanese Army on the north coast without having to make the climb over the mountains. Milne Bay was hardly a tropical paradise as it was surrounded by rain-clad mountains that received 200in of rain per year, and was described as humid, swampy and malarial.

The Japanese underestimated the number of allied troops defending Milne Bay. By late August there were nearly 9,500 soldiers, including about 7,500 Australians, as compared to a Japanese force of 2,400. The Japanese advanced usually at night to avoid the allied aircraft that now had complete command of the air.

The climactic battle occurred at dawn on 31 August 1942, with a determined Japanese assault on one of the air strips. They received heavy losses during their three attempts to attack across open ground against well dug-in defences. Over the next few days, the Australians gained the upper hand and pushed the Japanese back. It was during this action on 4 September that Corporal French was to win the posthumous Victoria Cross. Lieutenant Colonel C.J. Cummings, commander of the 2/9th, gave this description of the actions led to French being recommended for the decoration:

> On the afternoon of 4 Sept. 42, 'B' Coy. 2/9 Aust. Inf. Bn. attacked a Japanese position East of Goroni Creek at 146993 Ref. K.B. Mission, trace 3' to 1 mile. The Coy. Crossed the creek to the north of the enemy position and started to work south in an enflanking movement. At approx. 1600 hrs. the Company encountered terrific fire from enemy medium and light machine guns and rifles. The advance of No.7 Sec., of which Cpl. French was commanding, was held up by the fire from three enemy machine gun posts.
>
> Ordering his section to take cover, this N.C.O. advanced and silenced one of the posts with grenades. His supply of grenades being exhausted, he returned to the section, obtained more grenades and again advanced and silenced the second post. Armed with a Thompson Sub Machine Gun he then attacked the third post, firing from the hip as he went forward. He was seen to be hit hard by the fire from this post, but continued to advance. The enemy gun was heard to cease fire and the section then pushed on. It was found that all members of the three enemy gun crews had been killed and that Cpl. French had died in front of the third gun pit.
>
> By his cool courage and disregard of his own personal safety Cpl. French undoubtedly saved many casualties amongst the members of his section and was greatly instrumental in allowing the attack to continue.

In a statement by Private W.E. Derrick, (there were five witness statements), French was said to have fallen about 15 yards from the machine-gun post. When Derrick reached French, he examined him and found that he had been mortally wounded and died shortly after.

The Japanese eventually gave up and evacuated most of their troops. For the Japanese, the attack had been a disaster with 600 men killed, while the Allies lost fewer than 200 men. Milne Bay was to be a turning point for the Allies for, along with the victory at the Kokoda Track, it ended any Japanese hopes of taking Port Moresby.

The award of the Victoria Cross to French was mentioned in *The Australia Gazette* No.14, dated January 1943. His father and brother, Eric, received his Cross from the Queensland Governor at Parliament House, Brisbane, on 1 November 1943.

The Australian victory at Milne Bay at the beginning of September was a great morale boost and by the end of the month the Australians were advancing back along the Kokoda Trail while the Americans were getting the upper hand at Guadalcanal. The Japanese failed on the Kokoda Trail because the terrain was more difficult than expected, was tenaciously defended by Australian troops that allowed time for Australian reinforcements to arrive and forced the Japanese to use up their limited supplies. The Japanese diversion of resources from Papua to Guadalcanal greatly helped the Australians.

At first MacArthur used a combination of US–Australian forces to fight in Papua New Guinea but as the fighting moved further north, the Australian Army was relegated to mopping up operations. MacArthur further exacerbated US–Australian relationships by describing combined operations as 'US victories' and Australian-only victories as 'Allied victories'. He also inflamed an already shaky situation by declaring, 'I tell you these Australians won't fight'.

On 6 November 1942, MacArthur moved his forward echelon of his GHQ to Port Moresby. His crusade to recapture the Philippines had started and it was to be an American-only operation.

Months of fighting continued until the Japanese were finally defeated in Papua on 22 January 1943 and at Guadalcanal on 8 February 1943.

WILLIAM NEWTON VC

William Ellis Newton was born on 8 June 1919 at St Kilda, Melbourne, Australia, the only son of Minnie Newton (née Miller) – the second wife of dentist Charles Ellis Newton, whom she married in 1918. He had two stepbrothers and a stepsister. After living at St Kilda for a few years, the family moved to Melbourne and lived in rooms above Charles's dental surgery until the mid-1930s.

Bill, as Newton was known, was educated at St Kilda Park Central School and Melbourne Grammar. Though not gifted academically he excelled in sport. Considered to be an all-rounder, his skills in leadership, coupled with a strong temperament, were spotted by his schoolmasters – qualities that would be displayed with devastating precision in his later life. He represented the school in cricket, football and swimming. A natural candidate for being the senior prefect, he also led younger boys as a sergeant in the school's cadet corps. Melbourne Grammar also helped him to secure his Intermediate certificate.

In September 1936, any dreams Newton may have fostered had to be suppressed for the time being as tragedy hit the Newton family when his father died suddenly of a heart attack at just fifty-one. The family was split up – with his stepbrothers living with friends and a sickly sister Phyllis living with relatives. Minnie and Bill moved to a much smaller flat in Inverleith Street, St Kilda. With money short, Newton left school and found employment as a materials warehouseman at a cotton and silk merchants.

Even though he was now working, he continued his passion for sports with Australian rules football, golf and water polo. His prowess at cricket was unequalled as he secured places on the Victoria second XI cricket team and, as a fast bowler, picked up the Victorian Cricket Association bowling trophy for the 1937–38 season. In 1939 he opened the bowling against the NSW Second XI – his one and only match – taking 3/113.

His stint as a sergeant in the cadet corps propelled him to join the Royal Melbourne Regiment (RMR) militia on 28 November 1938, where he became a private in the machine section of the 6th Battalion. His immediate ambition was to join the Royal Australian Air Force (RAAF) and learn to fly. This wish came true when war broke out and he joined the air force on 5 February 1940.

Training took place at No.1 Elementary Flying Training School, Parafield, Victoria, where Newton was introduced to flying the De Havilland Tiger Moth as well as the basic workings of an aircraft and ground crew instruction. On 14 March 1940, after eight hours of instruction, he completed his first solo mission and nine weeks after that passed an assessment of ability test with an 'average' mark. He became an official pilot officer on 28 June 1940, three weeks after turning twenty-one. Advanced training followed on Avro Ansons at No.1 Service Flying Training School until 9 September where, spotted for his piloting skills, he was sent to Central Flying School, Camden, New South Wales, for tutoring in becoming a flying instructor. Up until Christmas 1940 he taught novice pilots, before being promoted to flying officer on 28 December 1940. However, in his heart he wanted some real action.

During most of 1941 he submitted many applications to move into an operational role but to no avail. Records show that by November 1941 he was still in his instructor post but the Japanese bombing of Pearl Harbor on 7 December 1941 meant that his wish would soon be granted. On 9 May 1942 he finally had a posting to an Operational Squadron unit – 22 City of Sydney Station Squadron at Richmond RAAF base. It coincided with the delivery of new aircraft – the Douglas Boston attack bomber – to replace the now outdated Wirraway. The Bostons, originally intended for the Dutch East Indies, came with practically no tools and even fewer spare parts.

Newton was described by a fellow pilot as being: 'Big, brash, likeable who could drink most of us under the table, was a good pilot, good at sports.'

Between July and September 1942, the squadron was engaged in convoy escort and anti-submarine patrols off Sydney before taking its

Bostons to Townsville, Queensland. Here the crews learned the dangerous art of ground attack, flying low over a target, planting bombs and strafing.

In November 1942, 22 Squadron was deployed to Port Moresby, under the leadership of No.9 Operational Group, RAAF. At Christmas 1942, Bill went home to see his mother. Minnie remembered her son's prophetic words when he told her that if he did not return, 'not to make a fuss'.

In early 1942, clashes between Allied and Japanese forces began with a Japanese attack on Rabaul – which became a springboard for other attacks, including the Battle of Buna–Gona. Incidentally, Newton's 22 Squadron had assisted in attempting to prevent the Japanese creating a beachhead in the Buna–Gona area of Oro Bay at New Guinea.

After the capture of Rabaul, the Japanese had fixed their attention on the north coast of New Guinea in March 1942 – at the large town of Lae and the small administrative town and port in Salamaua. These two towns became a battleground between the Allies and the Japanese. Casualties were many – 5,700 Australian and 2,800 US – with three times as many suffering from sickness in the jungles, which were saturated in malaria.

Newton's squadron was well utilised at the close of 1942. Japanese land forces were concentrated along the northern coast of Papua and Australian and USAF air units carried out a relentless barrage of bombing raids in this area. In early January 1943, Newton undertook the first of fifty-two operational sorties.

Lae proved to be one of the last bastions of Japanese resistance and they were intent on holding on to it. During January and early February, 22 Squadron flight records show an impressive tally of hits as custom sheds, bridges, runways, dock areas, fuel dumps, barges and villages were decimated. The salient facts that stand out reports is that, wherever possible bombs fell in areas targeted to cause maximum damage.

Newton had gained a formidable reputation at diving headlong into the target, swooping low to just above treetop level, taking advantage by bombing any target he could see and leaving a sea of flames in his wake. This had earned the fearless Newton the nickname 'Firebug'. His aircraft often paid the price and on landing the bullet-riddled machine was a mechanics nightmare! Flying these missions, Newton cut an instantly recognisable figure due to his penchant for wearing a soft blue cricket cap.

At 06.45 hours on 2 March, Newton flew one of six Boston aircraft from 22 Squadron down the Markham Valley and again attacked Lae – this time the airfield. This hampered the Japanese as they were now unable to land their aircraft. A sixteen-ship Japanese convoy was next to be attacked in what became known as the Battle of the Bismarck Sea.

By 16 March, Newton had amassed an impressive fifty sorties. On this day his objective was to hit supply dumps near McDonalds Road. He was accompanied by Flight Sergeant John Lyon and Sergeant Basil Eastwood, as navigator. By 07.56 hours they were airborne. The flight report was typically modest and did not recount the full story, merely stating:

> Stores and buildings of foreshore of Salamaua bombed ... Remaining bombs covered target area, starting four fires, which were converging into one general fire covering practically the whole area ... Flames were rising several hundred feet.

Although accurate, the attack on the Salamaua Isthmus was nothing short of death-defying. Ground fire peppered the fuselage of Newton's Boston, damaging both wings, repeatedly stabbing the fuel tanks and nearly killing the right engine. Newton had run the gauntlet through 800m of fanatical anti-aircraft fire, and he had to fly straight towards the guns as the battery protecting the target was in line with the best line of attack required.

At this point Newton had two choices (the plane had suffered four direct hits) – fly to Dobodura forty miles away to refuel or attempt a 180-mile flight back to base at Ward's Field. He chose the latter, knowing that the plane was vital to continuing future battles. Though the trip back was uneventful, more headaches ensued as one of the tyres had been damaged and on touchdown the plane ran off the runway but no injuries were recorded. The crew landed at 10.05 hours.

Newton, on alighting, said to the groundcrew in his jocular fashion: 'You blokes like problems, so here's a beaut for you.' His Boston needed two new wings, two engines, two propellers, elevators, tail ports and 142 patches. The now famous 'war horse' flew on until June 1944 before being destroyed in a take-off crash. It was on the strength of the events of 16 March and other similar exploits that lead Newton's CO to recommend him for the VC.

Thursday, 18 March, saw Newton and his crew of Lyon and Eastwood, together with six other bombers, leave Wards Airstrip, Port Moresby, at 09.02 hours to bomb his objective at Salamaua. Reports of the day showed that the bombings were accurate, starting many fires in stores and buildings. Eyewitness accounts attest to fires burning very brightly but only for a short duration. Sadly, on lifting over his target the anti-aircraft ground crew struck lucky and raked the fuselage and wings of the Boston. The 'Firebug' had been stung. RAAF records recount the next few desperate seconds:

> Aircraft A28-3 seen smoking after leaving target area, later caught on fire and landed in water approximately 1.5 miles south of Lapui Point and one mile out to sea and sank in a few seconds.

It is believed that Newton still had use of the ailerons and rudder, plus engine control, as he flew low south-east. Newton had battled to get his craft to the shoreline and away from the enemy so that his crew had a fighting chance of survival. The belly of the plane hit the sea at more than 120mph and skimmed the water for about 150 yards, finally coming to rest around 900 yards from the shore. The aircraft sank in a matter of seconds. Eastwood, in his position as lower air gunner, was susceptible to anti-aircraft fire and was believed to have been killed on impact or drowned. His body was never found.

On reaching shore Newton and Lyon ran into some natives, who agreed to lead them to safety. It is not known why the two flyers broke from their guides. One theory is that they may have seen friendly aircraft – which had flown around the area for more than two hours. They branched out on their own to find their own way to friendly forces. Luck finally ran out for the pair as they were captured by a troop of Japanese No.5 'Sasebo' Special Naval Landing Force and they were taken to Lae for interrogation.

The Japanese instantly recognised their prize (due to his cap) and Newton was interrogated by the feared Japanese military police – the *Kempeitai*. On the orders of Rear Admiral Ruitaro Fujita, Newton and Lyon were sent back to Salamaua and to the hands of the 51st Infantry Division of the Imperial Japanese Army, where they were tortured for almost a week. Lyon was executed by bayoneting through the back. Newton's fate was to be spun out even further until 29 March.

After the war, Sir William Webb was tasked with uncovering the fate of Australian soldiers due to war crimes. He devotes a section of his report to the fate of Newton. A captured diary from a Japanese eyewitness soldier entitled 'Blood Carnival' was taken in evidence by Webb to be genuine. Sections of the diary entry are relayed here:

> 29/3/43: All four of us assembled in front of HQ at 15:00 hrs ... one of the ... Douglas crew ... had been under cross examination by 7 Base Force for some days ... it has been decided to kill him. Tai Commander (Uichi) Komai ... he was going to kill the prisoner himself with his favourite sword. The prisoner ... is given his last

drink of water ... the prisoner with his arms bound and his long hair cropped and close, totters forward ... he is more composed than I thought he would be. (He is then taken on a truck for twenty minutes). I glance at the prisoner: he has probably resigned himself to his fate ... he looked about ... and seems deep in thought. (The truck stops). Komai says 'we are going to kill you' ... Prisoner says a few words in a low voice. Apparently he wants to be killed by one stroke of the sword. Commander replies 'yes.' Prisoner is made to kneel on the bank of a bomb crater filled with water (at Kila Point). He is apparently resigned ... but remains calm. He even stretches out his neck, and is very brave. It (sword) glitters in the light and sends a cold shiver down my spine. He taps the prisoner's neck lightly ... then raises it ... and brings it down with a sweep ... In that moment I closed my eyes ... With a sound as though something watery has been cut out, body falls forward. The head detached from the trunk, rolls in front of it ... The dark blood gushes out. All is over. A seaman ... takes a sword ... intent on paying off old scores ... cuts his abdomen open ... It is pushed over into the crater at once and is buried ... This will be something to remember all my life.

The body of the twenty-three-year-old Newton lay in the partially flooded bomb crater in Salamaua until September 1943, when the Allies finally took the town from the Japanese. The remains were located by an Australian who had lived in the area prior to the war. So as not to affect the morale of the remaining RAAF flyers, South West Pacific Area HQ did not release details of the execution until 5 October. Newton's body was initially interred with full military honours at Salamaua Military Cemetery. It was later moved to Lae War Cemetery, Papua New Guinea, in January 1946.

The VC recommendation was first made on 17 August 1943 by the Australian Governor General, Lord Gowrie. The award was gazetted on 21 October.

Some two-and-a-half years after his death, William's mother, Minnie, was presented with her son's VC by HRH The Duke of Gloucester in a ceremony in Melbourne. Interestingly, the date engraved on the reverse of the VC shows the date when the submission was signed by the King, and not the date of the action. His medals were presented to the Australian War Memorial in January 1966.

Newton was the only member of the RAAF to be awarded the VC in the South West Pacific on RAAF OPS. Other than Group Captain Leonard Cheshire VC and Wing Commander Hugh Malcolm VC, he is one of the few airmen to be awarded the VC for operations over a period of time rather than for one episode.

RICHARD KELLIHER VC

The seventh and youngest child born to cattle dealer Michael and his wife Mary Anne Kelliher on 1 September 1910 was christened Richard. He was brought up at the family home in Ballybrannagh, Tralee in County Kerry, Ireland. Educated at the Jeffries Institute, before leaving and training to be a mechanic, Kelliher worked for his eldest brother and attended the technical college in Tralee. In 1929, he and his fifteen-year-old sister emigrated to Australia and lived with their relations in Brisbane.

Having left Ireland because of the Depression, Kelliher found things just as bad in his new country. He left Brisbane and took any employment he could find but spent much of his time living in the open. Food was irregular and soon his health deteriorated and he suffered from typhoid and meningitis. He worked harvesting bananas and cutting cane, which he found difficult with the state of his health. Despite the hard times, he managed to send some money home to his widowed mother in Ireland. Somehow surviving the 1930s, he was saved when war broke out and he was able to enlist in the AIF on 21 February 1941. Despite his history of serious illness, he managed to pass the Army medical examination and began infantry training.

In June Kelliher embarked to join the 2/2nd Battalion at Tobruk, Libya. He landed at Palestine and after another spell of training, joined the 2/25th Battalion, which had been involved in beating the Vichy French in Syria. Private Kelliher did not see any action and his time in the Middle East was spent on garrison duty until Prime Minister John Curtin ordered the 6th and 7th Divisions to return to Australia to combat the threat from Japan.

On 21 February 1942, the 2/25th embarked for the long journey home. When the men arrived back they were sent to North Queensland to train in jungle warfare for nearly six months.

On 9 September they arrived in Port Moresby and immediately sent to the front to face the Japanese, who had taken Buna and Gona on the north coast. The Japanese were determined to hold on to these small ports and put up a stiff resistance as the 2/25th pushed them down the Markham Valley towards Lae. There was now an incident that was either a miscarriage of justice or flagrant cowardice and one that forever coloured Kelliher's reputation.

At 16.30 hours on 12 November, as his section was putting in an attack on the Japanese, Kelliher appeared at the Company HQ saying that his section leader had sent him to report on the situation. He also reportedly said 'It's too bloody hot for me,' and 'I'm not a bloody fool'. This resulted in him being accused of cowardice and not taking his position with his section.

The attack had gone ahead and Kelliher's section leader had been killed, thus he was unable to verify his statement that he had been sent back with information. Both the officer who accused him and Brigadier R. King of 6th Division based their case on the hearsay of the officers at the 2/25th Company HQ. Nonetheless, a court martial proceeded and Kelliher was taken to Cairns and then Ravenshoe to face the charges brought against him.

On 27 March 1943, he was found guilty of misbehaving before the enemy in such a manner to show cowardice. He was found guilty and sentenced to twelve months' detention. Kelliher suffered from the effects of malaria he had contracted in New Guinea and was hospitalised. On 25 June, the adjutant general read the finding of the court and because there was little first-hand evidence of Kelliher's guilt, he quashed the sentence.

Four days after leaving hospital, Kelliher re-joined his regiment at Townsville and on 17 August he returned to Port Moresby. On 5 September, a parachute drop by the US 503rd Regiment supported by Australian artillery resulted in the airfield at Nadzab in the Markham Valley being captured. Four days later, the 7th Division including Kelliher's regiment was flown in and sent to push the Japanese back towards Lae. At the same time, the 9th Division had landed by sea east of Lae and pushed towards the Japanese base.

For the first third of the advance there was little opposition until the 10th at Jensen's Copra Plantation. There about 200 Japanese resisted until pushed back by artillery. The following day the advance was again held up at Whittacker's Plantation by Japanese marines until they were forced back to the next objective; Heath's Plantation.

On the 13th, 11 Platoon of 'B' Company advanced but were soon pinned down by a well-sited machine-gun position. Five men were killed and three wounded, including Kelliher's section leader, Corporal William Richards, who had been hit three times.

Whether or not Kelliher was prompted by his recent brush with the military court, he did not hesitate in performing an action that neutralised the enemy position and saved his comrade. Arming himself with a couple of grenades, he ran down the hill towards the machine-gun, ignoring the heavy fire. Hurling the bombs into the nest, he killed some of the crew but not all, Dashing back to his line he picked up a Bren gun and dashed back to within 30 yards of the bunker and sprayed the position until all the crew were killed.

Kelliher then turned his attention to Corporal Richards. Ignoring the enemy's rifle fire, he reached the badly wounded Richards and half-dragged him back to safety. He also assisted in recovering two other wounded.

Kelliher later stated that his actions were to wipe out the stigma of the charge of cowardice. Whatever the motive, it was a display of outstanding bravery and was recognised by the awarding of the Victoria Cross.

Three days later, Lae fell and Kelliher succumbed to another bout of malaria. He was recovering in the base hospital at Port Moresby when, on 30 December 1943, he learned that he had been awarded the Victoria Cross.

Due to his reoccurring bouts of malaria, Kelliher was granted a year's convalescent leave. He was able at the war's end to come to London to be part of the Australian Forces in the Victory Parade. Along with Reg Rattey, he was presented with his Cross on 9 July 1946 by King George at Buckingham Palace.

In the post-war years, poor health and menial jobs kept Kelliher and his new family on the poverty line. Frail and older-looking than his forty-four years, he died of a stroke on 28 January 1963. His medal group is displayed at the Australian Memorial in Canberra.

THOMAS DERRICK VC

Thomas Currie Derrick was born on 20 March 1914 in the Adelaide suburb of Medindie to Derek and Ada Derrick. The Derricks were poor and the Depression of the 1920s and '30s made life very hard. Derrick often walked barefoot to Sturt Street Public School and later Le Fevre Peninsular School. In 1928, he left school and worked for a time in a bakery. He was keen on sports, particularly swimming, and his diving prowess earned him the nickname 'Diver'. In 1931, he lost his bakery job and was forced to look further afield for employment.

With some friends he cycled 114 miles to Berri and spent the next few months camped on the banks of the Murray River. He managed to get a job fruit picking, which lasted for nine years until the outbreak of the Second World War. In 1939, Derrick married his childhood sweetheart, Beryl, and on 5 July 1940, he enlisted in AIF and was allotted the 2/48th Battalion, 26th Brigade.

In October 1940, the brigade was sent to the Middle East and trained for desert warfare. In March 1941, it was transferred to the 9th Brigade in Libya. In April, the 2/48th ended up in the port of Tobruk, where it was besieged by the Afrika Korps for eight months. The garrison was celebrated as 'the Rats of Tobruk, borrowing propaganda broadcaster Lord Haw-Haw's description that they were 'trapped like rats'.

During this time Derrick acquired an Italian Breda machine-gun, which he used to good effect on the fighting patrols he led. When they were relieved, he was recommended for a Military Medal, which did not materialise. Instead, he was promoted to corporal and by the end of the siege he had been promoted to platoon sergeant. After a period of recuperation, the 2/48th returned to the front line to reinforce the British Eighth Army for the Battle of El-Alamein on 10 July 1942.

Diver Derrick took part in the 26th Brigade's attack on Tel el Eisa, in which he led an assault on three machine-gun nests, destroying them and taking 100 prisoners. That evening, the German's counter-attacked with tanks. Using sticky bombs, Derrick destroyed two tanks. This anti-tank grenade relied on the user getting close enough to the enemy tank without being spotted and planting it near the tracks. During this period of fighting in North Africa, six tanks were immobilised by this dangerous method. Derrick was recommended for outstanding courage and leadership and was awarded the Distinguished Conduct Medal. He was also promoted to sergeant.

On 28 July, he led a six-man reconnaissance patrol and pinpointed several German strongpoints that were vital for the success of the Second Battle of El-Alamein. The assault began on 23 October and Sergeant Derrick was in the thick of it. At one point, he jumped on a Bren gun carrier heading for the enemy. An eyewitness later said that:

> We could see Diver standing in the carrier tommy gun in hand, the top half of his body exposed. It was like a chap riding a horse into a hail of fire. You could hear bullets splattering on the metal sides of the carrier. I thought, 'God, he'll never come out of that'.

Under such intense fire, Derrick managed to silence three machine-gun posts, enabling his platoon to occupy the enemy positions. All who witnessed this act were certain that he would be awarded the Victoria Cross, but no recommendation was submitted. It would be in another quite different part of the world that Derrick would finally achieve the ultimate gallantry award.

With so many wounded officers and senior NCOs, Sergeant Derrick assumed command of his company. The brigade was again sent for a period of rest in Palestine before returning to Australia. Disembarking at Port Melbourne in late February 1943, he was granted leave before a lengthy period of jungle training.

In August, the 9th Brigade was sent to Papua New Guinea to take part in the capture of Lae, which was completed by 16 September. It was then tasked with seizing Finschhafen to clear the Huon Peninsula to the north of Lae and gain control of the Vitiaz Strait. The Japanese put up stiff resistance in the fight for Finschhafen and the 26th Brigade was transferred to reinforce the Australian position. Once this target was captured, attention focused on a densely wooded 3,300ft-high hill called Sattelberg.

The Australian advance started in mid-November and the Japanese were gradually pushed back up the steep slopes. Casualties were high and Derrick was acting as commander of 'B' Company's 11 Platoon after the loss of all its leaders. By 22 November, the 2/23rd and 2/48th Battalions had reached approximately 600 yards from the summit but a landslide had blocked the only road so the Japanese defences had to be taken by the infantry alone.

On 24 November, 'B' Company of the 2/48th was ordered to outflank a strong Japanese position sited atop a cliff face. The approach was extremely perilous as the Australians had to cross a wide strip of grass without cover beneath the cliff. For a couple of hours the Australians made several attempts but were driven back by machine-gun fire and grenade attacks. As dusk fell it seemed that position was impossible to take frontally and the company was ordered to withdraw. Derrick's response to his officer was:

> Bugger the CO. Just give me twenty more minutes and we'll have this place. Tell him I'm pinned down and can't get out.

Moving forward with his platoon, Derrick attacked a Japanese post that had been holding up the advance with grenades and ordered his second section around to the right flank. The attackers soon came under heavy machine-gun and grenade fire from six enemy positions.

Derrick clambered up the cliff face despite the heavy fire. Holding on with one hand, he lobbed hand grenades into the weapon pits. Climbing further up the cliff and in full view of the enemy, he continued his grenade attack on the Japanese positions, following up with accurate rifle fire. Within the twenty minutes he had told his officer he had reached the summit, having cleared the area of the enemy. Those survivors retreated to the building in the small village of Sattelberg about 150 yards distant.

Derrick returned to his platoon and prepared to assault three machine-gun nests that were holding up the advance. Again leading from the front, he rushed forward throwing grenades from close range until all three posts were silenced. With night falling, 2/48th held its position until morning.

On 24 November 1943, the battalion commander insisted Derrick personally hoist the Australian flag over the town. Derrick had practically captured this formidable target and single-handedly destroyed ten enemy posts. He was recommended for the Victoria Cross and his citation was gazetted on 23 March 1944.

The 2/48th returned to Australia and because of Tom Derrick's outstanding leadership qualities, he was recommended for officer training. He became a lieutenant on 26 November 1944 and requested that he return to 2/48th Battalion, contrary to normal Army policy that prevented officers commissioned from the ranks returning to their original units. After much lobbying, Derrick's application was granted.

Lieutenant Derrick had become a national hero at a time when the Australian Army was not enjoying the best of reputations. There was talk that some units were disobeying their officers and refusing to fight. There was also the feeling that the Army had been sidelined. The Americans had moved north and were 'island hopping'. This left the Australian Army to mop up pockets of Japanese trapped in the jungles, where they could not prevent the advance on their homeland. The Australian Navy and Air Force, on the other hand, were involved in aiding the US forces as they moved towards the Philippines and Japan.

One of these 'mopping up' operations was the amphibious landings at the island of Tarakan off the north-east Borneo coast. The landing on 1 May 1945 by 2/23rd and 2/48th Battalions was unopposed. Some 2,100 Japanese were dug in well-sited bunkers in the low hills behind the town of Tarakan. At the end of the first day, the Australians had established a mile-wide front as they approached the hills. The Japanese resistance was of predictably suicidal tenacity and Derrick was heard to comment that he had, 'never struck anything so tough as the Japanese on Tarakan'.

On 19 May, the 2/48th's objective was to capture a heavily defended hill code-named *Freda*. The first day was unsuccessful with two Australians killed for little ground gained. On 22 May, Derrick led his platoon and helped capture the position. Reinforced by 2/4th Commando Squadron, it dug in in anticipation of a counter-attack.

At about 03.00 hours on 23 May, a Japanese machine-gun opened fire on the Australian position. Derrick sat upright to see if any of his men had been hit and was struck by five bullets, wounding him from his left hip to the right of his chest. He lay until in great pain until morning when a stretcher arrived. He insisted that other wounded were evacuated first before he was finally carried off *Freda* in the late morning. He briefly spoke with his commanding officer before excusing himself as he wished to see the padre. At the hospital, it was found that the bullets had torn away much of his liver. On 24 May Derrick died while having second operation.

Derrick's death was widely mourned. He had gone through the war seemingly with a charmed life as he performed many outstandingly courageous acts. But, with the end of the war in sight and on a target with little strategic significance, his luck ran out. As if to emphasise how fruitless was the taking of Tarakan Island, the airfield, which was the object of the invasion, was not secured until 20 June and then found to be unusable. Including Derrick, 225 Australians lost their lives and 669 were wounded.

On 7 May 1947, Beryl Derrick attended an investiture at Government House in Adelaide to accept her husband's Victoria Cross and Distinguished Conduct Medal. Along with the rest of his medals, these are now displayed at the Australian War Memorial.

ALBERT CHOWNE VC

Born on 19 July 1920, Albert 'Bert' Edward Chowne was the son of Arthur James Chowne and Frances Ellen Dalziell of Willoughby, New South Wales. Educated at Chatswood Boys Intermediate High School and Naremburn Junior Technical School, he was an enthusiastic tennis and rugby union player. In 1935 he commenced work as a shirt cutter with David Jones Men's Store. Five years later, on 4 February 1940, now aged nineteen, he was working as a salesman when he was conscripted into the Australian Militia Forces as a private to train with 'A' Company of the 36th Battalion at Rutherford. Chowne transferred to the AIF on 27 May and three days later he was assigned to the 2/13th Battalion as part of the 20th Brigade of the newly formed 7th Division of the 2nd AIF.

In August, at the completion of his basic training, Chowne and 900 men of the 2/13th left their camp to march 200km to Bathurst. Here they trained for two months before embarking on 19 October for the Middle East. En route to Egypt the 20th Brigade was transferred to the newly formed 9th Division.

Disembarking in Egypt on 26 November, the 2/13th travelled by train to Palestine, where it went into camp. In early March 1941 the 9th Division relieved the 6th Division, which, on Churchill's orders, was moved to Greece to combat the German advance. The 9th moved to Benghazi in an attempt to prevent the newly arrived Afrika Korps stopping the Allied advance. However, with supply lines stretched, the Allies were pushed back. The 2/13th provided covering fire as the 9th withdrew eastwards from Benghazi into Cyrenaica. On 4 April the battalion had a firefight at Er Regima but, being outnumbered three to one, it fell back to Tobruk where it stayed besieged for eight months. The 2/13th was the only Australian Battalion to serve right through the eight-month siege.

Chowne left Tobruk on 25 October and was assigned to a carrier instruction course. He was attached to the British Eighth Army in mid-July before re-joining the 9th Division at Latakia, in Syria. Chowne, who had been appointed lance sergeant on 9 April 1942, returned from his transfer to the Eighth Army and re-joined the 2/13th. On 16 September he was promoted to sergeant.

The Afrika Korps advanced toward Alexandria until the British Eighth Army dug in on ground of its own choosing; El-Alamein. The Australian 9th Division was called up and in the course of the fierce fighting, Chowne's carrier was disabled. He then fought as an infantryman until 24 October, when he was wounded in the right leg and hand and was admitted to the 7th Australian General Hospital for twenty-three days. The Allied defeat of the Afrika Korps at El-Alamein, just seventy miles from Alexandria, was the turning point of the war in the Middle East.

After the battle, the 2/13th, along with other Australian units, was called back to its home country to combat the Japanese, who had advanced into Papua New Guinea.

After jungle training, Chowne embarked from Cairns on 26 July for Milne Bay, New Guinea. On 4 September the 2/13th boarded landing craft at Milne Bay and landed without casualty on Red Beach to the north-west of Lae. With Lae secured twelve days later, the battalion moved to Scarlet Beach near Finschhafen on 22 September, where it fought off Japanese counter-attacks.

On 25 October, as a mortar sergeant, Chowne was leading a detachment of mortars when they were halted by strong enemy defensive positions on both sides of a narrow ridge on top of the Kreutberg range, west of Finschhafen. Heavy casualties were inflicted on his troops as they sought a way past the Japanese. Chowne went forward alone with a telephone and cable to appraise the situation and was able to successfully direct his mortars in their attack. So close was Chowne to the enemy position that he was covered with earth from the exploding mortar shells on several occasions.

Chowne repeated this daring act a few days later with the same results. This time the destruction of the enemy posts allowed for the rescue of eight of his men who were lying wounded in front of the enemy position. For his actions he was awarded the Military Medal.

Chowne was nominated to attend an Officer Cadet Training Course, graduating as a lieutenant on 21 January 1944. He was then assigned to a Jungle Warfare Training Course at Canungra, but within days of commencing the course he was hospitalised with a hernia and flown to a hospital in Sydney. On 15 May 1944, he married Corporal Daphne May Barton of the Australian Woman's Army Service.

On 7 October, Chowne was transferred to the 2/2nd Battalion, part of the 16th Brigade of the 6th Division. As the Americans left New Guinea and moved north, General Blamey then issued orders to the Australian troops to clear the remaining Japanese out of the occupied territories of Bougainville, New Britain, Borneo and the Aitape–Wewak area in Australian New Guinea.

Leaving Cairns on 19 December, Lieutenant Chowne and 2/2nd Battalion disembarked at Aitape on 30 December. The 2/2nd, which had been given the task of driving the 18th Japanese Army, commanded by Lieutenant-General Hatazo Adachi, from the Aitape–Wewak region on New Guinea's north coast. 'A' Company of the 2/2nd was under the command of Captain Derbyshire with Chowne in charge of the 8th Platoon.

By 8 March, 'A' Company had cleared the Simba Creek area near Sowom village, from where the 8th platoon patrolled the enemy-occupied area as far as the Ninahau River. Chowne preferred to do his reconnaissance patrols on his own and on one mission he came upon a Japanese camp occupied by thirty-five to forty soldiers. In his report he wrote:

> Sighted 1 Jap washing clothes. Waited until he had finished and tailed him to a hut. The Jap hung out his clothes to dry and moved to the creek. In the hut were three beds, packs, grenades and rifles in good order. All equipment was good and one man had a brand new ground-sheet. A position in front of the hut was sited to north and had overhead cover. Then went to river and sighted 3 Japs washing cloths. Returned to hut to search for documents.

Entering the hut, he was on his knees looking through the possessions of the occupants when out of the corner of his eye he saw the feet of a man standing beside him. Chowne signed off his report, 'so I was compelled to shoot him and then withdrew'.

On 22 March, Captain Derbyshire led 'A' company in a successful attack on Magahen village. The following day Chowne was again in action as he led his platoon in an attack on a well-established Japanese camp containing several huts occupied by the troops and their Indian servants. After a brief skirmish, Chowne returned to camp with his prisoners late that night.

On 25 March, 'A' Company was confronted by a strong Japanese defensive position. Chowne's VC citation describes the attack:

> After the capture of Dagua, the main enemy force withdrew southwards from the beach to previously prepared positions on the flank of the Division. Further movement towards Waawak was impossible while this threat to the flank existed and the Battalion was ordered to destroy the enemy force.
>
> 'A' Company, after making contact with the enemy on a narrow ridge, was ordered to attack the position. The leading Platoon in the attack came under heavy fire from concealed enemy machine-guns sited on a small rise dominating the approach. In the initial approach one member of this Platoon was killed and nine wounded, including the Platoon Commander, and the enemy continued to inflict casualties on our troops. Without awaiting orders, Lieutenant Chowne, whose Platoon was in reserve, instantly appreciated the plight of the leading Platoon, and rushed the enemy's position. Running up a steep, narrow track, he hurled grenades which knocked out two enemy Light Machine-Guns. Then calling on his men to follow him, and firing his sub-machine-gun from the hip, he charged the enemy's position. Although he sustained two serious wounds in the chest, the impetus of his charge carried him 50 yards forward under the most intense machine-gun and rifle fire. Lieutenant Chowne accounted for two more Japanese before he was killed standing over three foxholes occupied by the enemy.

The following day the mountain stronghold was finally taken with the help of artillery and airstrikes. The offensive ordered by General Blamey to clear out the 35,000 Japanese from New Guinea cost 958 Australian lives. Lieutenant General Adachi surrendered on 15 August 1945; he was found guilty of war crimes and sentenced to life imprisonment. On 10 September 1947 Adachi committed suicide, believing that his lack of ability had paved the way for his country's defeat.

Both of Chowne's awards were presented to his widow by the Governor General of Australia, His Royal Highness the Duke of Gloucester, on 8 January 1947 and are now held by the Australian War Memorial.

EDWARD KENNA VC

The son of Bryan Kenna, Edward was born on 6 July 1919 at Hamilton in Western Australia. The fourth child of seven, he was educated at St Mary's Convent and when he left at fourteen he trained to be a plumber. He joined the Citizen Military Forces, the equivalent to the Territorial Army, before enlisting in the AIF on 9 August 1940.

The first three years were taken up with home service defending the Port Phillip area of Victoria and the much-bombed Darwin. Finally Kenna got to see some action when he joined the 2/4th Battalion, which embarked for New Guinea on 28 October 1944.

On 10–11 May 1945, 6th Division attacked Japan's last coastal base and airfield at Wewak on the north coast. The honour of seizing this target went to Kenna's battalion. The Japanese had already established a second defensive line in the rugged jungle-covered hills south of Wewak and were shelling the Australians at the Wirui mission post. After a sharp fight, on 14 May, the 2/4th had captured all but the north-western spur.

Unfortunately the supporting artillery and heavy mortars were unable to get into a suitable position due to heavy machine-gun fire. It fell to 2/4th to neutralise these troublesome bunkers. On 15 May, Kenna moved his section as close as possible to the bunkers to provide some covering fire for the flank attack by the rest of the platoon. When they began their attack, they became pinned down by heavy automatic fire.

Kenna was on the Bren gun and found that the position he was in could not give effective covering fire. Without orders, he stood up in full view of the enemy and began blazing away firing from the hip. The Japanese returned fire and miraculously Kenna was not hit as rounds passed between his arms and body. Kenna continued firing until the magazine was empty. Discarding it, he grabbed a rifle and managed to kill the machine-gunner with his first round.

A second machine-gun opened fire on him and Kenna, who was still standing, killed the gunner with his next round. Emboldened by this one-man display of bravery, the company surged forward and carried the position. Kenna's action was noted and he was recommended for the Victoria Cross.

The following month, Kenna was taking part in another action when he was hit in the mouth by an explosive bullet. Rather callously he was told that he was likely to die but a lengthy period in hospital saw him restored to health. It was here that he met and married one of the nurses, Marjory Rushberry. On 6 January 1947, he was presented with his Victoria Cross by the Governor General at Melbourne; the last VC awarded for the New Guinea Campaign late in the war.

Returning to Hamilton, he worked at Borough Hall and became curator of the Melville Oval Cricket ground. Funds were raised by the local population and a house was built for the couple. Kenna died on 8 July 2009 at the age of ninety-one, the last VC survivor from the Second World War.

Prior to the Second World War, both Bougainville and Buka were held by Australia under a League of Nations mandate and administered as part of the Australian Territory of New Guinea, despite it being geographically part of the Solomon Islands chain. In March to April 1942, the Japanese landed on the island as part of their advance in the South Pacific.

Once secured, the Japanese began constructing a number of airfields across the island. The main airfields were on Buka Island and Bonos Peninsula in the north, Kahili and Kara in the south and Kieta on the east coast. A naval anchorage was constructed at Tonolei Harbour near Buin on the southern plain along with anchorages on the Shortland Islands off the south coast. The bases on the south side of Bougainville allowed the Japanese to conduct operations in the Solomon Islands and to attack the Allied lines of communication between the United States, Australia and the South West Pacific Area.

It was not until November 1943, that the Allies began an offensive campaign. At that time the Japanese had between 45,000 and 65,000 men on Bougainville; mostly based in the south. They had neglected to station any troops on the west side of the island thinking that the Allies would concentrate their attacks through the main Solomon Islands and the New Georgias to the east. On 1–2 November 1943, the Americans made an amphibious landing near Cape Torokina in Empress Augusta Bay with the object of expanding a perimeter big enough to build airfields from which to attack the main Japanese base at Rabaul on New Britain and neutralise the Japanese airfields on Bougainville.

The operation was quickly carried out and more than 14,000 men were landed. Admiral Theodore Wilkinson, who directed the landing, was aware that the Japanese Navy would react quickly and wanted to quickly withdraw his vessels. The Japanese were on their way with 1,000 troops on board five destroyer-transports and escorted by cruisers and destroyers. The US Navy had anticipated this and sent four light cruisers and eight destroyers. The two forces met in the early morning of 2 November and fought what was to known as the Battle of Empress Augusta Bay in which the Japanese lost a cruiser and a destroyer and were forced to retreat.

By the 13th, the perimeter had expanded to 7,000 yards of beach front and a circumference of about 16,000 yards with two airfields operable. The Japanese did manage to land troops and by mid-December, the Americans had fought the Japanese to a standstill. From their newly built airfields on the perimeter, Allied attacks on Rabaul proved very effective. The US Naval historian Admiral Samuel Eliot Morison wrote:

> It is significant that the splendid harbour which in October 1943 had held 300,000 tons of enemy shipping, and had sheltered powerful task forces of the Japanese Navy, was reduced to a third-rate barge depot.

The Japanese made another all-out attempt to penetrate the perimeter in March 1944 but sustaining such heavy losses that they withdrew. By this time, the Japanese on Bougainville were isolated, sick and starving. They had lost 8,200 men in combat and 16,000 through disease and malnutrition. Morale fell and, rare for a Japanese soldier, there was even mutiny. Hundreds deserted and wandered off through the jungle, living on anything they could find.

The rapid pace of Allied victories in the Pacific brought forward the retaking of the Philippines. General Macarthur needed all the troops he could get to effect a successful landing. As part of this build-up, he withdrew the US troops from Bougainville to be replaced by the Australian II Corps, which was completed by 1 February 1945. The Australian commander, Lieutenant General Sir Stanley Savige, set out his objectives, the most important being that Australian forces were seen to be playing an active role in the war.

To this end, two more Victoria Crosses were awarded against a trapped Japanese force still capable of fanatical opposition.

SEFANAIA SUKANAIVALU VC

Sefanaia Sukanaivalu was born two months prematurely on 1 January 1918 on the island of Yacata, in the Fiji Islands. His parents reared him in a home-made incubator made from a coconut basket stuffed with old tapa pieces to keep him warm. They wrapped him in a banana leaf because of his sensitive and under-developed skin and gradually he gained his strength. His name means 'Return from War' in the Fijian language, for his birth, in 1918, coincided with the return of the chief of his island of Yacata from serving in France. Despite this unpromising beginning, Sukanaivalu grew up to be an unusually strong boy. He attended the Methodist school on the island of Taveuni, which was about 80km north of Yacata. In 1935, he moved to the main island of Viti Levu to learn carpentry at the Methodist Church's technical school. When he graduated, he started work as a carpenter at Vatukoula gold mine. He later moved to Mount Kasi mine to be with his two brothers.

When war broke out, he returned to Yacata to enlist with men from his home island, but found that he had missed the enlisting boat that was on its way to Taveuni. Undeterred and determined still to join the war, Suka felled two huge hardwood trees, cut them into shape to build a seafaring catamaran and set sail. He managed to catch up with his friends at Taveuni and he enlisted on 23 April 1942. He was promoted to corporal in the Fiji Infantry Regiment, where he was affectionately known as Corporal Suka. His commanding officer was New Zealander, Colonel Geoffrey Upton, later editor of the *Auckland Star* newspaper.

With America's entrance into the war in December 1941, it sought a forward training area and supply base against the Japanese advance. In June 1942, the US 37th Division was established throughout the islands that made up Fiji and the country's defence force was placed under control of the US Army. When the US forces started their advance through the Solomons, Guadalcanal became their main objective.

The Americans had become impressed by the jungle skills of the Fijian soldiers, which prompted them to send a party of thirty Fijian commandos to conduct guerrilla operations against the Japanese. A strong rapport grew between the American and Fijian soldiers and their bravery was recognised with the awarding of the US's second highest gallantry award; the Silver Star. Sukanaivalu was one who received this for bravery during the Guadalcanal campaign.

On 1 November 1943, the Allied objective to retake Bougainville from the Japanese 17th Army began. The successful establishment of a beachhead around Torokina (on the northern side of Empress Augusta Bay) allowed the Americans to construct an airfield within fighter range of a key location – Rabaul. Heavy fighting around the Torokina area into March 1944 caused more than 250 Allied fatalities, with the Japanese losing approximately 5000. All the while the Fijian Infantry Battalion, which was attached to US Division, had been lending patrol support and assisting in extending the US perimeter.

The fighting and the Allied takeover of the island saw the first of three VCs awarded for the Bougainville Campaign. On 23 June 1944, on the south side of Empress Augusta Bay (below Torokina) at Mawaraka, a US–Fijian force penetrated deep into Japanese territory in an attempt to locate and destroy the enemy's HQ. Taking the lead, the Fijians ran into overwhelming opposition, forcing them to withdraw.

As they attempted to fall back, the Fijians came under heavy automatic fire and those at the front became casualties. Sukanaivalu, who was in command of the rear section, volunteered to crawl forward under fire and retrieve his injured comrades. After the two leading scouts had been successfully rescued and brought back to safety the intrepid corporal embarked on another attempt to go further into enemy territory and rescue another soldier. With little thought for his own safety, and under heavy machine-gun and mortar fire, he crawled again to the wounded man's position. On the way back he himself was seriously wounded in the groin and thighs and fell to the ground, unable to move any further.

According to accounts given by a former officer from E Company, 164 Infantry Regiment (US Division) US Army, the Fijians were dangerously close to the Japanese position and the hand grenade blasts were deafening. The enemy had successfully foiled any attempt to rescue the injured corporal, and the relentless gun fire and further casualties made further efforts to rescue him impossible.

Caught in an exposed position where cover from fire was minimal (any movement resulted in bullets whipping the undergrowth around him), Sukanaivalu pleaded with his men to desist in any more rescue attempts and to leave him. However, the soldier's code of never leaving a wounded comrade to the mercy of the enemy was uppermost in his patrol's thoughts. His VC citation reads:

> Realising that his men would not withdraw as long as they could see that he was still alive and knowing that they were themselves all in danger of being killed or captured as long as they remained where they were, Corporal Sukanaivalu, well aware of the consequences, raised himself up in front of the Japanese machine gun and was riddled with bullets.

This deliberate act of self-sacrifice to save the lives of those around him is beyond all praise. So intense was the fighting that it was a full four months before the Australian troops (who took over the perimeter at Empress Augusta Bay from the Americans) came across his body and buried him with full military honours. Fijian, New Zealand, Australian and US serviceman attended the ceremony.

On 23 June 1944, permission was sought to withdraw forces and return to the perimeter. Under darkness the various companies made their way to the landing craft that were moored on the beaches. This was the last active operation of the Fijian forces in the Solomon Islands. Altogether Sukanaivalu's battalion lost four men and fifteen wounded.

Sukanaivalu was laid to rest at the Rabaul War Cemetery, Kokopo, East New Britain Province, Papua New Guinea. In 2006 the Fijian government warmly endorsed a proposal to bring back the remains of Sukanaivalu, one of its greatest war heroes, to Fiji. However, the ongoing political unrest that has bedevilled Fiji for many years halted this plan. There is a large and colourful mural of Suka above the main staircase of Suva's city hall and several roads and public buildings bear his name. In June 2010 a new war memorial project was launched. A National War Memorial is to be constructed together with a war museum at the new parliament complex at Veiuto. Some $500,000 has been earmarked for the project, which will include a statue of Sukanaivalu, water garden and pavilion.

Corporal Sukanaivalu's VC medal, which is privately held, was presented to his parents Lote Vulakaro and Kuva at a special ceremony held in Suva's Albert Park on 6 February 1945.

As this time, the Americans had moved further north and were island hopping towards the Philippines and mainland Japan. General MacArthur made no bones about relegating Australia's role to mopping up operations. The Japanese left behind by the American advance had no means of supply or reinforcements. They were depleted by starvation and sickness but still were capable of fighting to the last man. General Blamey, Australia's unloved commanding general, urged his men to fight on and clear the enemy from what were Australian's possessions.

Although Bougainville, like most of the Melanesia islands, is beautiful with masses of perfumed orchids and highly coloured butterflies and birds, it is also a hellish place in which to soldier. The loia vine, with its savagely barbed tentacles, can rip flesh from the unwary, while the bite of giant centipedes can bring three days of agony and blood-sucking leeches attach themselves to arms and legs of the unwary. All the time there is the whine of mosquitoes bringing the soldier's worst enemy; malaria. Of all the places to fight a war, the South Pacific was the least hospitable.

REGINALD RATTEY VC
Born in Barmedman, a small rural community midway between Wyalong and Temora, on 28 March 1917, Reginald Roy Rattey was the third of seven children of South Australian-born share farmer Johennis Albert Rattey and his wife Anna Elisabeth (née Damschke). As a youngster he travelled four miles to and from the small one-teacher

Bellarwi School. At weekends he worked on the family farm, while for recreation he played tennis.

When he was only eleven, the worsening of the depression made it necessary for the older boys of the family to leave home and find work off the farm. Rattey found work at the Gibsonvale open-cast tin mine at Kikoira and was working there when the Second World War started. He joined the 21st Light Horse Militia Regiment (The Riverina Horse) at Wagga Wagga, which was mechanised and redesignated as a reconnaissance battalion.

Rattey was promoted to driver mechanic and appointed as his commanding officer's personal driver. On 23 September his unit was designated the 21st Australian Cavalry Regiment and on 3 September 1943, it embarked for New Guinea. Rattey served at Port Moresby, Soputa and the Gusap area, where he was promoted to acting corporal before he returned to Townsville on 12 February 1944 to train as an infantryman.

On 9 June Rattey was assigned to the 25th Australian Infantry Battalion (The Darling Downs Regiment). It embarked for New Guinea on 20 July, disembarking at Madang on the northern part of the mainland. Four months later, as the Americans left Bougainville Island and moved to the Philippines, the 25th embarked from Madang for Torokina, on Bougainville.

On 24 January 1945, the 25th relieved the 47th at Tavera River. During a particularly bitter phase of the campaign on the 4 March, the 25th confronted elements of the Japanese 6th Division which, under the command of Major General Kanda, was advancing on the town of Buin at the southern end of the island.

Supported by mortar and medium machine-gun fire, 'A' Company of the 25th breached the Puriata River at Galvin's Crossing. While digging in 200 yards south of the crossing on the main road to Buin the men were surrounded by a large Japanese force who for the next three days gradually drove a wedge between the forward and rear companies of the regiment.

Promoted to acting sergeant, Rattey commanded a section as it and another section fought their way along the road until halted by an extensive system of Japanese pillboxes at a road junction. The enemy had to be cleared out of this position and Rattey's VC citation accurately describes his action:

> In the South-West Pacific, on 22 March 1945 a company of an Australian Infantry Battalion was ordered to capture a strongly held enemy position astride Buin Road, South Bougainville. The attack

was met by extremely heavy fire from advanced enemy bunkers, slit trenches and foxholes sited on strong ground and all forward movement was stopped with casualties mounting rapidly among our troops. Corporal Rattey quickly appreciated that the serious situation delaying the advance could only be averted by silencing enemy fire from automatic weapons in bunkers, which dominated all the lines of approach, by our troops. He calculated that a forward move by his section would be halted by fire with heavy casualties and he determined that a bold rush by himself alone would surprise the enemy and offered the best chance of success. With amazing courage he rushed forward firing his Bren gun from the hip into the openings under the head cover of the three forward bunkers. This completely neutralised enemy fire from these positions. On gaining the nearest bunker he hurled a grenade among the garrison, which completely silenced further enemy aggressive action. Corporal Rattey was now without grenades but without hesitation he raced back to his section under extremely heavy fire and obtained two grenades with which he again rushed the enemy bunkers and effectively silenced all opposition by killing seven of the enemy garrison. This led to the flight of the remaining enemy troops, which enabled his company to continue its advance.

A little later the advance of his Company was again held up by a heavy machine-gun firing across the front. Without hesitation Corporal Rattey rushed the gun and silenced it with fire from his Bren gun used from his hip. When one had been killed and another wounded, the remainder of the enemy gun-crew broke and fled. The machine-gun and 2,000 rounds of ammunition were captured and the company again continued its advance, and gained its objective, which was consolidated. The serious situation was turned into a brilliant success, entirely by the courage, cool planning and stern determination of Corporal Rattey. His bravery was an incentive to the entire company, who fought with inspiration derived from the gallantry of Corporal Rattey, despite the stubborn opposition to which they were subjected.

In all, Rattey killed seventeen Japanese. Due to his quick thinking and skill, this serious situation was turned into a brilliant success. During the attack, three of his men had been wounded. Within half an hour of capturing the last gun, Rattey had made himself a cup of tea. Noticing his shirt that had been torn by shrapnel, he pondered on how very lucky he had been to survive the action. Two days later Rattey was recommended for an immediate award of a Victoria Cross.

After three-and-a-half months of continuous fighting, the 7th Brigade was relieved on 13 April 1945, arriving back in Sydney on 9 May. On returning home on leave, Rattey did not tell his family of his exploits but spent the remainder of his leave helping his brother plough the fields in readiness for the autumn sowing.

Reporting back for duty, Rattey went down with a bout of malaria and was admitted to hospital. Re-joining his unit at Yerongopilly Staging Camp in Brisbane, Rattey read in the morning newspaper that Australia's recently appointed Governor General had announced that his award of a VC had been approved. To avoid any fuss, Rattey removed his sergeant's stripes from his tunic and mingled with the other troops in the camp. He was only discovered when a camp orderly read his name at the morning parade.

The Minister for Lands granted him a special lease of 2,400 acres on Lake Cowal.

Again suffering from malaria, Rattey returned to hospital and was discharged from the Army at his own request on 31 October 1945.

In 1946 Rattey joined 250 men and women who had received 162 Bravery Awards. As the Australian Victory Contingent, they represented Australia when the 'Fighting Men and Women of the Empire' marched in the Victory Parade through the streets of London on 8 June 1946. A month later, on 9 July, King George VI invested Rattey and Richard Kelliher with their Victoria Crosses at Buckingham Palace. In 1948 Rattey married nineteen-year-old Emily Joyce Café.

Acting Sergeant Reg Rattey again visited England in April 1953 with fellow VCs Edward Kenna, Richard Kelliher and Frank Partridge as members of the Australian and New Zealand Coronation Contingent.

Following the death of Joyce, Rattey married Aileen Delaney, on 11 January 1955. Unable to spare the time away from his property, he declined an invitation to attend the Victoria Cross Centenary Celebrations in London in 1956. The residents of West Wyalong, understanding his concern, raised the funds for Reg and Aileen to fly to London for the celebrations, thus avoiding the long sea voyage. On 1 July, during the celebrations, Rattey laid a wreath on the Cenotaph at Whitehall on behalf of the Australian contingent.

Reginald Roy Rattey VC died of emphysema, aged sixty-eight, on 10 January 1986.

FRANK PARTRIDGE VC

Frank John Partridge was born in Grafton, New South Wales, on 29 November 1924 to parents Frank and Mary. His father was a dairy farmer and banana grower at Upper Newee Creek, Macksville.

Partridge was educated at Tewinga Public School and left at the age of thirteen to help work on his father's farm. Despite his sketchy and brief schooling, he later self-educated himself and achieved great success on radio and television quiz shows.

Following service in the local Volunteer Defence Corps he enlisted on 26 March 1943 with the 8th Battalion AIF. After a year of domestic service in Australia, he and the regiment were sent to Lae, New Guinea, with the 23rd Brigade, of which the 8th was a part. Finally, the regiment moved to North Bougainville for the last stages of the campaign.

The Allies had forced the Japanese apart, with their main units in the south and the remnants in the north. General Savige's plan was to push the Japanese back on to the narrow Bonis Peninsula and either destroy them or force their surrender. By February and March, the Australians had driven the Japanese north past the Soaken Plantation. Advancing against fanatical opposition, the 8th approached Ratsua but was confronted by a ridge called 'Base 5', later renamed 'Part Ridge', after the heroics of Private Partridge.

On 23 July, the 8th launched an attack against Base 5 and successfully occupied it. Coming under very heavy fire from some well-entrenched machine-guns and rifles, they were unable to advance. Partridge was in a section carrying out a flanking movement when he was hit twice, in the left arm and thigh. His Bren gunner was killed and two others were wounded. Quickly summing up the situation, Partridge rushed forward, grabbed the Bren gun and passed it to another soldier to provide covering fire.

Then, dashing to the bunker, he lobbed in a grenade and before the dust had settled, followed up and killed the only enemy survivor with his knife. He then cleared the bunker of the dead crew before attempting to attack another bunker. By this time he was weak from loss of blood and called to his section commander that he was unable to continue. Although the platoon moved forward, more heavy fire forced them back. Later, the Japanese abandoned the position, which revealed forty-three enemy bunkers and other foxholes.

Partridge's prompt single-handed attack opened the way to taking of Ratsua. For his outstanding bravery he was recommended for the Victoria Cross. His citation was published in *The London Gazette* on 22 January 1946 and he was presented with his Cross on 13 April 1946 by the Governor General.

After the war Partridge made three visits to London; the 1946 Victory Parade, the Coronation in 1953 and the centenary of the Victoria Cross in 1956. He returned to farming and operated a banana plantation at

Upper Newee Creek. He married Barbara Dunlop on 23 March 1963 and they were blessed with a son that December. Tragically, Partridge was killed in a car accident in 23 March 1964.

Operations on Bougainville finally ended on 21 August 1945, when the Japanese surrendered. The final phase of the Campaign saw 516 Australians killed, another 1,572 wounded with 8,500 Japanese fatalities. Disease and malnutrition accounted for approximately 9,800 more deaths. The fatalities among the civilian population tend to be overlooked but it is estimated that out of a population of 52,000, up to 13,000 were killed.

The Borneo Campaign was the last major campaign in the South West Pacific. The battles for Papua New Guinea, Bougainville and New Britain had all but wiped out Japanese opposition. The only wholly enemy-occupied territory in the South West Pacific was the world's third largest island; Borneo. It had been captured by the Japanese in early 1942, mainly because of the oil fields, which produced a 'pure' form of oil that needed little refinement. By 1945, the war had moved further north, leaving the Japanese forces there isolated and without any hope of being supplied or reinforced.

The decision for the Allies to invade Borneo was mostly political. General MacArthur appears to have had some misgivings about his offhand behaviour towards Australia, for he planned the operation partly to alleviate concerns of the Australian government that its forces were being relegated to backwaters. The invasion of Borneo was intended to make Australia more visible again in pressing home the war against Japan. Although senior Australian officers had misgivings about the operation, they eventually threw their weight behind it by committing their two veteran infantry divisions, the 7th and 9th Divisions, to the invasion.

There were three separate operations, all amphibious. Code-named *Oboe 1*, the taking of Tarakan Island off north-east Borneo was in order to capture its oil field and airfields; the latter for use against the upcoming invasion of the mainland. It was during this operation that another Victoria Cross was won.

JOHN MACKEY VC

John Bernard Mackey was born on 16 May 1922 to Stanley and Bridget Mackey of Leichhardt, Sydney, where his father owned a bakery business. He was educated at St Columba's School and the Christian

Brothers High School. The family later moved to Portland in New South Wales and Mackey was apprenticed in his father's bakery, something he disliked. When his mother died, his relationship with his father became strained and he joined the AIF on 4 June 1940.

Mackey was posted to the 2/3rd Pioneer Battalion and served in Darwin in 1941. He was then shipped to the Middle East and took part in the battle of El-Alamein in 1942. Returning to Australia, the 2/3rd was sent to Finschhafen, on Huon Peninsular, New Guinea. He was promoted to corporal and was described by his commanding officer as an outstanding junior officer. All too commonplace for men serving in the jungles, Mackey was afflicted by reoccurring malaria, which resulted in months in hospital.

As part of the 9th Division, the 2/3rd embarked for the invasion of Tarakan Island, Borneo, in April 1945. Landing on 1 May, the 2/3rd came under heavy fire before forcing the enemy back to a strongly fortified position named *Helen* east of Tarakan town.

On 12 May, Mackey's section was moving along a narrow razor-backed ridge when it came under heavy machine-gun fire. With barely wide enough room for two men, Mackey and Lance Corporal Riedy scrambled up the ridge, throwing smoke grenades to mask their approach.

Charging the first machine-gun post, Mackey wrestled with the gunner until he managed to kill him with his bayonet. Another machine-gun opened fire just six yards away and Mackey rushed the post and killed the crew with grenades. Taking the wounded Riedy's Owen sub-machine-gun, Mackey attacked another machine-gun nest further up the slope. As he reached the position he managed to kill two of the crew until he fell mortally wounded. He had demolished three machine-gun nests and so enabled his section to advance. The Japanese were nothing if not tenacious and it took an attack from aircraft carrying napalm to dislodge them.

Corporal Mackey was recommended for the Victoria Cross, which was presented to his sister on 1 January 1946 by the Governor General in Sydney.

The Allies took Tarakan Island but found that the airfield had been so effectively bombed by their air force that it was unusable. The Japanese fell back and heavy artillery and air bombardments effectively neutralised them. By 15 May, Tarakan was declared secure. Attention now focused on Oboe 6, the invasion of Brunei and Northern Borneo. It was here that the sixth – and last – soldier of the 9th Australian Division carried out the action that led to him being awarded the VC.

LESLIE STARCEVICH VC

Leslie Thomislav (Thomas) was the third of ten children born to Croatian-born miner Joseph Starcevich and his English wife, Gertrude May. on 5 September 1918, in Subiaco, Western Australia. In the 1920s, the family moved to Grass Patch near Esperance, where Starcevich was educated at the local school. When he left, he followed his father and worked as a miner at the Norseman Gold Mine until he joined the AIF on 9 April 1941.

Starcevich was sent to join the 2/43rd Infantry Battalion and within six months had embarked for the Middle East. After a spell of desert training, he was involved in the battle for Ruin Ridge in the El-Alamein campaign in 1942, where he was wounded in the thigh. Called back to Australia in January 1944, he trained for jungle fighting. In August, he put his training to the test at Lae and Finschhafen. Although promoted to corporal, he later voluntarily relinquished the rank.

From May 1945 the 9th Infantry Division took part in the invasion of Labuan in Brunei Bay and British North Borneo. Part of the 9th Division landed on 10 June with the objective being the oil fields and the rubber plantations. On 27–28 June, the 2/43rd attacked the town of Beaufort, which was approached along a thickly wooded spur that made a frontal attack more hazardous. The leading platoon found the enemy well dug-in and putting down a heavy fire. Starcevich, on Bren gun, moved forward and firing from the hip, managed to silence the forward machine-gun. Fired on by a second machine-gun, he changed his magazine, coolly advanced on the enemy post and killed the crew.

A third machine-gun then opened fire and Starcevich and another soldier replied with accurate fire that silenced the enemy nest. The advance was able to progress and by the 29th, the fight was almost over and the day was spent mopping up. For taking the initiative and coolness under fire, Starcevich was presented the Victoria Cross on 27 May 1947 by the Lieutenant Governor of Western Australia.

On 10 December 1947, he married Kathleen Warr and on being demobbed, he worked as a car salesman in Perth. In the early 1950s he was granted a war service property where he farmed sheep and wheat. He divorced in 1969, moved to a 100-acre farm and lived in a small shack. A modest man, he was popular with the locals. On 17 November 1989 he died and was buried with full military honours in the local cemetery at Grass Patch. His VC is held at the Army Museum of Western Australia.

The war was drawing to a close. The Borneo invasion was Australia's last act and it now sought to be party to the Japanese surrender. The dropping of the atomic bombs on Nagasaki and Hiroshima caught the Australian government unaware (only the US and Great Britain knew). General MacArthur was sympathetic to Australia's wish to include its signature to the surrender but the general also wished to include New Zealand, Canada, France and the Netherlands. After objecting to the last three mentioned, Australia did agreed to the terms and, on 2 September 1945, General Blamey added Australia's signature to the surrender document.

The final recipient of the Victoria Cross in the Second World War was a Canadian flier and his posthumous award was somewhat controversial. The awarding of the Cross to a member of the Canadian Navy, as well as the Fleet Air Arm, concentrated the minds of the Admiralty's Honours and Awards Committee in the weeks that followed the end of Second World War. They had to examine the case of a posthumous award to a Canadian-born pilot attached to the Fleet Air Arm and bear in mind a memo sent by Vice-Admiral Sir Philip Vian (Flag Officer Commanding, First Aircraft Carrier Squadron, British Pacific Fleet) to the Commander-in-Chief, British Pacific Fleet. Dated 13 September 1945, it read:

> In recommending the award of the Victoria Cross Posthumous to the late Temporary Lieutenant R.H. Gray, DSC, RCNVR, I have in mind his brilliant fighting spirit and inspired leadership, an unforgettable example of selfless and sustained devotion to duty without regard to safety of life and limb:
>
> Secondly, that you may think as I do that a Victoria Cross is the just due of the gallant company of Naval Airmen who have from December last have fought and beat the Japanese from Palembang to Tokyo and:
>
> Thirdly, that the award of this highly prized and highly regarded recognition of valour may fittingly be conferred on a native of Canada, which Dominion has played so great a part in the training of our Airmen.

The question was clear: should a VC be awarded to a naval airman because he was a Canadian and serving in the Fleet Air Arm?

ROBERT GRAY VC

Robert Hampton Gray, nicknamed 'Hammy', was born 2 November 1919 in Trail, British Columbia, a town just 10km from the United States border. He was the oldest of three children born to Boer War veteran, John Balfour Gray and his wife, Wilhelmina. The family later moved to another border town, Nelson, where Gray enjoyed an unremarkable but happy upbringing. He graduated from high school in 1936 and enrolled at the University of Alberta, then transferred to the University of British Columbia in 1939, intending to go on to McGill University for medical training.

In the summer of 1940, Gray decided to enlist and applied to join the Canadian Naval Volunteer Reserve (RCNVR) as an officer cadet to serve on loan to the Royal Navy. On arriving in England, he saw that the road to officer status would be a long one, so when he saw an opportunity to switch to the Royal Navy Fleet Air Arm as an officer pilot, he made the transfer.

Gray was joining at the right time as the Fleet Air Arm was expanding rapidly and needed aircrew. Despite never previously expressing an interest in flying, Gray began his basic flying training at HMS *St Vincent*, Gosport, and was commissioned as a sub-lieutenant. He was awarded his wings on 6 October 1941 and sent to HMS *Daedalus* and HMS *Heron* for advanced training and operational preparation. Finally, he joined his first squadron, 757 Naval Air Squadron, on 10 March 1942. It would be three long years before he saw any action.

Gray was almost immediately transferred to 789 Squadron based at HMS *Afrikander* at Simon's Town in South Africa. The newly formed squadron operated Albacores, Sea Hurricanes, Swordfish and Walruses and was in South Africa to protect against any advances the Japanese Navy might make. After the American success at the Battle of Midway, the threat to South Africa eased and Gray was reassigned to Kilindini in Kenya with 795 Squadron.

Yet more transfers saw Gray move through 803 to 877 Naval Air Squadron. His new squadron flew Sea Hurricanes from HMS *Illustrious*. With the transfer, he was promoted to lieutenant and second in command. His final transfer was to *Illustrious*'s sister-ship, HMS *Formidable*, as senior pilot with 1841 Naval Air Squadron, which flew Corsairs.

After four years of training and operational flying, Gray was finally going to see some action. The target was the German battleship *Tirpitz*, still at anchor in Kåa Fiord in northern Norway after the daring X-craft attack the previous September. A series of carrier-borne strikes were planned but poor weather caused them to be cancelled. Operation *Goodwood III* finally got under way on 24 August 1944. The aircraft carriers *Furious*, *Indefatigable* and *Formidable* launched forty-eight bombers and twenty-nine ground attack aircraft in a mission that resulted in just two hits that caused minor damage. Another 1,600lb bomb did penetrate the upper and lower armour decks and came to rest in the No.4 switchboard room. Its fuse, however, had been damaged and it failed to explode.

Gray took part in a second raid five days later, but poor visibility prevented any accurate bombing. He did lead a close-in attack on the anti-aircraft batteries and received a hit on his rudder. His gun camera showed just how close he was in his attack on the German flak defences. He also led an attack on three enemy destroyers at anchor. For this display of bravery, he was Mentioned in Despatches 'for undaunted courage, skill and determination in carrying out daring attacks on the *Tirpitz*'.

By early 1945, the naval war against Germany was virtually won. In April, HMS *Formidable* had joined the British Pacific Fleet as the Japanese 'Greater Eastern Co-Prosperity Sphere' steadily deflated. Leaving Sydney at the end of June, *Formidable* and four other carriers joined the US Navy's Third Fleet. The enemy still held some nasty surprises and *Formidable* was on the receiving end of one of them. In operations south of Okinawa in July, the Japanese launched their Kamikaze attacks on the allied warships.

In one attack, a Kamikaze hit the flight deck of *Formidable*. Fortunately, the armoured deck withstood the impact and there was little interruption to her aircraft's operations against Japanese targets. Almost constantly in the air, the aircrew losses were heavy – the British carriers lost forty-seven aircraft to enemy fire and operational losses.

In July, Gray led strafing missions against enemy airfields and on the 24th led a strike against shipping and airfields in the Inland Sea area. On the 28th, he headed a strike against the naval base at Maisuru and made a direct hit on a destroyer (it was later reported sunk). His leadership against such well-defended targets led to a recommendation from Admiral Vian for an immediate award of the Distinguished Service Cross.

On 30 July, the Fleet withdrew for a couple of days for replenishment. This became extended due to a succession of typhoons that hit the operational area. It also coincided with the dropping of the atomic bomb on Hiroshima on 6 August, around the time that Gray's squadron was able to return to operations against Japanese targets. Captain Ruck-Keene, the carrier's commander, cautioned the pilots to avoid taking unnecessary risks and to restrict themselves to just one attack run on each target.

On 9 August, a second atomic bomb was dropped on Nagasaki and it could only be a matter of days before the Japanese surrendered. The 9th was also the day that 1841 Naval Air Squadron was tasked with three sorties against enemy airfields, for there was still the fear of Kamikaze strikes.

Gray took off with seven other Corsairs and climbed to 10,000ft. Each aircraft carried a pair of 500lb high explosive bombs in addition to four .50i wing-mounted machine-guns. They flew the 150 miles from carrier to landfall at the mouth of Onagawa Bay and Gray noted two destroyers and two escorts at anchor. Continuing inland, they found their intended target only to discover that it had been destroyed by some other Allied aircraft.

There seemed no point in wasting bombs on an airfield that was no longer operable, so Gray radioed that he intended to attack the ships he had seen in Onagawa Bay instead. All eight Corsairs turned towards the bay and their approach was covered by the surrounding hills. As they cleared the hills in a 400mph dive to almost sea level, they were met by heavy anti-aircraft fire from dozens of guns sited on the hillsides and the naval ships.

Gray aimed at one of the ships, an escort frigate, *Amakusa*, and closed at full speed, jinking to avoid the enemy fire. One of his bombs was shot off and he was taking hits. Undeterred, he managed to release his remaining bomb and hit *Amakusa* below the after gun turret, which detonated the ammunition locker and blew out the side of the ship. Very quickly, she foundered and sank immediately.

Gray, his plane on fire, continued flying for a few seconds. Then his plane rolled over, hit the water at high speed and broke up. The rest of the group continued their attack. Another Corsair burst into flames as its port wing petrol tank exploded and crashed into the sea. Re-forming, the group made another attack and badly damaged two of the other warships, before returning to the carrier. Sadly, they were to lose another pilot, Lieutenant Anderson, who crashed while attempting to land back on *Formidable*'s deck.

Just six days later, on 15 August 1945, Japan surrendered.

Captain Ruck-Keene wrote to Gray's father, concluding with the words that he was 'The best and bravest fighter pilot in the ship and everybody loved him. The tragedy is all the worse coming so close to the end.

Admiral Vian attached a record of Gray's active service showing that between August 1944 and August 1945 he had been involved several dangerous missions. He argued that these were as much for a 'periodic' Victoria Cross, similar to the case of Leonard Cheshire, as an immediate one for the Onagawa Bay attack. The Admiralty's Honours and Awards Committee debated the issue that similar cases had been considered and rejected. At length, they reached agreement that, in view of the success of the attack, Gray should receive a posthumous Victoria Cross.

Gray's citation appeared in *The London Gazette* on 12 November 1945. His Cross was presented to his family in February 1946 by the Governor General, Earl of Athlone, in Ottawa. His medal group is held by the Canadian War Museum

In Onagawa Bay, next to a memorial to those Japanese servicemen killed on 9 August (150 died) stands the only foreign military memorial on Japanese soil – a memorial to Robert Gray VC. This was placed by the Japanese military to honour what they saw as an extreme act of heroism. On a 2006 visit to Japan, members of the Canadian warship HMCS *Ottawa* placed a wreath at the memorial in Hammy Gray's honour.

The war in the Far East had been like no other. The colonial wars of the nineteenth century were fought against populations who were armed with unsophisticated weapons and were comparatively easily overcome by the forces armed with the latest weapons. In a century, Japan had progressed from a closed society armed with swords, bow and arrows and the occasional cannon into an industrial power. It absorbed the technologies of the West. Its armed services were modelled on the West. By the 1930s, Japan commanded a large army, an air force equipped with the best aircraft and one of the world's largest navies. All around it saw weakness and the temptation to exert its influence on its neighbours could not be halted.

When Japan began its expansion in the 1930s into the early '40s, it caught the colonial powers of Britain, France and Holland quite unprepared. The Germans and Italians seemed certain to overrun all of Europe, including Britain, and Japan spotted its chance to become masters of South-East Asia. With France and the Netherlands occupied and Britain fighting for its life, it seemed only a matter of time before Japan became the dominant force in the Far East.

After the defeats in Burma and Malaya, the British Indian Army under the leadership of Lord Wavell and General Bill Slim was significantly increased and underwent a thorough training in jungle warfare. When they went into battle, they were given flexibility by the increasing use of air drops, something the Japanese did not and could not use.

The jungle, in which much of the war was fought, was a leveller. Neither side could claim to be natural jungle-fighters even though, for a while, the Japanese were thus regarded. British, Australian and

American had to learn the hard way to fight in this hostile environment, as did the mountain-dwellers of the Himalayas and north-west India.

In the majority of the fights and battles, the protagonists could see the whites of the eyes of their enemy. Most clashes were hand-to-hand, as borne out by the citations of the forty-eight Victoria Crosses awarded. It is not an exaggeration to say that some of the VCs were awarded for action that bordered on the superhuman. With the exception of the VCs awarded to Lieutenant Ian Fraser, Leading Seaman Mick Magennis and a few Gurkhas, the majority have long faded from the memory. It is hoped that this book will remind us of the incredible sacrifice these men made in a war that is justifiably called the Forgotten War.

Bibliography

Beyond Their Duty – Heroes of the Green Howards by Roger Chapman, 2001.
Beyond the Chindwin by Bernard Ferguson, 1945.
Burma Railway Man – Secret Letters from a Japanese POW. Edited by Brian Best, 2004, 2013.
Burma – The Forgotten War, by Jon Latimer, 2004.
The Campaign in Burma. His Majesty's Stationary Office, 1946.
Chindit, The Explosive Truth about the Last Wingate Expedition by Richard Rhodes James, 1980.
The Chindit War, The Campaign in Burma by Shelford Bidwell, 1979.
Chindits – Long Range Penetration by Mike Calvert, 1973.
Defeat into Victory by William Slim, 1956.
Fighting with the Fourteenth Army in Burma. By James Luto, 2013.
Forgotten Voices of the Victoria Cross by Roderick Bailey, 2010.
For Your Tomorrow – Canadians and the Burma Campaign 1941–45 by Robert H. Farquharson, 2004.
From Alliance to Enmity: Anglo–Japanese Relations 1930–1939. A thesis by Jon C. Scully, 2011.
From Kent to Kohima by Major Stanley Clark and Major A.T. Tillott, 1951.
Great British Battles of the British Army. Edited by David Chandler, 1991.
Hirohito's War by Francis Pike, 2015.
The Journal of the Victoria Cross Society. 2002–2016. Edited by Brian Best.
Kohima by Arthur Swinson, 1966.
Leadership in the Indian Army: Biographies of 12 Soldiers by V.K. Singh, 2005.
Magennis VC by George Fleming, 1998.
March or Die by Philip D. Chinnery, 1997.
Malayan Postscript by Ian Morrison, 1942.
A Matter of Honour by Philip Mason, 1974.
Nemesis by Max Hastings, 2007.
Reporting the Second World War by Brian Best, 2015.
Short Stories from the British Indian Army by J. Francis, 2015.
Singapore Burning by Colin Smith, 2005.
Three Quarters of a Century or Seventy five Not Out by Brigadier K.R.T. Trevor, Burma Star Association, 2009.

BIBLIOGRAPHY

A Traveller's War by Alaric Jacob, 1944.
Valour and Gallantry by Chris Kempton, 2001.
Victoria Cross – Australia's Finest and the Battles they Fought by Anthony Staunton, 2005.
Victoria Cross Heroes by Michael Ashcroft, 2006.

Index

List of Victoria Cross Recipients

Allmand, Michael, **75-6**, 79
Anderson, Charles, **20-3**

Blaker, Frank Gerald, **81-5**

Cairns, George, **72-5**, 77
Chib, Prakash Singh, **136-9**
Chowne, Albert, **171-4**
Cumming, Arthur Edward, **16-20**

Derrick, Thomas, **167-71**
Din, Fazal, **143-4**

Fraser, Ian, **37-43**, 193
French, John, **156-9**

Ghale, Gaje, **55-7**, 94, 97
Gray, Robert, **188-93**
Gurung, Bhanubhakta, **128-32**
Gurung, Lachhiman, 81, **146-9**

Hafiz, Abdul, 66, **88-90**
Harman, John, **100-108**
Hoey, Charles Ferguson, **63-4**
Horwood, Alec George, **59-63**

Judge, Karamjeen Singh, **140-3**

Kelliher, Richard, **165-7**
Kenna, Edward, **175-7**, 183
Kingsbury, Bruce, **152-5**
Knowland, George, **123-8**

Lama, Ganju, 66, **91-4**

Mackey, John, **185-6**
Magennis, James, **33-7**, 39, 40, 43, 193

Newton, William, 159-65

Rai, Agansing, **96-7**
Ram, Bhandari, **116-8**
Randle, John, **108-12**
Rattey, Reginald, 167, **180-3**
Raymond, Claud, **132-4**

Partridge, Frank, **183-5**
Pun, Tul Bahadur, 76, **77-81**

Scarf, Arthur, 13-6
Shah, Sher, **120-3**
Singh, Gian, 119, 130, **139-40**
Singh, Nand, **64-8**
Singh, Ram Sarup, **114-6**
Singh, Parkash, **51-4**
Singh, Umrao, **118-20**, 130, 140
Starcevich, Leslie, **187**
Sukanaivalu, Sefanaia, **177-80**

Thapa, Netrabahadur, **94-5**, 96
Turner, Hanson Victor, **90-1**

Weston, William Basil, **144-6**
Wilkinson, Thomas, **24-32**